The Complete Guide to
USING A COMPUTER
FOR THE FIRST TIME

For a complete list of Management Books 2000 titles,
visit our web-site on http://www.mb2000.com

The Complete Guide to USING A COMPUTER FOR THE FIRST TIME

Bill Hall

2000

First published in 2002 by Management Books 2000 Ltd
Forge House, Limes Road
Kemble, Cirencester
Gloucestershire, GL7 6AD, UK
Tel: 0044 (0) 1285 771441/2
Fax: 0044 (0) 1285 771055
E-mail: m.b.2000@virgin.net
Web: mb2000.com

Printed and bound in Great Britain by Biddles, Guildford

British Library Cataloguing in Publication Data is available
ISBN 1-85252-391-3

Contents

5

Introduction

The scope of this book

This book is intended as a simple book, written for older people of average ability. Its purpose is to provide basic foundation instructions on using a personal computer for those people who have never used a computer before and who have no expert on hand to teach them. If you follow the chapters carefully and in their order, then the book will take you from the point of setting up a computer yourself and switching it on and off, through to the point where you can write simple letters, print and save them. You will also be shown how to play games on the computer and how to make simple drawings.

This book will not make you an expert in any sense about computers. It will not teach you about using the Internet or Electronic Mail – these topics are covered in subsequent simple books that you can follow up with at a later stage. It will, however, give you the early confidence and very important basic skills to use a computer keyboard and mouse pointing-device. It will also explain to you what you are seeing on the computer screen, so that you have the foundation knowledge to move forward later to more advanced topics such as the Internet. The book will also teach you how things are really organised and stored on a computer, so that you will always be able to find work that you have saved from earlier efforts.

You should be able to achieve all the aims of this book without needing additional external help. In fact, doing things for your self with computers is quite important. If others do them for you then chances are that you may miss, or forget, the basic reasons why we do some of the things in the way that we do. Doing and learning things for yourself also means you can progress at your own pace, and not be embarrassed or intimidated by the progress of others.

You will not require any special added computer programs on your computer to work through the book – you will only need the basic "Windows" type programs that generally come with every computer. The book will specifically discuss those computers that use the Windows 98 system, but most of the ideas and instructions will be applicable to earlier and later versions of Windows.

Take time to work your way through the chapters slowly and make sure you have understood them before moving to the next. Many people make the mistake of rushing to advanced things before they are really ready. This can be quite stressful and frustrating later on, particularly when you know that some task is possible, but cannot make it happen yourself. Also, rushing on to advanced topics too quickly will make you dependant on the advice of others to achieve your task. This is generally time-consuming for both parties, as well as maybe slowing you down by waiting, in connection with a job that you may be keen to get on with.

Computers are without doubt complex tools to use properly. The problem usually is not that they are inherently difficult – it is more the sheer number of new things that you need to get to grips with. Many of these things are simple if taken step by step, but the need to remember each of these things and their sequences can be daunting to the beginner. The real secret for success is to build your knowledge and skills slowly. Don't try and learn too much in one go. Don't be afraid to read and re-read sections over again. You will be surprised at how much more you take in and remember the second time. Do follow the chapters by practising on your own computer as you go along. You will retain more of the information you learn in that way.

Acknowledgements

In creating a book out of nowhere, it is not just the author's effort in writing it that makes it happen. I therefore would like to thank the following people for their valued contributions in making this book a reality.

I would first like to thank Elaine Watkins for her initial suggestion of taking the time to write it. I then should like to thank my three star pupils, Dilys Birkett, John Hall and Vic Reading, to whom I am much indebted for their diligence and patience in working through each of the chapters, as they were produced. I need also thank James Alexander, of Management Books 2000 Ltd, for his help and guidance in steering this book to its finished form. And finally, I must thank my wife Norma, who greatly deserves the credit for having faith and sharing the burdens of producing it.

1

Initial Preparation

1.1 Starting out

Congratulations on buying your computer. They say that laying out your precious cash is the hardest part of getting started in computing! Congratulations also on choosing this 'First Time' book to learn from. I hope to prove to you that by doing so you have made a good choice.

Learning how to use your computer can be another hard struggle, particularly for those of us who went to school before the personal computer (the PC) became popular. However, in this book, I will try my very best to make it less of a struggle by giving you explanations for all you need to know in plain and simple language. I hope to show you that the computer learning process can in fact be simple – if we take it at the right speed – and also enjoyable as we progress.

My method for reducing your learning trauma is to take you through the steps of various procedures in a very, very slow and very, very deliberate manner. If we take things slowly, and a little at a time, then your confidence will begin to build, and you will start to see the simplicity that lies behind everything that we do.

Computers are indisputably complex beasts to master. The complexity is not so much the difficulty of the task. It tends to be more the sheer amount of things that you have to first learn and then remember. Each of these individual things are relatively simple in themselves. But put them all together and to the beginner they seem formidable.

Perhaps, some time in the near future, computers may become less complex items to use. Maybe that day will be when we can easily speak to them directly and be fully understood by them. However, that time is not yet come. And if we are to avoid frustration today we must start out very slowly, and be sure that we really do understand why we are doing what we do. If we understand – then it becomes easier to remember.

Every now and then – in our journey along the learning route – we will need to use and understand some technical terms and some jargon. Computing is full of jargon – there is no way honestly of avoiding it. But if you are to be proficient in using your computer, then sooner or later you will need to communicate with others. It is probably at those times that the jargon is best appreciated for what it is – a shorthand way when communicating to economise on many more words. You may smile to yourself one day when you find yourself unwittingly using it in conversation!

For us and throughout this book, if we need to use a technical term or some jargon then I shall not assume you already know anything about it. We will occasionally take time out from the main thrust of things to explain terms and jargon in some detail. But we shall only do this once the first time it crops up. If you come across something that you think we haven't met before, or have forgotten about it, then look it up in the index at the rear of the book. Chances are that the simple explanation is given somewhere else earlier so you can re-read about it.

If during the course of this book you feel that I am going too slow for you, then maybe you know a bit more than an absolute beginner. If you find yourself struggling, then you need to keep your calm and perhaps read a section or two over again. More than likely in the re-read the penny will eventually drop.

1.2   The basic parts of a personal computer

Having now bought your computer, you need first to prove it is working okay and that you haven't wasted your money. We should start at the very beginning by running through the basics of connecting it up and getting it switch on. Then you will be ready to start learning how to operate it. However, before we get underway, you do need to understand that there are four basic parts to any modern personal computer so we will run through them now. Here they are:

First – A **display screen** looking a bit like a TV screen. Some people call this a 'monitor' or 'display monitor'. We shall just use the term 'monitor' throughout the rest of this book instead of display screen. Here is a typical monitor.

Second: A **processor unit**. This is a separate box and either lies flat on its broadest side, under the monitor; or stands upright upon one end, at the side of the monitor or under a desk. It contains all the real working parts of the computer. The one shown below left is typical.

Third: A **keyboard** looking a bit like a typewriter's keyboard, but without the rest of the mechanics.

Fourth: A small plastic round shaped device with a cable and plug attached, having two, maybe three, large buttons to click on it; and a small, heavy ball trapped underneath. This is the famous '**mouse**' pointing device. Small rectangular mats (called mouse-mats) go underneath the mouse to provide a flat smooth frictional surface for the ping pong ball to roll on. Here is a mouse and mouse-mat.

Later, as we progress through our learning process of using the computer, we will introduce other parts when and where necessary. These will be add-on, rather than basic parts. The key point to understand is that the four parts above are the fundamentals of the modern personal computer. With only these four parts you can at least make a computer do some work. Without any one of them then you will not be able to do even the simplest of computing tasks.

Occasionally, you will hear people use the word 'peripheral' to mean add-on bits and pieces to the computer. Computer peripherals are items of equipment to be connected to the computer, but are not themselves fundamental to its working. For example, a printer is a computer peripheral. The four parts we have described above are not peripherals – they are essential basic parts. A printer, on the other hand, is nice to have but not essential to make the computer operate.

When people first start to learn about personal computing, the first three of the above basic components don't seem to trouble them too much. However, the fourth component – the 'mouse' pointing device – always seems to cause a bit of consternation. For now, I want you to trust me. We will spend a lot of time on the mouse during the course of our learning. We shall learn how a mouse should be used properly, but if for reasons of dexterity (or the lack of it) the mouse starts to give you problems, then we shall discover simple ways to get around these using alternative ideas and methods. After much practice, you will probably become sufficiently competent not to need using the alternatives.

Hardware and software

Referring back now to our list of basic parts, this is known as the 'hardware' of the computer. It is called *hard* because you can physically touch it with your own hands! Later we will introduce you to using 'software'. This is something that you cannot touch. It is held on computer disks. The disks themselves are still called hardware, but the information that is held upon them is the software.

Get used to the idea that software means information. The historical meanings of the terms 'hard' and 'soft' in computing are to do with the ease of altering things. Hard things are those that cannot easily be altered (for example your monitor, or your processor unit, etc.). Soft things are those that can easily be altered (for example the information stored within the computer – the computer programs and such like). If you are ever unsure what is hard and what is soft, use a simple test – can anyone physically touch it? If it can be touched then it is almost certainly not soft in the computing sense of the word! For example, an idea in your own head is an example of software. Why is this? Well you cannot touch an idea with your finger. Can it easily be changed? For the most of us, yes it can … unless of course you are particularly stubborn!

This notion that some things are hardware and some things are software is strange for newcomers to computers. Throughout our life, we tend to think of objects as only those things that are physical and visible. The thought that an idea or information can also be an object doesn't seem to be a natural thought for us. However, if you are going to get your feet under the table with computers then you need to allow your imagination to stretch a little bit. Software is very much a real object, even though you cannot hold it in the palm of your hand. It is so much of a real object that it has made a few people amongst us some of the richest in the world – one being the legendary Mr Bill Gates, the main founder of the Microsoft Computer Software Company!

Computers need both hardware and software to do their job. If you don't have both then you cannot make the computer do anything at all. If either gets broken then you are in bother. These days, the hardware is pretty reliable. Usually, when people have trouble with their computers, it is because the software has somehow become 'broken'. Fortunately, repairing software doesn't usually involve buying new software. It is mostly a matter of reloading it into the computer from the original place where it was stored. Unfortunately, repairing software does usually need someone with expert knowledge. We shall avoid the subject of repairing software until you are much more familiar with the stuff. It is not something that 'first timers' should be getting into!

In my forthcoming description and explanation of the hardware, you may well find that your particular computer is slightly different in some respect or other. Don't worry too much about differences. The important and essential point is to find the part of your own hardware that closest matches that which I am describing. For example, the mouse that I will use in my descriptions will have two buttons that you can click with your finger to operate it. Your own mouse may well have three buttons, and maybe a wheel on it as well. Your mouse will still perform all the operations that I shall describe, but you need to make sure if I refer to the LEFT button that you find the corresponding button on your own mouse when you repeat my instructions.

Now to how the hardware should be laid out.

1.3 Laying out your computer equipment

Laying out your computer hardware for ease of use is a very important consideration. Take a bit of time to think about it. Don't just dump it on the nearest surface to hand. If necessary, maybe you should invest in another second-hand table or desk specifically for the job. After all, you have laid out many hundreds of pounds to purchase your equipment, so if you are going to get the best out of it you need to be comfortable. I personally am not too keen on purpose built computer furniture. I much prefer an older but well made table with a large surface to work from.

Now let me give you two sound tips to start with:

1. **Don't plug anything into the mains power supply until we are ready to do it!**

2. **Do purchase a four-way mains power extension lead to use solely for your computer set up. You can power all your computer equipment from one wall outlet socket and when you switch off you only have one plug to disconnect for safety.** (Note – There are four way mains power extension leads specifically designed for use with computing equipment that contain a 'Surge Suppression' device. This type of extension lead is good value for money. It will help protect your computer equipment from abnormal mains voltage conditions which can arise from time to time.)

First you must decide how the computer hardware is to be laid out on your desk or table. Choose a surface where you have plenty of space to put everything and have enough freedom to move the mouse around on it's mat without obstruction. It is also a good idea to leave a small gap between the desk or table and a wall so that you can run mains leads and other cables from the rear of your equipment down the back out of the way. The picture below shows an ideal layout with plenty of space on the table for manipulating the mouse with the right hand, whilst having space on the left for placing reference books (such as this one!).

The mouse mat needs to lay perfectly flat and immediately to the side of the keyboard (right or left depending on your 'handed-ness'). If the mouse mat is not absolutely flat and free to move at least 10 cm (3 inches) in all directions, then you will have major difficulties when you come to use it.

The keyboard itself should be placed directly in front of the monitor, and the monitor should be directly and centrally in front of the chair where you will sit to operate the computer. You are likely to spend many hours in front of your computer, so if you don't have things aligned centrally you will end up with a 'crick' in your neck!

Where you place the processor unit depends on whether it is designed to be normally stood upright or laid flat on the broadest side. Check this out by examining the processor unit for the four rubber feet that it normally sits upon. If the processor unit is designed for upright operation, you might wish to place it to the right or left of the monitor as in the previous picture (again depending on your handed-ness). An advantage of sitting it on the desk is that you can easily get to plug in additional equipment and computer disks when needed.

Alternatively, with upright designed units you may want to place it under the table or desk, facing forward, so that you have more space on the top of the desk or table. However, the cable lengths supplied for connecting things together might not be long enough to let you do this – you should beware of this point and not put the cables under any strain when we start plugging in. If the cables won't reach, then don't force them.

Some computers have processor units designed to lay upon the broadest side (if this is so then the four rubber feet will be found on this side of the processor unit). In this case, you may be able to sit the monitor on top of the processor unit and save space this way. However, be careful to check that the processor unit is manufactured with a metal case. If the case is plastic, not metal, it may not be capable of taking the weight of the monitor – the latest 17 inch monitor screens are particularly heavy! You will have to exercise your own judgement here.

This picture illustrates a processor unit designed to operate on its side under the monitor. Next we shall connect up the computer leads.

1.4   Plugging it together in preparation for switching on

Remember – Don't plug anything into the mains power supply until we are ready to do it!

If you already know how to connect up your computer, or someone has done it for you, you may want to skip forward to the next chapter at this point. If you want to do it yourself then read on.

First examine the rear of the monitor and find the lead attached to it with a plug that looks something like this:

This is the video lead and plug. Recognise it because it has three rows of electrical pins inside the plug shell. The outer shell surrounding the pins has one side slightly longer than the other and is often referred to as a 'D' type of connector. It is so called because the outline shell shape (I mean the bit surrounding the pins)

when viewed from the pins looks vaguely like the letter D. In this picture, the 'D' is laid on its side. As an aside, D connectors are a common type of connector used in computer equipment. Shortly, we may meet other D connectors that look very similar but are slightly different. Beware there are different numbers of pins on different D connectors! The one we are dealing with now is the only one with three rows of pins.

Now locate the socket on the rear of the processor unit which also has a 'D' outline shape and has three rows of – not pins – but holes for pins to fit in. This picture shows a typical socket of the kind that we are looking for.

 Prepare to plug the video lead from the monitor into this socket by positioning it just in front, but don't enter it in just yet. Observe the outer shell of both plug and socket carefully taking note of the longer and shorter sides for each. Make sure that you have the plug the right way around to line up the longer sides of both. When you are sure you have it the right way around then firmly push it **slowly** into the socket but don't try to force it. If the plug won't go in without forcing then there is something not right. If you try to use force excessively then you may end up bending a few of the pins and you will need to get them straightened out again! This applies to all plugs and sockets, particularly the small variety as used in computing – never try forcing them.

The secret with all plugs and sockets is this. If they are the correct ones which are meant to go together, then providing you get them aligned the right way round they should not require any force beyond that of a simple push. To make sure you get the right plug for the right socket, and to make sure they are the right way around, manufacturers usually have a design feature (it is called a 'key') that prevents you getting it wrong. If they don't fit together easily then this might be telling you either that they are no supposed to be connected together, or you have the plug the wrong way up.

With the video plug of the monitor now firmly into the socket on the rear of the processor unit, you should then screw clockwise the two retaining screws at either end of the plug (see the previous plug picture showing the retaining screws). These retaining screws are to prevent the plug falling out of the socket inadvertently. There are different types of retaining screws. Some have thumbscrews that you can twirl with your thumb and fingers and you only need to make them finger tight. Some others are slot-headed screws that require a small screwdriver to fasten up.

☑ **Okay, we now have the monitor and processor unit connected.**

Now take the keyboard and position it in front of the monitor. Then route the keyboard lead around to the back of the processor unit. The keyboard socket that the plug fits into can take a few different styles of connector. The older variety is a larger type of about 15mm diameter and is called a DIN connector. This is shown on the left in the picture below. Newer types are smaller about 10mm diameter and are called PS2 Style connectors. The PS2 style is shown on the right in the picture below. Notice on the PS2 type that the metal shell surrounding the pins has a small part of it cut back:

Whichever your type of plug is on the end of your keyboard lead, then you need to find the appropriate matching socket at the rear of the processor unit. When you think you have it located, rotate the plug so that the pins line up with the socket (look for another 'key' mechanism in both plug and socket) and then push firmly home. One tip to consider – many plugs have a 'pip' or line or other distinctive marker on the body of the plug which usually goes to the top (upper most) side if it is correctly aligned for inserting into the socket. Another tip is that often manufacturers will show symbols of the various parts that connect to differing sockets – thus showing you which plug should go where. On my own computer the plugs are **colour coded**, so it makes it very easy to identify the corresponding sockets.

☑ Okay, now we have the keyboard connected.

Now take the mouse and position it to right or left of your keyboard (whichever handed you are) and place the mouse mat underneath. Take the mouse lead and route it around to the back of the processor. Tip – it pays to leave a small amount of lead slack at the mouse end so that you can move the mouse around on the mat without dragging on the whole lead. On the end of the mouse lead is a plug connector for attaching to the rear of the processor unit. Connecting this can be a bit tricky, depending on the hardware you have bought, so we will cover the options here in a bit of detail.

As with keyboards, mouse plugs and sockets can also come in a variety of styles. The newer style is known as a PS2 type and is circular, about 10mm diameter. The PS2 plug has a small cutaway at the bottom of the outer metal plug shell and has pins. Older type mouse plugs have another D type connector attached, this time with only two rows of holes (note – holes not pins). Both types are shown below. The PS2 type is on the left and the D type on the right:

17

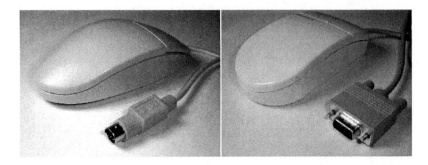

Identify the plug type on your own particular mouse lead. Is it of the PS2 type? If it is then the follow the next description relating to PS2 style plugs. If it is the older D type connector then jump forward to the description relating to D style mouse plugs.

PS2 style mouse plugs

Look now to the rear of the processor unit and see if you can identify the corresponding mouse socket (If your keyboard socket was also a PS2 style then the mouse socket will probably be close to it). If you can see a circular socket of about 10 mm diameter then hold the plug near to the socket and check if the plug pins and socket holes seem to line up. If you think they seem to, then gently but firmly try push the plug home to connect it.

Once connected then you are ready to move on to the next stage. Now skip forward to the next section in this chapter which deals with connecting power leads (miss out the bit about D style mouse plugs).

If you are unlucky and cannot see any suitable circular socket at all at the rear of the processor unit, then it may well be that you need to fit an adapter to the PS2 type mouse plug in order to convert it to the older style D type connector. Here is a picture of such an adapter:

If the mouse arrived in a box with your computer and it is intended to be used with an adapter, then there should be one somewhere in the box. However, have a little caution. Even if you have an adapter delivered with the mouse, it does not necessarily mean that you **need** to use it. Often the manufacturer of the computer processor unit may differ from the mouse manufacturer, so the mouse makers may throw in an adapter anyway in case some other users might need one.

Do check very carefully that there is no direct connection to a PS2 style socket before you resign yourself to using the adapter. If after an extensive search of the processor unit you still find that you cannot locate the mouse PS2 socket then you have no alternative but to use the adapter. Connect the adapter to the mouse plug. Now effectively the mouse is a D style plug and you should read and follow the next description.

D style mouse plugs

Before we start on this description, let me first give you an apology! Computer designers over the years have come up with quite a number of different ways of implementing D style connections on processor units. This fact means that, to cover all the possibilities of your computer, our description might get a bit involved. If I tell you that this bit is the always the most tricky for everybody – including the professionals – then you might not feel so bad when your head starts spinning! Please proceed with me. Take it slowly, and read carefully. Relate my words to your particular computer and find the corresponding bit that I am talking about. Use the pictures to compare against your actual hardware.

Older D style mouse plugs are usually of the 'nine hole' variety. The sockets on the rear of the processor unit to accommodate them may also be of the 9-pin variety to accommodate them – but they may not be. If the sockets are not of the 9-pin then they will almost certainly be of the 25-pin variety, and an adapter from 9-pin to 25-pin will be required. For connecting up a mouse, the 25-pin sockets are functionally the same as 9-pin sockets – they just are physically different in the number of pins which they have. Many of the pins of a 25-pin socket are not used when a mouse is connected.

> **IMPORTANT NOTE – To connect the mouse, we are only looking here for sockets on the processor unit that are of the D type and have pins. Ignore any D sockets on the processor unit that have holes instead of pins. They are for something else!**

Both 9-pin and 25-pin connectors have only two rows of pins or holes. A 9-pin will have one row of 4 pins and another row of 5 pins. A 25-pin will have one row of 12 pins and another row of 13 pins. This reminds us again why the connector is called a D type connector – because one side of the connector has more pins than the other side, and is therefore longer length, the 'end on' view of the outer connector shell surrounding the pins has the form of a long letter 'D'. The longer side represents the left of the D symbol and the shorter side represents the right. Get the idea? Now you should always be able to recognise a D connector no matter how many pins it has! And in computing we shall meet more peripherals that use D style connectors, so learning this snippet is useful information!

By the way, the D shape of the connector is the 'keying' mechanism for that connector. It just won't fit the wrong way around.

Now, back to the processor unit and to the rear of it. When we search for the correct socket to plug our 9-pin D style mouse plug into it, we need to take a little care. Chances are that there may be two D style sockets to choose from. One of these may be a 9-pin socket, the other may be a 25-pin socket. Let us have a little side discussion first before we make the choice.

The sockets on the processor unit we are dealing with here are called the COM sockets. COM is short for COMMUNICATION and if we are going to be really precise we should further describe them as SERIAL COMMUNICATION sockets. I won't go into the SERIAL aspect at this point. Let's leave that for another time.

These COM sockets are usually called and referred to as 'COM1' and 'COM2'. Look at the processor unit to see if these sockets are also marked as COM1 and COM2 at the side of the sockets. If yours are marked then you are in luck, the names will make life easier. Chances are though that they will not be. Another method some manufacturers have for marking COM sockets is to use the symbol '10101'. Yet other manufacturers will refer to 'A' and 'B' instead of COM1 and COM2. Fortunately there aren't two many of these!

Now, you may have two COM sockets on the rear of your processor unit, or you may have only one. If you do have only one, then it will be referred to always as the COM1 socket. If there is only one then chances are that it will also be a 9-pin socket. In this case you have found what you are looking for! This 9-pin D style socket is where you will plug in your mouse. Align the plug of the mouse lead with the 9-pin socket on the processor unit and go ahead and plug it in. That is the end of that! Move on to the next section about connecting power leads while your sanity is still intact!

Chances are however that you will have two COM sockets. One will be a 9-pin socket and the other will be a 25-pin socket. There might possibly be just two 9-pin sockets but that's not common with the older style processor units that use COM sockets for plugging a mouse in. Remember we are looking here at sockets which have *pins*, not holes. Ignore any D sockets on the rear of the processor unit that have holes.

If you do have one 9-pin COM socket and another 25-pin COM socket (a very common arrangement) then the chances are that the 9-pin one is COM1 and the 25-pin one is COM2. If your computer is very unusual, then these could be the other way around, but a penny to a pinch of salt, it is as I first said.

If you do have two 9-pin COM sockets instead, then they are likely to be marked up as COM1 and COM2.

Does it matter whether we use COM1 or COM2 to connect up a mouse to? Well, actually no, they both will work OK. The only advantage of choosing one against the other will arise when you want to connect other computer peripherals to your basic machine. If this doesn't bother you at the moment, then go ahead and choose either. You can always adjust things later if need be.

The simplest thing to do is to plug the 9-hole mouse plug into the 9-pin processor socket. It's easiest because they fit and you won't need a further adapter. If they are both 9-pins sockets then again, either will work – the choice is up to you.

My own preferred option is to use COM2 as the mouse connector, and use a 9-pin to 25-pin adapter to accommodate the different sized plug and socket, if this is the case. The reason behind this preference is that COM1 is then left free for future use. COM1 is often used as the 'default' option for other equipment, and if it is left free, it becomes nice and simple for connecting up other such equipment.

> **Note – If you haven't met the term 'default' before then perhaps it is a good time to pick up this bit of jargon. It is used a lot in computing. The default option is that option to which something is initially set at. It is the 'normal' condition. If you prefer, the default setting is that setting which the makers of something left it set to when they sold it to you!.**

So, finally, you should have reached the point where you can connect up the mouse to the processor unit. You have made your choice of the COM socket that you intend to use, whether it be COM1 or COM2. Line up the mouse plug with the appropriate socket and go ahead and plug it in – again firmly but don't force it and bend the pins.

☑   **Okay, we now have the mouse connected (phew!)**

Connecting power leads

It is time now to address the mains power leads.

At the beginning of section 1.3, I gave you the tip to use a four-way mains extension lead for supply power to all your computer hardware (preferably the kind which has 'surge suppression' built into it, but not essential). The description that follows assumes you haven't got one of these to hand and that you are going to plug power leads directly into the mains sockets in the wall. As you are no doubt keen to get your hardware up and running, we will continue on this basis. However, if you get chance to use one later on then you can simply unplug all mains plugs from the wall and plug them into your new four-way extension, using the single plug of the extension lead then to then plug into the wall. The advantage of this latter arrangement is that you then have a single plug to switch off and disconnect from the wall when you shut down your hardware at the end of using it.

A standard computer mains lead looks like this:

The end of the cable shown on the left has what is known as an IEC connector attached to it, and the whole lead is sometimes known as an IEC type mains lead.

There should be one standard mains lead amongst your hardware to connect into the mains socket at the wall and to connect to the processor unit to provide power. Go ahead and plug this in at both ends, but make sure the power is off – and leave it switched off – when you connect at the wall socket.

What should you do if the power was accidentally left on and you connected it? Switch it off promptly. The prompter the better!

The next lead we need to connect up is the final one for getting the basic parts of the computer working. This is to provide a power connection to the monitor. There are two possible alternative ways that your hardware may use for doing this.

1. The first way is to use another standard IEC type power lead identical to the one you have just used for the processor. If you have another of this lead type then connect one end to the power socket on the monitor, and the other end to a second mains supply wall socket. Remember don't switch any power on yet.

2. The second way employs an unusual style of mains lead that generally is quite short in length. It has one end (the plug) identical to that used at the processor unit end of the standard mains lead, but a socket of the reverse style to the plug at the other end. The following picture shows such a lead:

This second type of lead fits directly from the processor unit to the monitor instead of from a mains wall socket to the monitor. If you have such a lead then you might already have noticed that the processor unit also has an additional but strange power connector with 3 holes instead of pins. Opposite is a picture of a processor unit with this added connector type:

Connect up this second power lead from the second power connector on the processor unit to monitor's power connector.

This latter method of powering the monitor is quite handy. It means that you only need to have one mains wall socket for the operation of the basic computer. Your delight though is likely to be short lived. Invariably, you will need to fix up other computer peripherals and they will probably each need a power connector.

Well, here we are. We now have the basic parts of the computer connected up and ready to try out. In chapter 2 we will go through the detail of the power up stage and learn that there are some tests that the computer itself will do as part of the power up process. We shall learn what these tests are. We shall learn how to detect if things are not as they should be, and how also to recognise if they are.

However, just before we leave the detail of connecting up hardware, there will be some readers fortunate to have a printer to use (the first of those peripheral devices we described in section 1.2!). If you do then we had better describe setting this up before we move on. We will do this in the next section – section 1.5. Also, your computer may have the capability to produce sound through external speakers. If it does then you should read section 1.6.

If you have neither a printer nor external speakers, then you can skip forward at this point to chapter 2.

1.5 Connecting up a printer to your computer

These days there are three different kinds of printers in general use for personal computers; these are the Dot Matrix, the Laser, and the Inkjet. Of the three, the Inkjet is probably becoming the most favourite because it is fairly cheap to buy and it is capable of printing very good quality colour pictures as well as ordinary printed text.

Here is a typical Inkjet printer:

Even though we have listed three different kinds of printer, the connections on them are fairly standard, so our description of making a cable connection from the printer to the computer will be the same in all cases. The connectors are to be found on the rear of the printer.

Most printers that you will encounter today are of the type known as 'parallel port' printers. What on earth does this mean? The word 'port' means 'connector'. A parallel port printer is a printer that uses a 'parallel' type connector to join it to the processor unit. The word parallel here is indicating that there are eight information wires in the cable joining the printer to the computer, and that information is flowing down each wire individually. This method contrasts with the older 'serial port' printers where only one wire carried all information going to the printer. The word 'serial', by the way, means information is flowing one bit after the other. Eight wires operating at the same time – that is, in parallel – is obviously much faster than just one, if the speed of flow is the same.

Well why just eight, you might ask? Why not ten or twenty? The answer is that eight is a magic number in computers for grouping individual bits of information together, as you will find out later. It is known as a 'byte'. Transferring information in whole bytes at a time was the easiest thing to do when the parallel port was first designed. The printer connector also has some extra wires for the control of information flow, so the connector used has a few more pins to it than just the eight information ones.

Recently, there has appeared on the market a newer type of serial printer employing something called 'USB' – Universal Serial Bus. This refers to the brand new method of connecting the printer peripheral (you know what a peripheral is now) to the processor unit. It's the hottest thing in the printer world, and its very good news because it can transfer information even faster than the parallel port connections. The reason is that technology has moved on since the old serial and parallel connections were first invented, and modern chip designs can operate at much faster speeds these days. So just to contradict the idea that eight wires are better than one, designers have gone back to the old serial idea, but have considerably increased the speed of sending. Well, you might ask, why not use this higher speed down eight parallel wires instead of just one serial channel? The answer here is that serial connectors are simpler and cheaper to make, and when you are working at the very highest speeds – as with the USB connector – it becomes tricky with parallel wires to guarantee that information all arrives at precisely the right moment. So, for the time being, the

USB connector has been adopted as the faster common method of connecting up a printer.

So now we know. There is a possibility that you have a printer using a parallel port style connection to the computer, or a USB style. Either of these can be used satisfactorily. But how do you decide which type you have, or which type you should be using? To complicate matters even further, you might have a very new printer that has the capability to do both parallel and USB choices of connector – mine does!

The easiest way to decide how you should connect up your printer is to examine the type of lead supplied and recognise the type of plug and socket connectors. Shortly, we will examine illustrations of each type in turn. If you have a printer that can do both then the decision may still be determined by the type of lead supplied, and the settings that your supplier has already made for you within the computer. Today, the most common printer setup is for parallel port connections but the USB method is becoming more popular. If your printer can do both, and you have been supplied with leads for both, then the deciding factor will still be how the internal computer settings have been set up. If after reading this chapter you are still unsure which of the two connection methods has been pre-set for you then you should check with your supplier.

Connecting up using parallel ports

A parallel port printer uses a parallel port cable to connect to the processor unit, and a parallel port cable looks like this:

Notice that the connector on the left of the above picture is somewhat different to that on the right. The parallel port on the printer is not quite the same as the parallel port on the processor unit. The parallel port on the printer itself is called a CENTRONICS connector and looks like the next picture (just to be confusing it is also known as a IEEE 1284 connector):

25

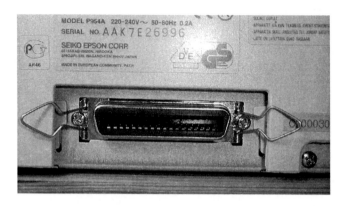

The parallel port on the processor unit is called a 25-way D type connector (remember D connectors from section 1.3 on connecting up the mouse!) and looks like this:

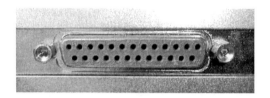

Examine the leads that you have been supplied with. Can you identify one as being the parallel port type? If so, plug the CENTRONICS plug end of the printer cable into the printer CENTRONICS socket. It will only fit one way round because it too has a D type shell surrounding the pins. You should then 'click' the two wire retaining clips (those wire things at either end of the socket) onto the cable plug shell so that they prevent the cable plug from inadvertently shaking loose in the future.

At the processor unit end, at the rear of the unit, find the 25-way D type connector that looks identical to that in the above picture. You will recognise it because it has holes not pins in two rows – one row of thirteen holes and one row of twelve. Now plug the other end of the printer cable into this connector socket. The retaining devices this time are likely to be screw devices that may need a small screwdriver, or have small twirl knobs that can be tightened using your fingers. Don't over tighten or cross thread these retaining screws – just screw them so that they are fully home.

If you cannot find a parallel port lead but you have a lead of another style, then it is probably a USB type lead. We will now discuss how to recognise this alternative method of connecting the printer to the processor unit.

Note – if you have been supplied with both types of lead, then it may not be obvious how the computer settings have been preset. In this situation try using one of them first and see if your printer works correctly. If you get a printer error message on the monitor screen during printing, then you should try the other lead. You will not cause any physical damage to the computer or printer by trying them out.

Connecting up using USB connectors

A USB socket on a printer rear panel looks like this:

Note the symbol shown above the label USB in this picture. This is the standardised symbol to show a USB connector, and you may come across it in other places on your computer.

A USB plug on the end of a cable to plug into a processor unit looks like this:

Note that the plugs for the printer end and the processor end of the cable are different. The processor end plug is wider.

If you do have a USB printer cable, you simply plug the narrower printer end USB cable plug into the printer, then plug the wider processor end cable plug into any USB socket that you can see on the processor unit rear panel. You will note from the design of the plugs and sockets that again they will only fit one way around. I say any USB socket on the processor unit, but generally speaking you have a choice of just two on most new processor units. Choose either. It's as simple as that.

Note that USB plugs and sockets don't have retaining screws or clips. We shall see why in a moment in the following added note about using USB connection.

You may find at some later stage that you want to connect up other computer peripherals such as scanners, digital cameras and the like, and you don't have enough separate USB sockets on the processor unit. Now USB connections are special. They are the only type of computer connections that are specifically designed to be 'pluggable or un-pluggable' with the computer switched on! Yes, you do not have to switch anything off in order to remove a plug, or plug in a new plug. This feature of the USB connector is known as 'Hot Swappable' – and the hot bit means that you can do it when the power is on! So, if you want to connect another peripheral but have already connected up something else to the two USB sockets on the processor unit, then you can simply unplug something you are not currently using, and plug in the device that you now want to use, at any time.

Note – This 'Hot Swappable' feature is only applicable to USB connectors. Don't assume you can do this with any other type of computer connector (unless of course you have specific information to the contrary). You may get away with it in some cases, but you should not do it as a general rule for reasons that we won't go into just now. If you want to disconnect other computer connections, then shut the computer down correctly first and turn the power off before you disturb the connection.

So now we can appreciate why USB connectors don't have retaining screws and the like. The general idea is that they can be plugged and unplugged fairly frequently. If they had retaining screws then this would make the plugging/unplugging operation more cumbersome.

One last word about Parallel and USB printer leads

I mentioned earlier that the deciding factor of connecting up your printer is how the supplier has previously set up the computer for you. If the computer is not set up to use USB but you connect up a USB lead at both ends anyway, then you will probably see a monitor screen message that says something like 'New Hardware Found' or 'Add New Hardware Wizard'. This is a sure sign that the software to use a USB connection to the printer has not been previously installed on your computer. You will not have caused any damage by connecting up the USB lead, but you should therefore assume that the computer and printer are set up to use the parallel port method.

If your computer and printer is already set up for a parallel port style connector and you desire to change to using a USB style, then providing the printer has a USB socket (and the computer processor unit does too) then this can be arranged fairly easily. However, it is not a job for the 'first-timer' to do and you will need to enlist the help of someone more expert.

Final power connections for the printer

Printers usually have their own power supply connectors. Now is the point where we plug the mains cable into the IEC connector at the rear of the printer, and the mains plug into a source of mains power (see section). If you are using the tip I gave you about a four-way mains extension lead, then you will plug this in here. Otherwise, you will need to find another mains outlet wall socket.

Again, don't switch mains power on just yet – we will do that as part of the power up sequence in the next chapter.

1.6 Connecting up external speakers

Many personal computers these days are fitted with peripherals called 'sound cards', or have sound capability built into the basic processor unit. This allows sounds to be played by the computer through external speakers. If your computer has internal speakers fitted, then you may have no further connections to make.

External speakers may be powered by a mains adapter unit, internal fitted batteries, or may need no external power source. For those speakers requiring a mains adapter then you need to find yet another power outlet to plug into. Connect up the power supply as necessary but don't switch on just yet. When you power up the main processor unit as outlined in the next chapter, remember to switch power on to these speakers at the same time. Your computer will then play a 'fanfare' sound as part of the power up sequence.

The sound signal connection lead from the external speakers to the processor unit usually has a miniature stereo type jack plug as shown in the next pictures on the left:

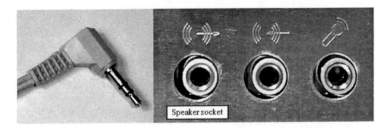

This needs plugging into the appropriate jack socket on the processor unit. If the computer has built-in sound capability, you should see a series of jack sockets at the rear of the processor unit looking like those in the above right picture.

The speaker socket is identified by either a symbol or labelled 'Spkr Out'. My own computer has it colour coded pale green. If your computer has a sound card fitted then it will look something like the picture on the left. The speaker socket is normally the one nearest to the D-type connector (for a games joystick).

2

Powering On and Off

2.1 Starting up the computer

Turn on the mains supply at the wall sockets for the processor unit and the monitor (and any other equipment such as a printer or external powered speakers). If the monitor has mains power coming via an additional connector on the processor unit then you have just one wall socket to switch on for these two items. Similarly, if you are using a four-way mains power extension lead then again you have only the one wall socket to switch on. Some four-way power leads have an extra switch on the extension box itself so what out for this and make sure it is now switched on.

Now locate the mains power switch on the processor unit itself and turn this on. Many use a push button these days – give the button a firm push in until you feel it click, then let go. Do likewise to the mains switch on the monitor itself. As a guide to which switch is the power switch, they often show a symbol looking something like this:

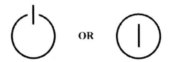

We should now have applied mains power to both processor unit and monitor. If you have a printer or externally powered speakers, make sure that these too are switched on at the equipment end.

If all is well you should notice some indicator lights (usually green these days) illuminate on the processor unit front panel and monitor. You should also begin to hear a bit of a whirring noise coming from the processor unit too. This is caused by an internal component called a 'hard drive' spinning up to speed (it has a spinning magnetic disk inside it). We will talk about the hard drive in more detail later. The hard drive has to reach a set speed after switch on before it is operational. It sorts this out by itself so you don't have to concern yourself. Just be aware that things don't happen instantaneously. The power up process itself can take a minute or two to fully complete.

If your indicator lights are red instead of green, or in fact any other colour, then don't be surprised or concerned. You will have to re-interpret my words accordingly. The important issue is that some lights are illuminated somewhere.

The purpose of these green indicator lights is to show you that mains power is actually getting through to the various pieces of hardware – the processor unit and the monitor (and printer). It is difficult to generalise about these lights because of the wide variety of designs of computer hardware. In most cases, you will have two separate indicator lights for the monitor and the processor unit. However, don't be at all surprised if your hardware only has one. The benefit of two indicator lights is that you can tell when the processor unit and monitor are individually receiving power.

The indicator light on the monitor might even change colour during the powering up process, for example between orange and green, or vice versa. We will explain why this could be so in the next section.

On the processor unit, there will be an additional indicator light and you will probably see this flashing on and off somewhat erratically. This light is a very useful one to know about and you should study it carefully. It lights to show you that things are happening internally within the processor unit. Specifically it tells you that the whirring hard drive component we previously mentioned is being 'read', that is, information is being accessed from it. The flashing occurs during the power up process because the computer is 'reading' a series of instructions that are permanently stored upon the hard drive and it is carrying out these instructions to get to the stage where you as a user can operate the computer. Every time this particular light goes out, then the reading of that instruction is finished. When it comes on again, it is reading another instruction. There are many instructions that need to be read and therefore the light is flashing on and off extensively.

You might now correctly deduce from this description that the hard drive is a form of memory unit where instructions (and other things) are stored, but as we said before, more about it later.

Quite soon after powering on, you will start to see things happening on the monitor's screen. In almost all cases, you can ignore most of what is happening there during the start-up process. However, if anything doesn't go right, then it is on the screen that error messages will be displayed, telling you what is wrong. Computers tell you what is wrong in a very detailed way. Don't expect to always understand what error messages really means – they are written for experts and sometimes in a very terse style. For absolute beginners, it is sufficient that you recognise what is an error message and what is not an error message.

The computer should by now be powering itself up. It is going to be a few minutes before it has reached the final 'ready' stage, where you the user can start to operate it. Let us now consider a few points along the way so that you get assurance that things are going well.

When the monitor first starts to display any information, it will spend a few seconds writing messages in white lettering on a black background. The hard disk indicator light will be merrily flashing away. After a minute or two the black background on the monitor screen will disappear to be replaced by a wonderful, colourful picture of the 'Windows' logo on top of a blue sky background and fluffy white clouds. Here is an example of this logo display – yours may not be identical but should be something similar:

You may notice at the bottom of this display that a small thin band acts like a 'wave' of blue colour (of differing blue shades) and appears to be moving across the screen. The wave is an indicator to you that events are still happening as part of the start up process.

The movement of the wave is the crucial part of the indicator. When it is moving then things are still happening and all is well. Occasionally, the wave will stop moving, but this should not be permanent. If ever the wave stops permanently, and stays that way for a long length of time (by a long I mean, for example, 5 actual clock minutes) then things have gone wrong and the start-up process has failed. Should this unfortunate event happen to you then switch off all mains power at both the computer end and the wall sockets and retry the start up process over again. However, if this problem happens repeatedly then you are not likely to be able to resolve the problem yourself and you will need to enlist the help of an expert.

Assuming that all is well and the start up process is continuing OK then the 'wave' shown on the monitor will still be moving right to left.

Some minutes after the Windows logo picture has appeared, the monitor will change its display yet again. Then you are likely to see another coloured background (your own specific computer could in fact display any one of several colours, or even pictures) and an hourglass symbol somewhere in the middle of your screen.

The hourglass is a representation on the monitor screen of your mouse pointing-device. If at this point you move the mouse from side to side on its mat, then the hourglass should also move in a corresponding manner. If you move the mouse forward (away from you) on the mat then the symbol goes upwards on screen; if you move the mouse backwards (towards you) then it goes downwards on the screen; and so on … Don't click any buttons or press any keyboard keys at this stage.

Very soon you will start to see many little pictures appear on top of the background. These little pictures are known as 'icons'. We shall talk much more about them in the next chapter. Near to the end of the power-up sequence, the hourglass symbol may itself start to flicker from a pure hourglass to a combined hourglass and arrow pointer.

Finally, your monitor will reach the end of the power up sequence. This is shown by the mouse pointer hourglass changing its shape permanently to an arrow-pointing symbol. When you see the mouse arrow pointer symbol appear on the screen, together with a number of icons, then you are at the stage where you can use the computer for whatever task it is that you want to do.

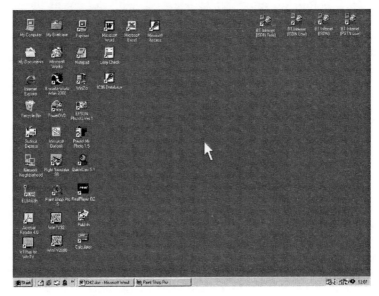

This screen display shown on the monitor at the end of the power up sequence is known as the '**Desktop**'. It is always from the Desktop that we shall start to use any of the specific computer programs that are installed on your computer.

> **Study the above picture and remember that this whole thing – the coloured background and all the icons – is known as the Desktop. We shall be using this term 'Desktop' many times throughout this book, and if you forget what it means, then you are going to make life difficult for yourself!**

The Desktop is a concept created by computer designers in an attempt to make computers easier to use. Use your imagination to think of this particular screen as though you were looking down on the surface of a real desktop. As such, here are various objects sitting upon it ready for you to use, manipulate and even to move about. Small pictures, known as '**icons**', represent the separate objects. We shall learn in more depth later that these objects are actually representing individual computer programs. They can be used independently from each other, or collaboratively if we want to exchange information from one to another.

When we first see an icon like this on the Desktop, then that object is currently closed and not being used. We shall learn throughout the other chapters of this book how to open, to use, and then to close these objects on the desktop.

The Desktop is the neutral condition that we always start from when the computer first powers up, and it is good practice to always try to return back to this neutral condition before you shut the computer down and power off.

> **So now, before we move on to learn how to use any of the computer programs installed on your computer, we shall first learn the correct way to switch off a computer. It is particularly important that you learn to do this correctly, or you are going to have trouble over and over again.**

Next, the shut down process...

2.2   Shutting down the computer properly

Shutting down a computer **in the proper way** is a very important action if you want to avoid the possibility of losing information stored on the computer.

In the early days of personal computers, it was quite acceptable simply to switch the power off at the mains supply almost whenever you felt like it – you just waited for any hard disk activity to stop and then you just turned the power switches off. However these days, and particularly with Windows type computers, **it is very important that you do not do it this way** – if you can avoid it. There may be times when you have no other alternative, but these occasions should be the exception not the rule.

The 3 correct steps in the procedure to turn off your computer are as follows (but don't do them yet until I ask you to!):

Step 1 – Close down any programs that you may have started yourself after powering up and are aware are still running. This should put you at the stage where you are looking at the Desktop on the monitor (see section 2.1 if you need a reminder what the Desktop is).

Step 2 – While looking at the Desktop, activate the 'Shut Down' command, and let the computer complete all the tasks that it automatically will attempt to do.

Step 3 – Finally, switch off mains power using switches at the hardware end (processor unit, monitor, and any other peripherals you might have), then switch off power at the wall sockets. Many of the latest models of computers can switch the processor units off automatically at the end of step 2.

To give you some experience of doing this job properly, we shall now go through the actual shut-down process in detail and turn the computer off completely.

First we examine Step 1. In the last section during the power up process, we reached the stage where the 'Desktop' was shown on the monitor screen. We have not as yet started any other programs running on the computer, therefore for now, we will not have to close any programs down that we are aware of which are still running. In later chapters we will be starting up programs and then we will have to remember to do this step.

We move on to perform step 2. Because we have not yet learnt how to use the mouse-pointing device, we shall carry out this step using only keyboard keys. With the help of the next picture, find the key on your keyboard known as the **Windows Key**. This key is marked with the 'wavy windows' symbol (⊞) and is usually on the bottom row to the left hand side If you cannot see this key on your keyboard, you may have one of the older style keyboards, in which case you need to read the note in italics following the picture:

Note – If you are using one of the older style keyboards, you may not have a Windows key on the keyboard. If so then you need to read Appendix I which describes how you can achieve the same effect as pressing the Windows key by using a combination of keys.

Now that you have found the Windows key, we ought have a word about key pressing in general before we get started. Though pressing and releasing keys on a keyboard might sound a simple enough action to do, it is surprising how many mistakes beginners make and this gets them into all kinds of trouble.

One of the most common problems is holding a key down for far too long. The correct way of pressing and releasing a key for computer keyboards is a short simple 'jabbing' action. The actual time that a key should be kept down is in fact very short indeed. If you hold a key down too long, then an automatic 'repeat' action takes place and it is as though you have pressed and released the key several times. This won't occur if you 'jab' the key, but you must learn to do this gently. Jabbing the keys too hard will hurt your fingers after a while, and may lead to repetitive strain injury if done over prolonged periods. As with many things, practice makes perfect, and you need to acquire an action that feels natural for you.

The action of swiftly pressing and releasing a key is known as 'hitting' a key. I shall use this term through the rest of this section to remind you of this correct swift action, but remember there is no real force needed – do it gently.

We are ready now to hit the Windows key. Go ahead and do it.

Notice now that a change occurs on the monitor display whereby something 'pops up' in the left hand corner of the screen as shown in the next picture:

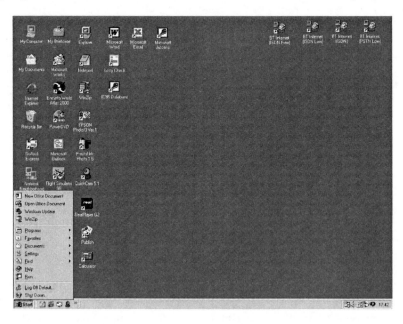

This 'grey' panel that popped up is called the **Start Menu** and is another item that you need to remember well because we shall refer to it many times in the course of this book.

Now we shall learn how to <u>undo</u> pressing the **Windows key** and cancel the **Start Menu**. Quite often beginners will inadvertently make mistakes, so it is as well to learn how to undo things as well as to do them.

We need now to locate the **ESC key**. This key is in the extreme top left hand corner of the keyboard as shown below:

Now hit the **ESC key**. Notice as soon as you do that the **Start Menu** disappears.

Tip – This action of the ESC key can be useful in other problem situations. If you should find that you are faced with a grey menu that you were not expecting, and you really want to make it go away, then hitting the ESC key is one possible way of getting out of trouble. ESC is an abbreviation for the word ESCAPE, and this key is very useful if you need to 'escape' from a situation without making any changes to things. Occasionally you may need to hit the ESC key two or three times in succession to get back to where you want to be.

Now hit the **Windows key** once more to bring the **Start Menu** back again. Then hit the letter U key (located on the top row of the letter keys just right from centre).

If you have done things properly and in the correct sequence, you will see the following changes on the monitor screen, as shown overleaf:

Three things happened fairly quickly. First, the Desktop background colour went slightly dark. Secondly, another grey panel popped up in the centre of the screen – the **Shut Down Menu** appeared. And thirdly, the **Start Menu** closed itself.

These grey 'things' that pop up are all known as menus. To give them their full titles, they are Pop Up Menus. Later in the book we shall learn of other kinds of menus.

Notice from this pop up Shut Down Menu that of the various options listed, the 'Shut Down' option will probably be shown 'selected'. This 'selection' is indicated by the dot inside the circle on the left side (the other little circles don't

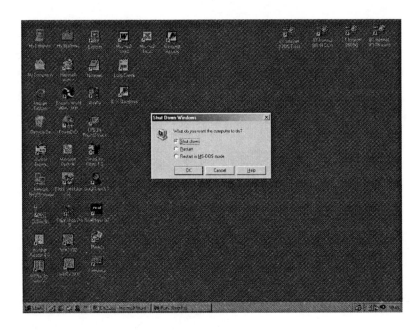

have a dot). If it is not selected, but one of the other options is, then we will have to do some manipulation.

Look carefully at the wording for the three options shown on this menu. Notice that for each one of them, a different letter is shown underlined on the wording for that option. You can manipulate which option is 'selected' by now hitting the letter key of the letter that is underlined. For example, to select 'Shut Down' you hit the S key. Let us now hit the R key to see what happens. When you have done so, you will notice that the 'Restart' option becomes selected. Now hit the S key and the selection goes back to 'Shut Down'.

Now for the final part of step 2, we need to locate and hit the **ENTER key**, but first a few words about this extra special key.

Sometimes the ENTER key is called the RETURN key because it is the equivalent of the carriage return key on a standard typewriter – we will always use the term ENTER key in this book and never call it the RETURN key. When we get to the point of doing things with word processors and the like, you will see that it does precisely the same job as a typewriter; that is, it terminates one line of writing and moves us on to the next line.

However, with computers it has another important function, as we shall shortly describe. The ENTER key is most often a peculiar shape, being normally a 'double height' key (compare it to the others and see it appears to take up space in two rows!). It is always located at the right hand edge of the standard keys of the keyboard, usually in the centre or slightly above centre. Some keyboards have it marked with the word 'Enter' on the key itself – some keyboards just use a symbol looking like a left arrow with a curious vertical 'tail' on it (↵) – some have both of these. The following picture shows us where to locate the ENTER key:

The important extra purpose of the ENTER key for a computer is to cause it to make an 'action' of some kind or another. What I mean here is it causes the computer to actually go ahead and do something. The 'what it does' depends on what takes place just before we press it. Most often, the beforehand is the setting up of the particular action that we want to happen. In our case now, we have just gone through the preliminaries for step 2 of setting up the option to be the 'Shut Down' option. But the activating of the 'Shut Down' option has to wait for some kind of trigger. This trigger is the hitting of the ENTER key. If you like, the meaning of the word 'Enter' in this context is to enter a 'command' into the computer. First we set up the command ready for action. Then we execute the command. Hitting the ENTER key is what causes the execution of the command.

Now hit the ENTER key on your own keyboard. This activates the selected option and will put the computer into an automatic shut down sequence.

Two things happen as part of the shut down sequence. First, the display changes to show you a screen telling you that the computer is shutting down, like the screen on the left picture following. Then, a few seconds afterwards, you automatically see the screen on the following right saying that you can now turn the mains power off:

The very end of the shut down sequence depends on how clever your particular computer is. Some of the latest computers can automatically turn off the power on the processor unit. You will know this if you see all the indicator lights go out on the processor unit, and see the monitor screen go blank. Other older computers just leave you with the message shown on the right above, and it is up to you to turn off the mains power yourself manually. If yours is of the latter type then switch off the mains supply to both processor unit and monitor (if it has separate power supply) using the switches on the equipment.

Finally, we have reached step 3. Switch off all mains power on wall sockets and now you are finished.

☑ **Congratulations! You have now successfully learnt how to switch a personal computer both ON and OFF.**

One last cautionary note – there are exceptional situations where sometimes you cannot follow the correct computer shut down process. This may be because your computer is experiencing a 'crash' situation (see Appendix 3 at the end of the book for more information about computer 'crashes') and it is not responding to anything that you try to do via the keyboard or mouse. Or it may be that some other event has occurred beyond your control. You might even get part way through the shut down process, and then everything appears to have frozen on the monitor screen.

If this happens to you don't be too alarmed. At some time in your future work with the computer *it will happen – believe me!* When this happens, read the section 'Appendix 2 – Not switching the computer off properly' and take the appropriate actions described therein.

The next and final section of this chapter is not so much something that you do as part of the power on and power off process. It is a few words to warn you about something that can happen at any time, and may cause you to think that the power has gone off ...

2.3 If the screen is blank but the mains power is on

Sometimes when operating your computer, you may be faced with a situation that you consider to be somewhat unusual. It may be that the power is switched on to both the central processor unit and to the monitor, and has been so for quite a while, but either:

(a) You cannot see anything shown on the monitor screen (that is, it is completely blank) ... or

(b) You have some unusual pattern or picture displayed on the monitor.

Both of the above conditions can arise on your computer if you haven't used the keyboard or the mouse for some pre-set period of time. They are nothing to worry about, but you need to know how to revert from these conditions back to the normal working state.

These conditions are known as either 'power saving' or 'screen saver' conditions. They happen if the computer has been configured (more jargon really meaning 'set up') so that the power saving or screen saving feature options are active, and you have left the computer alone without performing any action for a time greater than a pre-set value. It just switched part of itself off – very economical! The virtue of these features is to protect your computer from wasting power unnecessarily or to prevent your monitor screen from getting something known as 'screen burn'. Screen burn is a rare condition where a fixed display has been constantly showing on your monitor screen for an excessive period of time, and the image has burnt a permanent impression on the physical coating of monitor tube. Power saving is particularly important for lap-top type computers running on battery power.

When you purchased your computer, the manufacturer or supplier may have set these options for your computer as what is termed the 'default' options (remember 'default' is more jargon meaning pre-set or factory set). The setting of these options can be adjusted, but we will not attempt to cover this in the book as a first-timer. When you have more experience about how to operate the computer, you may want to explore changing this for yourself (later in the book we learn how to use something called the 'Help' feature, and this will give you more information about most aspects of the computer and changing settings).

The first action you should try in order to revert your computer back to normal state is to just to simply slide the mouse around on its mat a little without pressing any of its buttons! Watch the lights on the front of central processor unit when you have done this to see what happens. If one of these lights starts flickering on and off, then this will be the supervisory light for the hard disk unit, and it indicates that the computer is responding to the mouse movement by 'waking up' from a 'sleeping' or 'saving' condition.

Waking up takes a few seconds to occur. If the computer is in fact waking up, then eventually you will see the monitor go back to displaying the normal type of images – that is, those images that were on the screen when you last did anything with it.

The power saving or screen saver conditions are exactly this – they are a form of putting the computer to partial sleep, in order that either power is conserved or the monitor screen is protected from screen burn. Screen burn will not occur if the images on the monitor screen are frequently changing (or it is blanked out). Therefore, the screen saver active condition is one where your normal static display is temporarily replaced by another specialised self-generated display, designed to show a permanent moving image, or merely a blank screen.

41

3

The First Things to Know

3.1   About computer programs and the like

From chapter 2, we now know how to start up a personal computer and to stop it properly. Before we go any further, we need to be clear about a few more bits of jargon.

Most of us will have heard that computers use things called computer programs. However, we may not actually know what a 'program' really is or how it works. Because we will be using the word throughout the rest of the book, it is quite important that we are clear about its meaning right from the outset. We shall not need to go into any depth of technical detail about computer programs, but we shall need to appreciate what they are and what they do.

Let me also say before I throw any new jargon at you, there is going to be quite a bit of it in this section. Don't be worried that you need to memorise it. My real intention is only to get the ideas and concepts of computer programs over to you. I am going to attempt to do this by introducing the jargon at the appropriate moment in the discussion. You may then use this section as a future reference if you forget what a particular bit means. Here we go.

Programs
A **computer program** is a set of written instructions. It is a *complete* set of written instructions to achieve a particular task on the computer. We shall say more about the meaning of 'complete' shortly. A computer program is an example of **software**. It meets the test of not being able to touch it physically. You cannot touch an instruction. You might touch written symbols that convey an instruction, but you cannot touch the instruction itself!

These program instructions are written down with the intention of telling a computer processor unit what it must do as a series of steps, one step after another, in a set sequence. If I as a person were to give you the reader a series of instructions (do this, then do this, then do... etc.) I would need to use a language that we would both understand. So it is with computers. The computer processor unit has to be given instructions in a language that it understands. Not surprisingly, this language is foreign to the average person in the street, and there are several variations of different **computer languages** that programs can be written in.

Computer programs are written and stored as codes on the surface of disks. Common types of disks that you will meet today that store coded program instructions are:

- small, portable, magnetic disks inside a thin plastic jacket known as **Floppy Disks** (the word floppy is mainly historical – the outer jacket is fairly rigid)

- larger, metal cased magnetic disks inside the processor unit that we call the **Hard Drive**

- plastic disks with a metalised coating known as **CD-ROMS** -the underside surface of these reflects sparkling rainbow colours in the light.

The above pictures show examples of these forms of storage. They are (left to right) Floppy Disk, Hard Drive and CD-ROM.

With a modern computer, the number of individual instructions in a computer program that is required to achieve all the effects we can see on the monitor is vast – hundreds of millions. The computer processor unit can carry out these instructions at a very high speed (less that one millionth of a second for each one), so the effects we see on the monitor, as a consequence of performing these instructions, can appear to be continuous movement of images.

The action of carrying out the instructions of a computer program is said to be the '**running**' or '**execution**' of the program (they mean the same thing), and is the function of the central processing unit. Every program has a first instruction and a last instruction, and some others in the middle that may tell the processor unit to jump around the sequence and loop back through previous instructions. The total number of instructions from first to last makes up what we refer to as a complete program.

Programs are normally held and stored long term in a computer on the Hard Drive, which itself is in turn located inside the processor unit. New programs are initially purchased on CD-ROMS or Floppy Disks and the act of transferring the programs from these transportable disks to the Hard Drive is known as '**installing**' the program on the computer.

The clever bit that actually decodes and carries out each individual instruction of the program is the '**processor chip**', and like the Hard Drive, this chip resides within the processor unit. You may hear of various manufacturers' names used for these magical microchips, such as 'Pentium' or 'Celeron' and such like.

When running the program, the processor unit does not normally carry out the instructions by fetching them directly from where they are permanently stored on the Hard Drive. Arrangements are made when you start the program to automatically copy them to another area of temporary intermediate storage called **RAM Memory** (Random Access Memory). The following diagram illustrates this preliminary process, and the arrow represents instructions being transferred.

This first copy process is said to be '**loading**' the program. We say that the program is '**loaded**' into memory when all of the instructions for the complete program have been copied from the long-term storage place of the Hard Drive into the temporary storage space of RAM memory. Only when the program has been loaded into RAM will it run, and the start of running is automatic on completion of loading.

This next diagram illustrates the program actually running. Instructions (represented again by the black arrow) are taken one at a time from the RAM and copied inside the processor chip where they are executed. After the processor chip has finished with an instruction it discards it and gets the next one. Execution of the program continues in this way until the last program instruction has been completed.

Often, the processor chip will process an instruction and create new information that it wishes to save for a later time. It does this by writing the information back into RAM for short term saving. If the information is to be saved for long-term storage, then this will also be copied from RAM back to the Hard Drive.

When we have finished running a program, all its instructions are generally discarded from the temporary RAM. There is no need to copy program instructions back from RAM to the permanent store of the Hard Drive. After all, the original copy on the Hard Drive will still be there.

RAM memory is used in this way as an intermediate storage place for running the program because it is can be accessed at very high speed. Instructions in RAM can be 'read' (we really mean copied) into the processor chip itself at much higher speed than directly from the Hard Drive itself (like about 10,000 times faster). Because RAM has this higher access speed, then reading and executing each individual instruction takes place much faster, and the whole program 'runs' faster on the computer overall.

One other important difference between RAM and the Hard Drive is that the Hard Drive remembers things when the power is switched off, whereas RAM does not. *This is the reason why it is important to shut down your computer in the correct way – you need to action the processor unit to save all required information back from RAM to the Hard Drive, before the mains power disappears! It only knows to do this as part of the shut-down process.*

Data

We have now discussed quite a bit about computer programs. We started by saying that programs are software and that they consist of sets of instructions. We then discussed in general how these program instructions are manipulated inside the major parts of the processor unit. The time has now come to learn about another form of software that is not the same form as programs. This other form is known as computer '**data**'.

Computer 'data' is also software. If you are new to the term 'data', it simply means information. Computer data is information held in a computerised form. Such information might be the numerical figures used within calculations, or it could be the words of a written note or letter. If you type your own data into a computer it will be converted into computerised form by the keyboard and may then be stored as a code in one of the various types of storage we have previously discussed. Even picture images can be converted into computer data, as with digital cameras and document scanners. When any data it is stored within the computer, we also consider it to be software.

Having two forms of software – computer programs and computer data – we should explain now how these fit together.

A computer program on its own, as we have described it, is generally of little or no use to anyone. If a processor unit has no starting information upon which to operate, then executing the instructions of a computer program would not achieve a great deal. However, if the processor unit first finds some starting information, and then uses this as **input data** for an executing program to work upon, then the running of the program can achieve a lot. Running the program now generates what is known as **output data**.

This output data can be used in a variety of ways. The processor unit may create it in order to display it directly onto the monitor screen, or it may decide to save it for longer-term storage back on to the Hard Drive. An example of using output data directly on the Monitor screen is during the playing of a computer game. Here, the data takes the form of images, which can be quite complex in colour and shape. An example of output data saved as longer-term storage is when we create written notes and letters that we write back onto the Hard Drive. We can get even more sophisticated and use the output data from one program as the input data to another program, but we are getting into things a bit too deep for this stage of a absolute beginner's education!

Files

Before we leave the topic of computer programs and other software, I finally want to mention some final jargon by using the term '**computer file**', or '**files**'. A computer 'file' is the method by which all software is held and kept upon the Hard Drive. Let us understand this in a little more detail …

Before computers were invented, most of us had some idea of what a ordinary office 'file' was in everyday language. It was usually a buff cardboard-type folding envelope that we could tuck papers and other documents inside. In the computer world, the word 'file' has a slightly different meaning, and it is important from the outset to get this meaning clear.

In our everyday world, the words of a paper letter are collected together on a number of sheets of paper; the letter as a whole is the full collection of all sheets, and it may or may not be grouped together inside an envelope. The grouping together of the paper sheets is the complete 'thing' that we refer to as the letter. Sheets can exist on their own if we should want them to, but we often clip or staple them together to avoid them getting lost or mixed up. In the office file, we can then place several letters together inside the file. However, the smallest grouping of words in this everyday example is the paper sheet. Words cannot exist on their own. They can exist on a paper sheet and the paper sheet can exist on its own, but words by themselves cannot exist on their own.

In the computer world, here lies the difference in the meaning of the word 'file'. In computing terms, if we convert words into codes as data then the smallest grouping where we can hold the data together is called the 'file'. All computer data is held in containers called files, and the file is the smallest container we can ever have on the Hard Drive. The term file here is more equivalent to the paper sheet, if you like, but I wouldn't want to press this analogy too far because it may confuse us later when we come to look at word processing programs.

The key point is that for a computer, a file is the only thing that can exist by itself, on the storage device we call the Hard Drive. It is a container, and it is the smallest container we can have. That is not to say that files always hold small amounts of data. Far from it! They can in fact hold very large amounts of data and frequently do. But, should we wish to hold small amounts of data, then we must always use a file as the place to put it, if we want to save it on the Hard Drive.

Now if we want to group computer **files** together in some way, then we put files together inside a **folder**. You may therefore wish to think to yourself that the computer term 'folder' is more equivalent to the normal office term 'file' and you would be right. However, we shall leave this subject of files and folders until later in the book (section 8.2).

Returning to the topic of computer programs, we are now in a position to understand that a file is a container for any computer software, be it computer programs or computer data. We can now appreciate that all the instructions for a computer program will be kept in a file also. Exactly what kind of things are kept in which files is decided and dictated by the full name of the file. We shall look again into this later in chapter 8.

Résumé

Well, we have now covered quite a few bits of jargon in this section. It will pay us to just go over again through the important ones to get things clearer in our minds.

A program is a complete set of written instructions for the computer to carry out. What we mean by complete is that all instructions exist in the program to do all of a particular job in its entirety. We don't need any additional ones from anywhere else.

We might have several different types of jobs that we want to do. In which case we may need more than one program to do them. How much one program can actually achieve depends very much on how it is written, and how generous the program creator has been in the facilities provided within it.

If we have a number of programs that are supplied as a group together, then we often say that we have a **software package**. A software package does not refer to some physical item such as a parcel that might have disks inside it! It is referring to the fact that the software is a collection of programs grouped together because they have some common relationship between them. However, defining what is an individual program and what is a package of programs is becoming a tricky thing these days.

Computer programs are **software**, but they are not the only type of software. Computer '**data**' is also software. Data simply means information. Such information might be figures used in a calculation, perhaps the words of a letter, or the elements of a picture. All computer software, be it the largest program or the smallest collection of data, is held in **files** when stored on the Hard Drive. The word file in computer terms means something slightly different to its normal everyday meaning. If we want to group files together on the Hard Drive, because they are associated in some way, then we can pop them into a thing called a **folder**.

Installing a program is the action that humans perform to transfer programs from the supplied form (**CD ROMS** or **floppy disks**) onto long term storage inside the processor unit – the **Hard Drive**.

Loading a program is the action that the computer processor unit performs in copying the program instructions from permanent storage (the Hard Disk) into higher speed temporary storage called **RAM memory**, prior to running.

Running a program is the action of the computer processor unit actually carrying out the instructions of the program to do the job we want to do.

The **processor chip** is the magic device inside the processor unit that actually performs the execution of individual instructions, and it takes instructions one by one from RAM Memory as and when it needs them, starting with the first and ending with the last.

3.2 What is this thing called Windows on a computer?

When you purchase a PC (Personal Computer) these days, the chances are that something called '**Windows**' – Microsoft's operating system – will already be fitted on the computer. Our discussion will be limited to Windows-type computers. There are alternatives to 'Windows' (that is, non Windows-type computers) but we shall not cover these alternatives in this book. Today, nearly 100% of the computers that you will encounter will be Windows-type computers. It will be unusual if you come across a non-Windows-type computer.

What on earth is this thing called 'Windows' when used in the context of computers? The full answer to this seemingly simple question can get quite involved. However, in order to get started using the computer quickly, we shall give a brief initial explanation. We shall expand on this further at a later stage when we need to.

Windows is the name of a very special computer program. It is therefore software, not hardware. It is the one computer program that always automatically begins working when we power up the computer and it continues operating all the time that the computer is switched on. It never stops operating until the power is switched off. It is such a special computer program that we have a special term for a program of this type. We use the term '**operating system**' to describe this special program. *We can consider Windows to be the most fundamental computer program on which the computer relies to get all of the component parts working together as one whole unit.*

It is the 'brains', if you like, of the computer.

In the last chapter we discussed the process of powering up and the chapter ended when we had reached a stage where we could see the Desktop on the monitor screen (as shown in section 2.2), with a mouse pointer symbol also visible. It is the Windows program that is responsible for creating this screen display of the Desktop. It is also Windows that keeps track of what you do with the mouse and moves the mouse pointer symbol around accordingly. If you press any key on the keyboard, it is the Windows program that detects that a key has been pressed, and makes the appropriate response within the computer. In summary, Windows is the most fundamental program that runs on the computer and controls everything else that goes on.

In chapter 2, we discussed hardware and software and spoke of a test to determine the difference. The test was that hardware was something that could be physically touched whereas software could not be. Although we can never see, feel or touch software *directly*, the view we are given on the monitor of the Desktop is the nearest thing we can get to 'seeing' the thing called Windows itself. When you see the Desktop, you should say to yourself that you are really looking at the visible face of this fundamental program called Windows. Most of the views you will see on the monitor other than the Desktop are to do with other programs – they are not the special Windows program.

Why use the word 'Windows' for this special computer program? There is a very good reason. We shall take care here in our explanation and we need to appreciate three separate points in order to have the overall understanding …

First point. Every time we want to use the computer to do any practical work, we must employ a particular computer program written specially for the task that we have to do. Although the Windows program controls the computer itself as a whole unit, it is not the Windows program generally that will do a specific job for us. Usually, we will have another 'secondary' program for the specific task in hand. If we have many different tasks – for example writing a letter, making a drawing, working with the Internet, or maybe something else – then we need several different programs for these different jobs. That is the first point.

Second point. How is it that we can have other programs working when we know that the Windows program is always working all the time that the computer is switched on? The answer is that Windows not only controls all the hardware components of our computer, it also controls things that we should think of as 'software components'. A software component is precisely what its name says – it is software and it is a component. As we learnt in chapter 2 that a computer has multiple hardware components, so we now learn the point that we can have more than one piece of software working at any one time on the computer. Programs are software. A program is a piece of software that is complete in its own right to do some specific task or series of tasks. The Windows program is the master controlling program. It can allow other programs to run at the same time but the Windows master program is always running, keeping an eye on the overall status of the computer. Windows can even allow two, or three, or an even greater number of secondary programs to run at the same time. Now we have the second point complete – we can have more than one program working at once, and the Windows program is the master program that controls the running of any of the other programs. All the running programs appear to us to be running at the same time.

Third point. If several programs can be working at the same time, and if the master Windows program is always working, then how do we humans, as users of the computer, sort out one program from another? How do we know when we type something on the keyboard which of the many running programs might be affected by our typing? How do we know on the monitor which part of the screen is being created by which programs? The answer to these questions leads us to the third and final point. The master Windows program only allows another program to operate by creating something new on the monitor screen that we call a 'Window'. This something is squarish in shape; this something has a frame around it; and this something allows you another 'view' inside its frame – the view is the workings of the secondary program. Below is a picture of the thing that we call a window, when it has first been created by Windows to run a secondary program on top of the Desktop:

This window has been created to run a secondary program called Notepad. We do not see anything yet inside the window's 'view' so the inside of the frame appears blank white. This illustration is useful because it shows us what the basic window created for any secondary program actually looks like on its own, before that secondary program has started to do anything of its own.

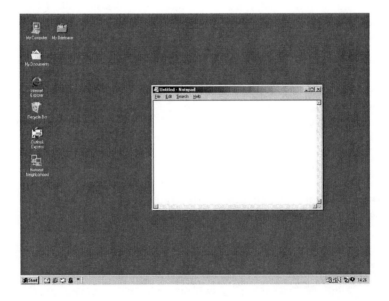

Each secondary program that we choose to set going on the computer needs its own separate 'window' in which to work. Therefore, if we have two secondary programs working at the same time, we should see two of these windows like this:

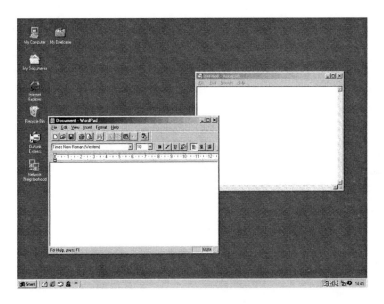

However, enough now of our brief explanation of what this thing called Windows actually is. Let us now use the computer to do some simple practical work and get a better feeling and appreciation of what we have been talking about.

4

Getting Started with the Keyboard

4.1 Using your computer for the first time – writing a note

We shall now use the computer to do the first simple job. The task is to write a shopping list in the form of a simple note.

- To make this note, we shall use a program already on your computer called 'Notepad'.
- When we have finished, we want to save the note to the Hard Drive for permanent storage, and then stop the Notepad program from running.
- Later in the chapter, we shall restart the Notepad program and learn how to edit the note that we previously saved.
- Finally, for those who have a printer available, we shall cover the action of printing the note on a printer.

Before we proceed, let us spend a few moments again discussing the computer keyboard. In section 2.2, we talked about using keys, and we said that the combined action of first pressing then releasing was known as 'hitting' a key. Whilst this term is very descriptive of the action, and it also conveys the desired swiftness of movement, it sounds a little aggressive for repeated use throughout the remainder of this book. I therefore propose, from here onwards, to use the word 'press' in connection with keys to mean both press and immediate release. If I want you not to release the key immediately, I will say 'press and hold'. Sometimes I will also use the word 'type'. By this I mean the same as 'press', but if we 'type' a key then usually you can expect that a symbol or alphabetic letter will appear on the monitor screen as a consequence of pressing it.

Now we begin our task

If you followed the instructions in section 2.2, your computer will now be switched off. Start it back up again as described by section 2.1 and reach the stage where the monitor is displaying what we call the **Desktop**. If you don't remember what the Desktop is then re-reading section 2.1 will explain and show you.

Now press the **Windows key** and the **Start Menu** should appear again. If you need a reminder of these two terms see section 2.2.

Don't forget the little trick we learnt should your keyboard be of the older type and not have a Windows key. See Appendix 1 for a reminder of what to do in this situation.

For safety, we shall now quickly refresh the action needed to reverse the effects of pressing the **Windows key**. Press the **ESC key** and observe that the **Start Menu** disappears. Okay, press the **Windows key** once more to bring up the **Start Menu**. With the **Start Menu** showing, now press the **R key**:

Your monitor should now show a new pop-up display titled **Run** as shown next.

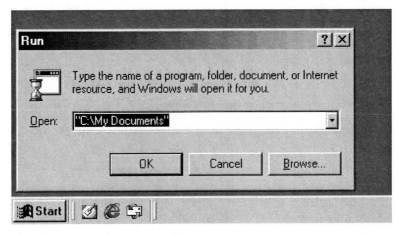

Note. Throughout this book, the illustrations are in black and white. But the Desktop on your computer has a range of colours showing. We presume

that you will be working through the various exercises as you read the book, so we say 'the blue band ...' or 'the yellow warning sign ...' because that is what <u>you will be seeing</u> on your screen, even if the book picture that illustrates the point only shows shades of grey!

If the white **Open box** in the center is empty of any words or lettering, then don't be concerned. However, more probably it will show one or more words from the last time that this feature was used by someone. If such words are shown, then they will be displayed in what we call 'reverse video', meaning that the background of the words is shown dark and the lettering is shown lighter, as in the illustration overleaf. Another term for 'reverse video' is 'highlight' (they mean the exactly the same). Take care whenever you see something 'highlighted'. It is a special state that is primed to magically make the highlighted words disappear if you then follow by typing any further alphanumeric key – as we shall very shortly see. Alphanumeric by the way is jargon to mean alphabetic or numeric. We shall learn more about 'highlight' when we come on to editing in section 4.3.

Now type the **N key**. Notice that if there was a highlighted word, it disappears completely and the Open box now shows the letter 'n' inside it. Follow this by typing the **O key**, then the **T Key**, then the **E Key** and so forth, until all the other appropriate keys for the word 'notepad' are shown inside the open box as we see in the picture below:

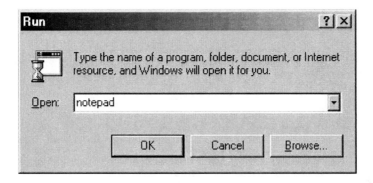

Notice that when we type words by simply pressing the keys directly, all the letters appear in non-capitals. We call non-capitals 'lower case'. Not surprisingly, we call capital letters 'upper case'. In most instances that will arise with a computer, there is no material difference if you use lower case or upper case, or even some mixture of the two. The computer will always interpret words as meaning the same thing in general (clever things are computers!). The only times that the 'case' matters is when we are writing letters and the presentation quite rightly should be as in normal written English, or if we are typing something called a 'password'. Passwords are very special words and usually case *does matter*, but more about passwords some other time.

Our actions to this point have prepared the computer by specifying which program we want to run – we have specified that we want to run a program called 'notepad'. The computer has not yet taken any notice of what we have typed, other than to present the letters on the monitor screen in the **Open box**. We now need to tell the computer to treat our actions as a command. This job is the one of the functions of the **ENTER key**. If you need to refresh your memory which is the **ENTER key**, here is where it is located:

You may also notice that there is another key on the extreme right of the keyboard which also says it is the **ENTER key**. This alternative key and the normal ENTER key (shown in the above picture) do the same job. This second key is part of the numeric keypad grouping and is for the convenience of speedy typist operators when entering columns of numeric data. We shall not normally use this second alternative key, but use the more general one shown above.

Press the general **ENTER key** and wait for a few seconds. The computer now activates the request we have made to 'run' the program called Notepad. Suddenly, a large window will pop up on the screen and the previous pop up displays will disappear, leaving the Desktop as a background apparently behind it. Don't be concerned if the exact size and position of this new large window is slightly different on your own computer, however. Your monitor screen should now look something like the picture over the page:

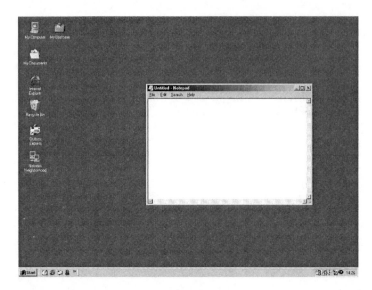

There are quite a few important things that we can learn from this new large window that has popped up, but we shall leave most of it till later. Remember though how we spoke in section 3.2 of running secondary programs while the Windows program itself was still running and was keeping master control of all the hardware and software of the computer. It is the Windows program that we effectively see in the background, represented by the **Desktop**. It is the Notepad program that we now see in the foreground, represented by this new large object called a window.

Notice in the large white area of the Notepad window that there is a flashing black vertical line. We call this line the 'cursor' and it shows us where any letters that we type will be placed. We shall now start to do this.

Type the **S key**, then the **H key** and so forth until you have completed typing the word 'shopping'. Notice that we are not getting concerned about 'upper case' lettering (capitals) yet. Now press the Space Bar key once. This is the very long key in the bottom middle of the keyboard shown below:

Space Bar Key

Now continue the line of type by typing out the word 'list'. Press the **ENTER key** once and you will notice that the cursor now moves to the start of the next available line. This is the second function of this special key, that is, to act like the carriage return key of a typewriter. Your monitor should display something like the picture below with the cursor flashing at the start of the second line:

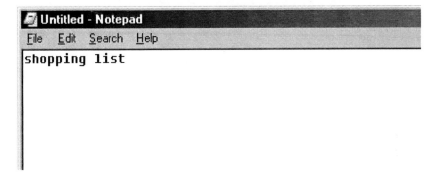

Now press the **Minus key** (the '-' key), which is located just to the right of the number zero key as shown in the next picture:

Press this key repeatedly several times. We are now forming a crude underlining for the above line. Press the **'-' key** until it has underlined up to the letter 't'. Now press the **ENTER key** again to go to the start of the third line. Press the **ENTER key** yet again to go to the start of the fourth line.

Now we will use a capital letter. If you have used a typewriter before, you are probably familiar with the fact that pressing and holding down the **SHIFT key**, whilst at the same time typing the desired letter key, is the way to form capital letters. As there are two ENTER keys, so it is with the SHIFT key – there are in fact two of these, also. One is the **Left SHIFT key** and the other the **Right SHIFT key**. Both of these are shown below:

If you are right-handed then press and hold the Left SHIFT key down with the left hand and type the L key with your right hand. If you are left-handed, hold the Right SHIFT key down with the right hand and type the L key with your left hand. Observe that you now have a capital 'L' displayed on the screen.

Continue typing the line to read 'Large tin of baked beans', and complete the line by pressing the **ENTER key**. The cursor should now be flashing at the start of the fifth line, and our Notepad window should show something like the following picture:

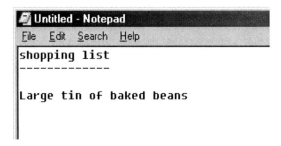

We shall now see how to correct or alter any text that we have previously typed. We are going to change the word 'Large' into the word 'Small'.

Locate the group of four arrow keys on your keyboard, which are situated as a group on their own just to the right of the Right SHIFT key.

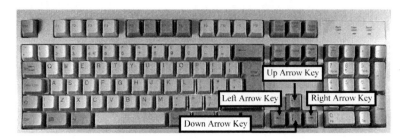

Press the **Up Arrow key** once and see the 'cursor' on the screen move up to a position just before the capital L letter in the word 'Large'. Now press the **Right Arrow key** several times to position the cursor to just after the 'e' in the word 'Large', but just before the space which follows it. We are now going to use a key called the **BackSpace key**. This key is shown below and is normally a large key just above the normal ENTER key:

Press the Backspace key several times to remove all the letters from the word 'Large'. The cursor is now positioned back at the start of the line. Now type the word 'Small', remembering to use the appropriate SHIFT key for the capital 'S' letter, but don't press the ENTER key when you have done so. The cursor should be flashing just after the last 'l' but in front of the space that follows it.

At this point, we have completed text editing using the BackSpace key to 'rub' letters out. Now we shall use a similar but slightly different key to also rub letters out, called the **Delete key** (your keyboard may have it marked just as Del instead of Delete). It is the way it does the rubbing out that is the slight difference. The location of the Delete key is also shown in the previous picture.

From the group of four arrow keys, press the Up Arrow Key repeatedly to move the cursor upwards to the start of the word 'shopping', that is, to position it to the very beginning of the first line. Now press the Delete key. Notice that the letter 's' in the word 'shopping' disappears and all the other letters move sideways to the left by one position. Now type a capital 'S'. Notice that all the letters move back right again one position, and the cursor is positioned between the 'S' and the 'h'.

We have now witnessed the subtle difference between using the **BackSpace key** and the **Delete key** in operation. They both achieve a similar effect, but the **BackSpace key** will always delete the letter that is immediately to the left of the cursor position, and the **Delete key** will always delete the letter to the right of the cursor position. You should practice the use of both these two keys yourself (later in your own time) until they are both familiar and second nature to you.

See if you can now complete your shopping list to include 'Large tin of peas' and 'Small white loaf' on lines following the beans. Use the arrow keys in the group of four arrow keys to move to the positions where you want to place the words, and then type the letters you are trying to add. If you make a typing error, you now should be able to use either the Backspace key or the Delete key to make corrections. Your completed work should look something like this:

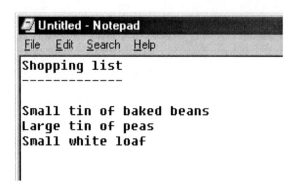

In moving the cursor around the lines, you may have noticed that you can only move the cursor to places where either a letter or space has been previously typed. You cannot, for instance, move the cursor to the far right of the word 'beans'. It looks as though you should be able to, but try it now and see what happens. Use the appropriate arrow keys to move around the lines.

Well, you probably noticed that as soon as you tried to move further to right of the word 'beans' then the cursor jumped to the start of the next line! This is a limitation of the simple program called Notepad. When we start to use more sophisticated word processing type programs, then you will see that this limitation is not present.

In our example with Notepad, if you really wished to move to the space to the right of the word 'beans', you can do it but you need to add blank spaces first. Try this now by positioning the cursor just to the right of the 's' in 'beans', and then press the SpaceBar key five times. When you have inserted the five spaces, then type '(Heinz)'. You will need to use the appropriate **SHIFT key** (according to your handed-ness) and the number **9 key** and number **0 key** in order to achieve the bracket symbols.

By the way, if you haven't spotted it by now, it is another rule of the book from here onwards that when I want you to type something specifically then I shall put the exact text within quotation marks. I therefore am asking you to type the brackets in '(Heinz)' but not the quotation marks themselves. Should I want you to type something including quotation marks, then I shall explicitly say so.

Your final note should look something like the following picture:

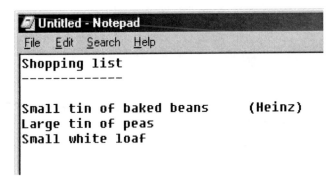

Don't fuss if it is not identical but you should endeavour at some later time to polish your keyboard skills so that you can create the precise presentation you wish to make.

Now that we have the note complete, we will learn how to save it to the Hard Drive for retrieval at any subsequent time we wish.

4.2   Saving the note to the Hard Drive

We will now save the note that you have created in section 4.1. We will do this by following a series of direct instructions without explaining the reasoning behind them. When we have finished we will review the process and give some reasoning.

Before we save the note, just take a second to observe your monitor and at the very top of the Notepad window, in the dark blue line that forms the top of the window, the words 'Untitled – Notepad' are shown. This line is known as the Title Bar for the window. We will come back to this point later.

Now we follow the saving procedure. Start by pressing and holding the **Left ALT key**. This key is located to the left of the spacebar as shown below:

With the **Left ALT key** held down, now press and release the **F key**. Now release the **Left ALT key**. Notice that a **drop down Menu** appears as shown below:

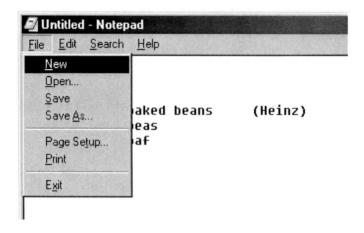

Now press the **A key**. This causes the 'Save As' selection from the menu to be activated, and a **Save As menu** then pops up like the follow picture.

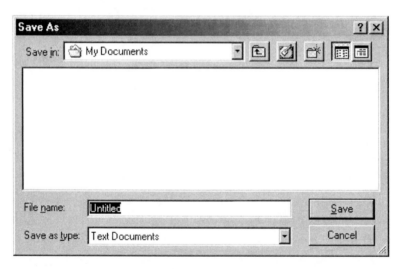

Notice that the word 'Untitled' is highlighted in blue in the **File name box**. Now type the following phrase exactly as shown, but remember not to include the quotation marks (as per our new rule!) ...

'Shopping List Number 1'

Make sure you use the correct capital letters and spaces, but no space after the number one at the end of the line. If you make a typing mistake, you can use the Arrow keys, the BackSpace key or the Delete key – as you wish – to make corrections.

Now press the **ENTER key**. Observe that after a second or two the **Save As pop-up menu** now disappears and the monitor shows the Notepad window again just as it was before we started to save the note. The note that we created is now saved permanently to the Hard Drive.

Let us now return to the subject of the **Title Bar**. If you are keen observer, you might have noticed there is one tiny difference – but a very important one – to the state of the Notepad window, from the way it was before we saved it. At the very top of the Notepad window, the phrase 'Shopping List Number 1 – Notepad' has appeared in the Title Bar, whereas previously you may remember it said 'Untitled – Notepad'. This change to the Title bar does in fact tell you, as a user of the computer, that the note has now been 'saved'.

But in what form has it been saved on the Hard Drive?

Well, if you remember our discussion at the end of section 3.1, you might recall that we talked about the meaning of the term '**computer file**'. We spent a bit of time explaining that the word '**file**' in computing sense has a slightly different interpretation to the same word when used in ordinary everyday office language. We concluded by stating that a computer file is a container. It was the smallest container for any computer software, be it computer programs or computer data, if we wanted to save such software to the Hard Drive. We are now in a position to answer the question about in what form was our note saved.

Returning to our note, it should be appreciated that this is a very good example of **computer data**. It actually started as a collection of physical key presses, which the keyboard converted into internal computer codes. These codes were gathered and collected by the Notepad program, and translated and displayed again in human-readable form as letters and words in the Notepad 'window' on the monitor screen. By running the Notepad program, the computer processor unit was able to take keyboard codes as **input data** and link them all together, one after the other, to display them again as **output data**. When we see them displayed on the monitor screen, they are actually stored in a part of **RAM Memory**, and the program is looping around several program instructions, continuously picking the codes up and displaying them inside the Notepad window. We humans cannot see the tremendous speed that this is happening at, and we simply think that there is a permanent display all the time on the screen.

When we saved the note, all the processor unit had to do was to create a new file somewhere on the Hard Drive, open it up and copy the letters and words sequentially (one code at a time) into this open file, then close the file when it was finished. Our computer data file therefore is nothing more than a sequence of computer codes strung out somewhere on the Hard Drive. It is the clever bit of creating the file, however, which keeps track of which code follows another, and of associating a name to the file (in our case we named it 'Shopping List Number 1'). There are times when files can get corrupted and things get very mixed up. Fortunately, these occurrences are not as frequent today as in the early days of personal computing. And today, we have special computer programs designed to sort such mix-ups out. But this is getting into a bit more detail than we should be doing for absolute beginners! We shall leave it at this point.

Résumé

Before we conclude this section on saving the note, let us now quickly review the key presses we did to save the note so that we have a clear understanding of what went on.

Having first completed entering words for our note in section 4.1, we began section 4.2 at the point of seeing them in the Notepad window. Let us list our actions from that moment forward...

Action 1

First we pressed and held the **Left ALT key**. Then we type the **F key** and released it. Then we released the **Left ALT key**. This combined action caused a **drop down Menu** to appear. What we were actually doing here was to activate one of the '**Menu Items**' listed on the grey '**Menu bar**' of the Notepad window. The Menu Item in question is called the '**File Menu**' (don't be confused with our previous use of the word file, though there is a connection). Let us just see where this actually is. In this next picture, observe the horizontal grey strip just under the blue strip:

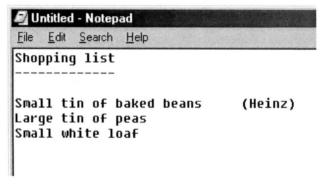

This grey strip (in the jargon we call it a bar) has four words written on it – '**File**', '**Edit**', '**Search**' and '**Help**'. Each word has the first letter underlined.

The underlining indicates a special feature. It means that used together in conjunction with the **Left ALT key**, the key corresponding to the underlined letter will activate that specific **Menu Item**. We used the **F key** with the **Left ALT key**. We therefore selected the '**F**ile' menu option – and not the '**E**dit' one, not the '**S**earch' one, nor the '**H**elp' one. After we did so, we saw the **File Menu** in its full glory as a **drop down Menu** list. This is shown again below:

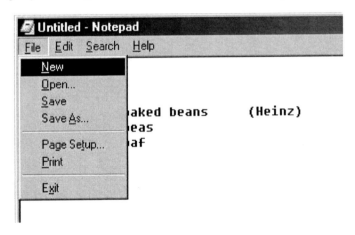

Action 2

Next, we pressed the **A key**. If you look carefully at the above picture, you can see that of each possible option in the **drop down list**, the only one with the letter 'A' underlined is the one which says '**Save As...**'. This is telling us that we can activate this option by pressing the **A key**. We don't need to the use the **Left ALT key** now. Once we have activated the **drop down list**, the computer knows that we are not typing the letter 'A' as a part of the text of our note and it will interpret the pressing of the A key as a command instead – clever little computer! (By the way, in Action 1, if we had not used the **Left ALT key** in conjunction with pressing the **F key** then the computer couldn't have known whether we wanted to use the **File Menu**, or whether we intended the letter 'f' to be typed into the note itself.)

Action 3

This action is naming our file. The pressing of the **A key** in Action 2 activated the '**Save As...**' pop-up menu and we now show that again over the page.

There are a lot of things on this pop-up menu that we don't really want to get into at this early stage of our learning. To fully understand what we are looking at, we need to know more about files and folders, and I am covering these in Chapter 8.

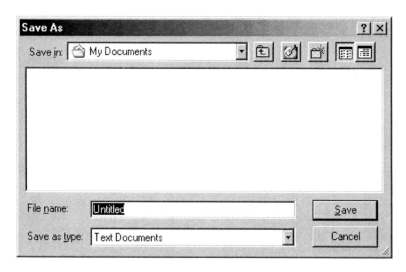

The only important bit to review is that when this pop-up menu first shows, the word 'Untitled' appears highlighted in the **File name box**. We recall from a former discussion in section 4.1 that 'highlighted' things must be treated with a little care. If we immediately follow by typing in any letter or number key from the keyboard, then whatever was highlighted instantly disappears, and we see only the symbol of the typed key. That is okay for us in this case, because we really want to get rid of the name 'Untitled' and replace it with our own name for the file we are creating. We therefore went ahead and typed the phrase 'Shopping List Number 1'.

Simply typing the name in the **File name box** didn't by itself finish the job. We had then to press the **ENTER key**, which we recall is the key that issues the command to tell the processor unit to go ahead and save our note in a new file.

We have now concluded our review of the actions for permanently saving our work to a file on the Hard Drive. We can safely at this point leave our work for the day and shut the computer down if we wish. I recommend that you do so, because we have learnt quite a lot in these first two sections of Chapter 4. It is better not to try take too much in all at once. However, if you do have an appetite for further work then you might like to close the Notepad program and start section 4.1 over again – but this time you can create your own note or letter, and save it using your own title for the **File name**.

Whether you choose to shut the computer down, or you try making your own notes, you first need to know how to close the Notepad program. We know that the Notepad program is still running because you can see its window on the monitor screen.

A very quick way to close any program window is to use the **Left ALT key** in conjunction with pressing a special key called the **F4 key**. The location of the **F4 key** is shown in this next picture:

We start by looking at the monitor screen. We should notice that, after saving the note to the Hard Drive, all of the **drop down Menu lists** and **pop-up Menus** have disappeared. The Notepad window is back to showing us just the words and letters we have typed from section 4.1.

Now press and hold the **Left ALT key**. Then press and then release the **F4 key**. Now release the **Left ALT key**.

There we have it! The Notepad window has now vanished completely from the monitor screen. We are back looking at the **Desktop**.

This last action of closing the Notepad window is something important that we mentioned in the computer shutdown process of section 2.2. In that section we stated the <u>three correct steps</u> needed for shut down. Step 1 was that we should first close down any particular programs that we know are currently running. Well, now we know how this is done. Later in the book we will have more than one program running. We will therefore need to repeat the closing action using the **Left ALT key/F4 key** combination for each of the programs individually.

If you do want to shut the computer down, follow on now with Steps 2 and 3 of section 2.2. Re-read that section again if you are unsure of the procedure.

In the next section, 4.3, we learn how to edit a note that was previously saved.

4.3   Editing a previously created note

We begin by assuming that you had a rest after section 4.2 and shut down the computer correctly. Start up the computer again to reach the **Desktop** stage.

Start up the Notepad program once again. We did this in section 4.1 by pressing the **Windows key**, then the **S key**, in order to get the **Start Menu** to appear. Then we pressed the **R key** to get the **Run Menu**. In the **Open box** we then typed the word 'notepad'. (Refer back to the beginning of section 4.1 if you need reminding about this sequence of events).

You might notice when you first see the Run Menu this time that the word 'notepad' already exists in the Open box. The computer usually remembers this word as the last command that you used in this box, providing that the computer shut-down process occurs correctly.

With the word 'notepad' showing in the Open box, we only need then to press the **ENTER key** in order to get the Notepad window to pop-up, and we can then start using the program.

When Notepad first starts running, it always starts with a clean window. Our next job is to reload the note we created previously, so that we can start to edit it further. We do this using the same **File Menu** as we did in section 4.2 when we saved the note. If you have correctly managed to get the Notepad window showing on the monitor it will look like this next picture:

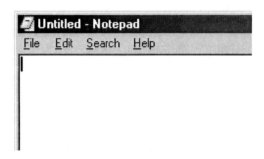

Press and hold the **Left ALT key**. Now press the **F key**. Now let go of the **Left ALT key**. The **File Menu** now drops down, as it did before when we saved the note to the Hard Drive in section 4.2. Your monitor now looks like this:

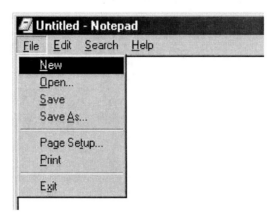

By the way, it is time for us to make another rule. It gets very tedious to say '*Press and hold the **Left ALT** key. Now press the **F** key. Now let go of the **Left ALT** key*'. Instead, we will introduce the following simplified notation of '**ALT+F**' to mean the same thing. Similarly, if I use '**ALT+E**' then I am really meaning '*Press and hold the Left ALT key. Now press the E key. Now let go of the Left ALT key*', and so on.

In the same way, if I use '**SHIFT+S**' then I am asking you to '*Press and hold the **Left SHIFT** key. Now press the **S** key. Now let go of the **Left SHIFT** key*' (or if you are left handed, you can use the Right SHIFT key instead, but don't try swapping the Left ALT key for the ALT Gr key – that won't do!).

From the point where we have the **File Menu** dropped down, press the **O Key** to activate the '**Open…**' menu list option. As before in section 4.2, we did not need the ALT key once we had started using the File Menu.

Now we should see the Open pop-up Menu screen appear as in the next picture:

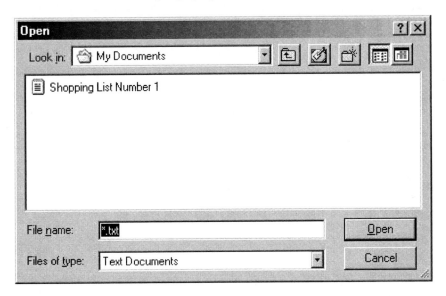

Your own monitor may show something slightly different to the above picture, if there are more **files** that have been previously saved. However, you should be able to see somewhere in the large white central area a little icon like the above one with the words 'Shopping List Number 1' written to the right side of it.

Both the icon and the title words jointly represent the **file** which we created in section 4.1 and which was saved to the Hard Drive in section 4.2. This file is actually saved inside a **folder** called 'My Documents'. You may remember from section 3.1 that we said that folders could be used to group computer files together. We know the name of the folder because it is given to us in the '**Look**

in box' just underneath the blue **Title bar**.

We shall learn later that **folders** can also be placed together inside other **folders**. Such a hierarchy of a file inside a folder, which in turn is inside yet another folder, is called a **file structure**. The placing of one thing inside another in computing is called **nesting**, and it is very similar conceptually to the 'Russian Dolls' idea with the exception that you can have more than one 'doll' at any level of the structure.

One of the biggest and most frustrating problems that absolute beginners have with computers is finding work that they have previously saved on their Hard Drive. If you get to grips with understanding the nature of files and folders and the idea of nesting, then you will make life a great deal easier for yourself (and less stressful!). We shall cover this more in chapter 8.

Returning to the previous picture of the **Open Menu**, you should also notice that the **File name box** underneath the large white central area is 'highlighted' and is displaying the symbol/letters '*.txt'. Now type the phrase 'Shopping List Number 1' from the keyboard. Observe that as soon as you start typing, your new lettering replaces the previously highlighted text.

If you make a mistake in your typing, don't forget to use the **Arrow** keys, **BackSpace** and **Delete** keys to correct it.

Now press the **ENTER** key. Remind yourself that by doing so, you are effectively issuing your command to the computer saying 'Open the file called 'Shopping List Number 1''.

If you did things correctly, you should now see your former note again displayed in all its glory as in the next picture:

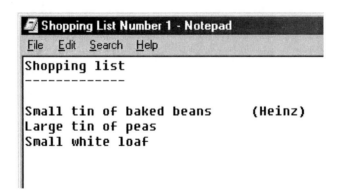

Note that the blue **Title bar** at the top this time has the name we gave to the note already displayed. If we make any more changes to the note, we cannot now assume just by seeing this title that the computer has saved these changes, as we did in section 4.2. However, from this point onwards, the computer itself will give us a warning message if we try and close down the Notepad program without saving them (as we shall shortly see!).

Okay. Let us imagine that we have just remembered some more items that we want to add to the shopping list.

At this point, the cursor should be flashing in the top left corner of the displayed text. This is always the case when we first open a file that we have previously saved (notice that we can now talk about our 'note' as a computer file because we know that this is how our computer deals with it!). Now press the **Down Arrow** key several times to place the cursor at the start of a new line, after the 'Small white loaf'. When you have arrived there, type the phrase 'Jar of strawberry jam' and then press the **ENTER** key.

Follow your new added line with two more saying – 'Tub of butter' and '4 slices of ham'. Remember, to always press the **ENTER** key when you need to complete the line and start a new one. We recall that this is the second way in which the **ENTER** key can be used, that is to act like the 'carriage return' lever of a typewriter in positioning us at the beginning of a new line.

Okay, so much for editing our note. Now we reach the moment where we want to save the changes we have made back into the original file as it is stored on the Hard Drive.

We need to again use the drop down **File Menu**. Therefore we press **ALT+F** (remember our last invented rule for using the ALT key in combination with the F key!). Again we see this appear on the monitor, as in the following picture:

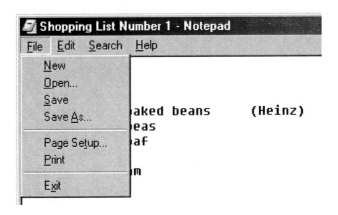

Now press the **S key** and watch carefully what happens! You might at first think that you have not done it right. What happens is that the drop down File menu just seems to disappear, and you are back at the main Notepad window looking at the note again.

This all happened so quickly. Why didn't we see anything more? Well, from an absolute beginner's point of view, it might have been nice if we had received some better indication that our recent changes had been saved back to the Hard

Drive. However, from a more experienced user's viewpoint, the argument is that it is unnecessary to show anything more. The computer already knows what the name of the file is to hold our note in, so it very, very quickly does the 'saving' and then goes back to the point where we can carry on making changes if we want to.

Having now done the editing to our note that we wished to, we could at this point close the Notepad program and get back to looking just at the Desktop. However, I am keen to demonstrate to you, before we finish our editing, what happens if you make some changes and you don't save them.

You may remember I said earlier in this section that we couldn't rely on seeing the name of the note in the blue Title bar as proof that all changes to the file have been saved to the Hard Drive. Let us now make one last change and see what happens if we forget to save the changes.

Add a final line to the end of the shopping list – 'Box of matches'. Remember you should always press the **ENTER** key to finish off the line cleanly, and position the cursor back at the start of the next line (it is bad practice not to do this for all your letters and notes).

Now we shall try and close down the Notepad program without saving this last line. Press **ALT+F4** at this point.

You should now see a warning message appear over the top of the note, which looks something like this:

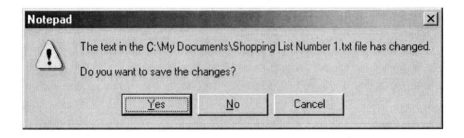

The actual message you get might be slightly different in its wording. Don't concern yourself if it is. However, you ought to notice that the yellow and black exclamation symbol appears on this message. This symbol is telling you that the message is a 'warning' and if you don't take appropriate action then something undesirable could happen. The undesirable 'something' in this instance is that we might lose any changes to the note that we have made since the last time it was definitely saved correctly.

Notice also in the above warning message that we are presented with three buttons that are different options we can take. When we become experienced at using the mouse-pointing device, we can point and then 'click' the mouse over the top of these buttons to select the option we want. However, we have not reached that stage yet, so we shall make our choice using keys from the keyboard.

The underlined letters on the first two buttons are indicating to us that we can use the Y or N keys, as appropriate, to choose the option we wish to select. Now press the **Y key**. Almost instantly, the warning message disappears and the Notepad window closes down. What has now happened is that the latest changes were first saved back to the file on the Hard Drive, then our **ALT+F4** command to close the Notepad program was recognized and carried out.

We have now successfully edited and resaved our shopping list. If you have a printer attached to your computer, we will now print this out in section 4.4. If you don't have a printer attached then skip forward to chapter 5.

4.4   Printing the note on a printer

If you are fortunate enough to have a printer attached to your computer, you can print out the shopping list note using the procedure outlined in this section. However, the printer must previously have been correctly installed on your computer in respect of both the hardware and the software requirements. There is a little test that we shall shortly describe, which should give you some indication if this has been done or not.

Setting up a printer from scratch is beyond the scope of this book, and not recommended for the absolute beginner. If it has not been done for you when you purchased your computer then you will need to either read the printer manual very carefully, or enlist some expert help from your supplier. I recommend the latter! Section 1.5 of this book does tell you how to connect the printer to the processor unit, but it assumes that all the general preparation of the printer, such as inserting ink cartridges, loading software and the like, has already been done.

Check now that mains power for your printer is turned on. You should see some indication that it is receiving power, probably by a green indicator light on the front panel. When a printer is first powered on, it usually has a preparation routine of its own that it goes through before it is ready for use. You may hear some whirring and clicking noises taking place automatically while this occurs. The green power indicator light usually flashes on and off during this stage to indicate that the printer is not yet ready for use. After a few minutes, the printer will settle down and go quiet, and the green indicator light will stop flashing and be permanently illuminated.

If printer paper needs inserting then you should do so at this point, in accordance with the printer manual.

Okay. We will assume now that the printer is primed and ready for action.

To begin printing our shopping list, you need to have the Notepad program running and the note opened and displayed in the Notepad window. If you have followed the editing exercise in section 4.3 then Notepad will currently be closed down. You therefore need to open it again using the same instructions given in section 4.3 up to the stage just before we started editing the text.

With Notepad running again, and the shopping list note loaded, your monitor will be showing something like the following picture:

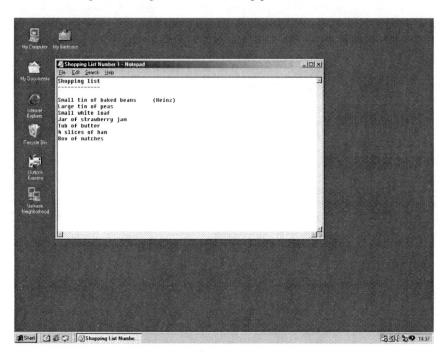

The cursor should be flashing in the top left-hand corner of the Notepad window.

Now press **ALT+F** and you will see the drop **down File Menu** appear again, as seen on the opposite page:

Notice that the fifth and sixth options listed in the menu are '**Page Setup…**' and '**Print**'. We should appreciate at this point that we can select these options by pressing either the **T key** or **P key** respectively (we know this because we see that these letters are underlined in the wording of the menu).

You should also be able to see the wording of both these options clearly as black writing on a grey background, as shown in our picture above. If for any reason the **Print** option appears unusual in that the wording is shown in a strange grey/white lettering instead of black, then this means that the printer and its software have not yet been correctly set up on your computer. This is the little test we mentioned at the start of this section to indicate whether or not the printer has been previously set up ready for use. If your computer is in this

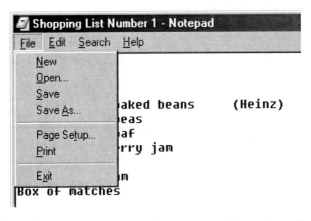

unusual condition then you cannot use the printer until you have it properly installed.

Incidentally, you may come across other menus in the future where the wording of a particular option is shown in a grey/white lettering instead of black. We say that options are 'greyed out' if they appear like this. Any option that appears greyed out is not available for you to select at that moment, and there will be some specific reason why not. If you really need to use a greyed out option then you must first resolve the cause of the why the computer is displaying it in this way. After you resolve the cause, the option will then appear in black and be available for use.

We presume that your printer has been set up correctly and we continue the discussion.

The **Page Setup...** option allows us to make some preliminary settings to alter how the printing will happen on our printer – if we want to – before printing takes place. The **Print** option is the one that actually does the printing.

Just a small point to discuss in passing, you may notice that some of the options in the drop down File Menu have three little dots shown at the end of the wording. For example the Page Setup... option has them, but the Print option does not. The significance of these three little dots is that these options have even further pop-up menus for you to make choices, whereas the others have not. This is a general rule with menus and you may notice this in other circumstances that we will come across.

Before we go ahead do the printing, let us take a quick look at the **Page Setup...** option. At this point, with the **File Menu** showing, press the **T** key. A **Page Setup Menu** should now pop up looking something like this next picture:

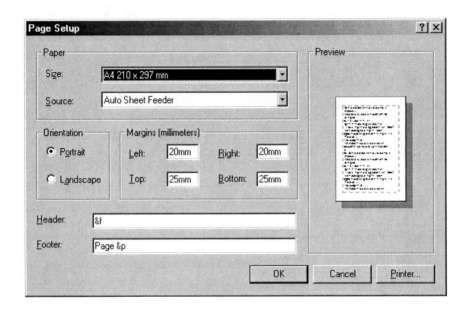

The menu displayed on your own computer may be slightly different. However, it should have similar features to that shown above, so we will briefly look at these and you may need to re-interpret the discussion for your own particular menu.

Notice first of all that different aspects of setting a page have groupings made by drawing rectangles with a grey/white outline. These groups have the titles – '**Paper**', '**Preview**', '**Orientation**' and '**Margins**'. Within each group there are a number of controls that can vary different choices of value for that control.

Notice also that each control has a name, and we see that in every name that one of the letters has been underlined. If we use the **ALT key** in combination with the letter key, for example, if we use **ALT+A** or **ALT+P** then we can vary the choice of which control we have selected (read section 4.3 if you have forgotten our rule about using the **ALT key** and the '+' symbol). For example, if we went ahead and pressed **ALT+A** then this would change the selection of 'Orientation' to **Landscape**. If we then pressed **ALT+O** this would change it back to **Portrait**.

By the way, if you haven't met the term Landscape before it means that the paper is printed with words appearing left to right across the widest width of the paper (the paper being wider than it is tall), rather than across the narrower width (which is known as Portrait). Effectively, these are ways of turning the printing around on the paper, so that we get the finished result in the direction that we would like to see it on the paper.

That is really as much as I want to say about the Page Setup Menu at this time. Making adjustments to control values becomes easier when we learn how to use the mouse-pointing device, so we shall leave such tasks until that time.

At this point, press the ESC key once (the key in the very top left-hand corner of the keyboard) to 'Cancel' and make the Page Setup Menu disappear. This will return you to seeing just the text of our shopping list note in the Notepad window once more.

Now press **ALT+F** to drop down the **File Menu** again. Now press the **P key** to select the **Print** option. Things will probably happen very quickly after the key press. If you fail to see all the things that I shall now describe, then the reason might be that they happened far too quickly for you to witness. Don't be concerned if you miss them. The only important event is to see the printed page produced at the end.

If all is well at this point, you will first see the **File Menu** disappear and then something will quickly flash up on the Notepad Window only to vanish just the same. This something is a message telling you that your note is now being printed. It may seem a bit pointless disappearing so quickly, but that is only because our note is very short. In the future, when you come to print much longer documents, then this message will be visible for a longer period and it provides you with feedback that your command to print is being accepted by the computer. Also, down in the right-hand corner of your monitor screen, you might see a pop-up display that shows you the 'progress' of the printing.

On the printer itself, you may notice the green indicator light begin flashing on and off again. The flashing is a signal that the printer is receiving data from the processor unit down the cable at that moment. The printer has some **RAM Memory** of its own, and it saves up the data (we call it '**buffering**') so that it can receive it all from the processor unit even before it has actually printed it out. In this way, the printer will not lose any printing information, and it allows the processor to send at high speed even though the physical printing process is much slower.

Very soon, you will hear the printer's mechanical bits jump into life. The top sheet of paper will be drawn inside the body of the printer, and then eventually re-emerge again with text now clearly visible as printing on the page. When all the text has been printed then the paper will be ejected from the printer body, and voila! – there is your shopping list now neatly presented as the printed word!

This concludes our discussion of printing the shopping list for the time being. All we need to do now is close down the Notepad window and return to the Desktop, which we do by pressing **ALT+F4**.

The next topic we shall cover in Chapter 5 is how to use the mouse pointing device.

5

Getting Started with the Mouse

5.1   Using a mouse pointing-device

So far, we have learnt a little about working with a computer using just the keyboard.

Although you can achieve quite a lot using the keyboard on its own, there are many tasks that become simpler and quicker if you also learn how to use the mouse pointing-device. You do need to learn how to get the best from both of these methods of interacting with the computer, if you are to become truly proficient.

The term 'mouse pointing-device' is somewhat cumbersome, so from hereon we shall simply refer to it as the mouse. With its thin flexible cable connecting it with the processor unit, and a small shaped body to fit the palm of your hand, it is not hard to see why it is so-called.

The main idea behind the mouse is that we have a gadget that we can control by hand in order to move an image of a pointer symbol around on the monitor screen. We can then use this pointer on the screen to point at, select or to manipulate many kinds of other screen objects, like icons for example.

When we are displaying the **Desktop** on the monitor, the pointer symbol takes the shape of an arrow like the following:

However, we know that it can, under different circumstances, take the shape of different symbols. For example, we always notice during the power up procedure for the computer that it first appears as an hourglass symbol, changing shape into the arrow symbol when the computer is ready to use. As we shall see later, there are a number of other shapes that the pointer can take. These other shapes are to assist the computer user in doing different tasks according to the context.

The mouse works in the following way. On the underside of it is a rubber ball that is retained internally but is free to rotate in any direction. In normal use, we slide the whole body of the mouse over the flat surface of the mouse-mat and friction of the ball against the mat causes the ball to rotate. Electronic sensors inside the mouse pick up this ball movement and transmit signals back to the processor unit. The processor unit reinterprets these signals and causes the pointer symbol to move about in sympathy over the display area of the monitor screen.

By carefully controlling the movement of the mouse with one hand, we can make the mouse pointer travel almost anywhere over the monitor display area. When we slide the mouse in a direction away from us, then the pointer moves up the screen and when we slide it towards us then the pointer moves down the screen. If we slide it to the left side then the pointer will also appear to move left, and vice versa. The actual distance travelled by the pointer depends directly on how far we move the mouse. The whole system is adjusted so that the pointer can move from one side of the screen to the other by a relatively small movement of the mouse within the area of the mouse mat. Just occasionally, we might run out of room on the mat and have to pick the mouse up completely and reposition it towards the centre. If we pick it up complete, then the rubber ball stops rotating and the pointer remains stationary on the screen. When we put the mouse down again we can continue the movement. After a while, such repositioning becomes second nature.

In the next section we will start our first practical exercises with the mouse. There we shall learn the fine art of how to control the movement of the screen pointer in just the manner we want it. First, though, we should describe some more controls on the mouse, and how to hold it correctly.

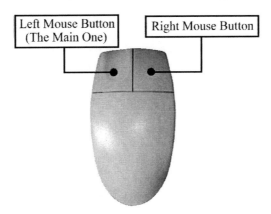

| Left Mouse Button (The Main One) | Right Mouse Button |

On the shaped body of the mouse there are usually two click-type switches that we call buttons (some models have an extra third button in the centre). To distinguish these from each other, we shall refer to them as the **left mouse**

button and the **right mouse button** (if your model has three then the middle one is the **centre mouse button**). As a beginner, we shall concentrate mainly on the left mouse button. This is the main one and is used for ninety-nine per cent of the time, when doing tasks with the computer. Let us now discuss the correct way to hold the mouse. In what follows, the over-riding consideration is that it should be comfortable. If your own personal way is slightly different to my description, then don't worry, but do make sure that you don't start with bad habits that cause you to have trouble with clicking the buttons. If you start to struggle with next section's exercises, then the chances are that you are not holding the mouse properly.

The very first thing to decide is with which hand are you going to hold the mouse. Make your choice according to your handedness and ensure that the mouse and its **mouse-mat** are placed to that same side of the keyboard. Re-route the mouse cable around the monitor if you need to.

For the next part of the discussion, we shall assume you are using the mouse as a right-handed person. However, there are some important differences for a left-handed person, and we shall come back to this point when we have the main points expressed clearly.

Place your hand now over the body of the mouse so that your index finger is lying gently over the top of the left button, and your second finger is over the right button (ignore the central button if your mouse has three). Place the wrist of your hand just off the body and in front of it, resting it actually on the mat rather than the mouse body itself. Grip the sides of the mouse body loosely with your thumb and the inside edge of your third finger. When you have the right sort of grip, then your index finger should have complete freedom of movement, touching the top of the left button, and not actually touching the mouse body. This grip is illustrated in the following picture:

Beginners have a tendency to grip the body of the mouse too tightly with the palm of the hand, or to place too much of the weight of the hand on the mouse itself instead of letting your wrist take the strain, resting on the mouse mat.

When you think you have the correct sort of grip, you should be able to move the mouse side to side just by flicking your wrist. The wrist joint should not have to leave contact with the mat.

Go ahead and try this now, with the computer switched on and showing the Desktop. Watch the screen **pointer** move side to side as you slowly flick your wrist across to the left and then to the right. See if you can make the pointer go off the display at either edge of the screen, and watch what happens when it reaches it. Well? Did you notice that when you get to the screen edge, the pointer stays put no matter how much further you move the mouse. But the instant you start to reverse the direction then the pointer starts moving in the opposite direction.

Centre the **pointer** on the screen and then try pushing the mouse away from you then towards you, a few times. Notice what happens now when the pointer reaches the top and bottom of the screen. If you are very observant, then you will notice that at the top of the screen the pointer stops – but you can still see the all of the arrow symbol – however when you reach the bottom of the screen, the pointer almost disappears from view.

> **There is a very important point to learn from this last observation, where the pointer almost disappears when at the bottom. It is the pointed tip of the arrow that is the 'active' part of the pointer symbol, not any of the rest of it. This 'active' bit always remains visible on the screen, even at the bottom. In the exercises of the next section, when we come to point at things on the screen and click buttons, it is the pointed tip that must be pointing precisely on top of the targets we will be aiming at.**

After a lot of 'wagging' the pointer back and forth between the extreme edges of the monitor screen, you may find that you start to run out of mat space, towards one of its edges. If the rubber ball underneath runs over a mat edge, then the movement of the pointer movement becomes erratic and unpredictable. This is the kind of circumstance where you might need to lift the complete mouse up, move your hand, and reposition them both towards the centre of the mat.

This whole business about using a mouse comes with lots of practice. Our discussion in this section has been more for guidance rather than rigid rule making. As I said earlier, the overriding consideration is to get comfortable and be able to move the pointer in a precise and predictable manner.

Left-handed?

Now some additional comments for those people who are left handed. As with many other things in life, the equipment designers often give you a raw deal. With the factory standard settings of a computer, it will still be the **left mouse button** that you will be using ninety nine per cent of the time in your work. This gives you a bit of a problem in terms of the way you may need to grip the mouse, so that you can click the correct button easily.

There is a technique where you can change some settings within the computer software to swap over the function of the left and right buttons, but that needs a bit of expertise that you don't have at this exact moment. You may choose to get a friend to do it immediately who has more expertise – or you can wait until the exercises in the next section, where we shall learn how to do this as part of an exercise in using the mouse itself. However, you may still be faced with the same problem in the future if you use someone elses computer who is right-handed. They may be none too happy if you keep swapping the button function over for them, and forgetting to switch it back again!

If you are left-handed, then you might find it easier to learn to operate the left mouse button by adapting your grip, and to leave the computer settings at the factory standard ones. One person I know who is left-handed has chosen to swap them over on her own personal computer, but has also learnt to use a standard mouse with her right hand when she needs to. The choice really is yours. Think about it carefully before you finally decide. It can affect you for the rest of your computing life. Once you have begun to acquire some skill with using a mouse in a certain way it may not be so simple to undo it!

Okay. We are now ready to move on to try out some exercises.

5.2 Windows exercises with a mouse

Before we begin, let me say this. For first timers, the **mouse** can be quite tricky to master. It takes quite a bit of practice to learn how to properly manipulate it to make it do what you really want it to do. Don't be dismayed if you have trouble at first. There are a few tips and tricks I will tell you of in due course that can make things easier. If it is of any consolation, I can tell you that almost everybody has some degree of difficulty with a mouse when they first begin.

Okay, let's get started. You should begin from the point where the computer is powered up and showing only the **Desktop** as in section 2.1. Place your hand on the mouse in the way we discussed in the last section. Your index finger should be resting on the left mouse button, but gently so that you are not activating the internal switch.

Exercise 1 – Moving the mouse pointer around the monitor screen
Here is a simple exercise sequence to get you used to moving the mouse around on the mouse mat. The rules for mouse movement are these:

a. Slide the mouse forward and the pointer goes up the screen.
b. Slide the mouse backward and the pointer goes down the screen.
c. Slide the mouse left and the pointer goes left on the screen.
d. Slide the mouse right and the pointer goes right on the screen.

The first task is to position the **pointer** roughly in the centre of the screen by moving the mouse using the above rules. Next, lift the whole mouse body up completely and place it in the centre of the mat. By doing this, the ball underneath doesn't rotate and the pointer will remain roughly in the same place. When you are done, then you are ready to start the exercise with both mouse and pointer lined up more or less in the middle of mat and screen.

If at any stage of these exercises you find that the mouse is drifting over the edge of the mat then, again, lift it up completely by the body and place it back in the centre.

Now begin by moving the pointer around clockwise repeatedly in a small circle (say a few cm. diameter). Try to make the circle as near perfect as you can within reason. While you are doing this, you should be able to keep your wrist resting in the same spot on the mat, and using a slight flexing of the wrist and bending of the fingers to make the circular motion. The following picture demonstrates what we are trying to do with the pointer.

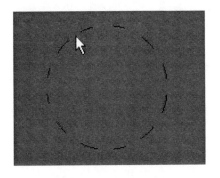

When you get tired of going clockwise, start to do the same but anti-clockwise. Keep an eye on how your hand is achieving the movement. If you see that you are moving your whole hand, wrist and forearm for this movement, then you are holding the mouse too rigidly, and you should let your hand, thumb and fingers flex more. The inside palm of your hand should be barely touching the mouse body, not rigidly gripping it or placing weight on it. Think of the way you hold a pen to write and how relaxed that is – well the grip of the mouse should be similar; it is as though you are writing with the mouse on the mat, and the rubber ball underneath is an imaginary pen nib.

When you have mastered small circles, start to move the mouse around clockwise repeatedly in a small square, stopping at each corner to change pointer direction. After a while, do the same in the anti-clockwise direction.

Okay. When you think you can do small circles and squares well enough, try now to do larger circles. How big can you make them without moving your wrist from its spot?

Now we have reached the point where we learn to make large screen movements of the pointer. In order to do this we shall need to start moving the wrist from its fixed spot. For large screen movements, it is permitted to move your hand, wrist and forearm in a more rigid style. But you will discover that by doing this we lose the precision of placing the pointer in an exact position.

Move the mouse repeatedly clockwise to trace out the largest circle that you can fit on the monitor display. Make sure the pointer extends right to the very top and bottom of the screen. After a while, reverse the direction to anticlockwise.

Then try the largest rectangle shape you can make, but without any part of the pointer symbol actually disappearing from sight, again both clockwise and then anti-clockwise. This bit is a lot harder to do than the earlier small circles, is it not?

Now, I want you to try combining the two differing types of movement. Use a large movement to place the pointer near the top right hand corner, then trace out repeated small circles in that corner by keeping your wrist still on the spot where it ended up. After several circles, move the pointer near to the bottom right hand corner, and repeat the small circles there. Next, move to the bottom left hand corner and repeat them there. And finally, move up to the top left hand corner and repeat them once more.

This last exercise sequence is a good way of acquiring the type of skill needed for normal everday use of the mouse and pointer. It has the mixture of first moving the pointer roughly to an area where we might wish to be, and then using more precise control when we have reached that area, so that we can prepare to do detailed manipulation of various objects that we will work with.

Round off this first exercise now by making out other imaginary shapes with the pointer of your own design; say for instance triangles, stars, alphabetic letters and such like.

Finally, a good test of your control is to try to imagine you are writing your surname as a signature on the screen in continuous writing.

Before we leave this exercise in learning mouse movement, I want to give you a few tips. Throughout all the things we have just done, you should have found the movement of the mouse and the pointer to be completely smooth and not jerky. The first tip is to make sure that the surface that you rest the mouse mat upon is completely flat. If the mat is not perfectly flat, then you will find that the rubber ball underneath doesn't rotate smoothly but starts skipping and the pointer appears to be somewhat 'sticky' on the screen. The next tip is to keep the mat surface free from dust and bits of debris. Again, if the rubber ball runs over just a small amount of debris, then it will not rotate smoothly and again the pointer movement will appear jerky. The last tip is to keep the rubber ball itself clean. If you look at the underside of the mouse, you will notice that a small plastic ring retains the ball. With care, you can depress and twist the ring and it drops free from the body. The rubber ball can then be removed, washed under the tap, dried off and refitted. You will also be able to blow out any dust or hair that might have accumulated in there. All these factors can prevent the ball rolling smoothly. By attending to them you will be amazed how different the movement can be after cleaning.

Exercise 2 – Learning how to single 'click' on an object

On the Desktop you should be able to see an **icon** with the title '**My Computer**'. It is usually placed in the top left corner of the monitor. Move the pointer so that the tip of the arrow is anywhere over the actual picture of the little computer, like this:

Now, without moving the mouse (not even just a tiny bit), 'click' the **left button** once with your finger. Give it a swift press and release. Your finger should remain over the button throughout. When you have clicked it, you should have felt the button 'give' just a bit under pressure, then pop back up automatically when you released the pressure.

After the click, the icon changes colour and looks like this:

This simple action of positioning the **pointer** and then making a single click of the **left mouse button** is a very important action to learn and remember. It is of such importance – and we shall use it so often – that we shall from hereon refer to it by the special term 'click'. Whenever I ask you to click on something, then what I really mean is – first position the very tip of the arrow pointer on the 'something', then swiftly press and immediately release the left mouse button, doing it without moving the pointer not even just a fraction!

If we ever need to use the **right mouse button**, then I will use a second special term of '**right-click**'.

There we have two new definitions for you – click and right-click.

It is important to note in these two definitions that they are single click actions. There is another action that we shall introduce in the next exercise where we press the left mouse button twice in rapid succession. You must be careful to avoid accidentally clicking twice for either click or right-click, or you may get unexpected results.

Note – One of the biggest faults that beginners make when trying to click on screen objects is that they move the mouse body, just ever so slightly, when they try to press the button. This mistake often shifts the pointer, ever so slightly, on the screen before the button has registered. Though small this may be, the shift is sometimes significant enough to move the pointer off the boundary area of the object that they are trying to click on. Now if you don't know it already, computers are not very forgiving devices. They are extremely precise about what they do, particularly when it comes to use of the mouse pointer. If the tip of the pointer is not exactly on the object when you press the button, then the computer will not understand your command – and you will get an unexpected response. Be warned!

Okay. We have learnt how to **click** on **My Computer**, and it changed colour. What does this mean, and how do we **un-click** it if we need to?

First: the un-click

To **un-click** an **icon**, we simply move the **pointer** to anywhere on the general background of the **Desktop** and make another **click**. I really do mean anywhere, providing it is not on top of any other type of screen object. Try this now. Move the pointer so that the tip of the pointer is just above the little picture of the icon of **My Computer**, as shown in this next picture:

Now make another click. Because the pointer is no longer pointing at the icon, when we click, we are effectively clicking on the background, and not on the My Computer icon. The effect of this is to un-do the original click action. You should now see the icon go back to its original colouring. Next we will discuss what the colour change means, but first, I want you to click again on My Computer so that it has changed colour, otherwise the next bit won't work properly.

Now the meaning of an icon that has changed colour

Whenever we see an **icon** on the **Desktop** that has changed colour in this way (most often to blue, but not always – it depends on the overall colour scheme in use), then we say in computer jargon that it is 'selected', or alternatively, we say it has the 'focus'. The real meaning is that the icon is 'selected to have the focus of attention for whatever action we do in the next forthcoming action'.

What on earth does that mean?

Lets learn by a practical experiment. **My Computer** should now be in the 'blue' or colour-changed state. If not then simply click on it, to make it so.

Now press the **ENTER key** on the keyboard.

If all is well, then a new window should pop up on the monitor looking like this:

If your window has a slightly different shape and arrangement, don't be concerned.

Okay. Why did this happen?

Well, we learnt in section 2.2 (and again in section 4.3) that the **ENTER key** is a special key and one of its jobs is to make the computer do a 'command' that has been set up beforehand. The **ENTER key** is the 'now go and do it' key (literally it 'enters the command'). In our example here, we had the My Computer icon selected by our click action. When we pressed the ENTER key then we were effectively saying to the computer 'do it' – that is, open up the My Computer window. Our command that we set up, if you like, was the 'open it up' command. And consequently that is what we now see, as in the last diagram.

So, to recap – if we **click** on a **Desktop icon**, we are then selecting it to have the focus of our attention. That is really what is meant when it changes to the 'blue' (highlighted) colour. Following this, when we do another action (in this case press the **ENTER key**) we are then sending that keystroke to that icon which has the selection (the icon has the focus).

This idea of something having the 'focus' is a very important point to grasp in modern personal computing. You will see this crop up all over the place, particularly when you start to work with other windows type programs and menus to do specialised jobs. Because we shall meet it again frequently, we had better now add a new term 'focus' to our collection of special terms. When something '**has the focus**' it is the thing that will get the attention of our next action, whatever that action might be.

Let us now round off this exercise on 'Learning how to single-click on an object', by closing the My Computer window, and getting back to where we began with no icons selected at all.

In the very top right-hand corner of the **My Computer** window, there is a group of three 'screen' **buttons,** one of which has an '**X**' marked on it (see the following picture to recognise this group). We call these grey objects buttons because they are very much like the mouse buttons, that is, you can press them. However, you don't press them with your finger but by using the screen pointer and doing a click. You will see this specific group of three buttons time and time again in almost every window that you meet. Here is a close up view of them:

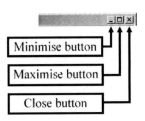

The one on the right (the **X**) is known as the **Close button** for the window. Its job is to do just that – to close the window. We will come back to discuss the function of the other two buttons in Chapter 6.

Go ahead and click now on the Close button. Remember to take care and make sure that the tip of the arrow pointer is on the button image. The instant you click on it then the My Computer window will disappear.

When you are back at the Desktop, the My Computer icon will still be selected (highlighted). We can even say with our new term that it has the **focus**. You should now **click** anywhere on the background to achieve the **un-click** action and lose the focus. When you have done it, we are now back where we started at the beginning of the exercise.

To gain further confidence with the click action, you should go through this exercise again on your own several times, repeatedly selecting the My Computer icon, pressing the ENTER key, and finally closing the window with the Close button.

When you think you have this sequence completely mastered, try then selecting these two alternative icons from the Desktop instead of My Computer (but not any others just yet), and doing the same cycle of actions:

- **My Documents**
- **Recycle Bin**

Finally, this whole exercise has been an important one in your learning of mouse skills. We have also learnt quite a lot of new definitions and ideas. Don't be afraid to come back to this exercise later if you become a bit unsure of these new items.

Exercise 3 - Learning how to 'double-click' on an object

If ever there was an Achilles heel for beginners learning computers, then the double-click action has got to be it. Brace yourself for an interesting exercise – but don't panic! This is where we might need to throw in a few special tips!

We begin again with the computer at the **Desktop** stage, and all other windows are closed.

Start by positioning the pointer well away from any icons and simply pointing to any part of the expanse that is the background of the Desktop, as in the picture opposite.

Now click the left mouse button twice slowly, without moving the mouse body. Don't worry – nothing is meant to happen. I just want you to get some practice in trying to perfect the action that we will come to call the **double-click**.

Try clicking twice again, but slightly quicker this time, leaving a longer pause between pairs of clicks than between the two clicks forming the pair. Keep repeating this double clicking motion over and over again, lets suggest twenty times, but picking up speed the more you do it. Don't worry about the timing between the pairs of clicks, it's the speed of the second click following on from the first one that we are trying to increase.

How fast can you achieve? Have a go at doing it very quickly – as fast as you can – but make sure you actually press the button twice, not just think that you might have done. Be quite positive when you are pressing.

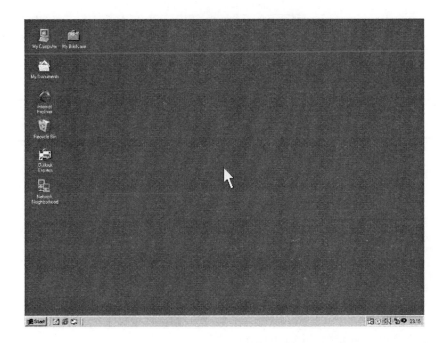

Okay – how fast do we need to achieve? This is a difficult idea to get across on paper but here's a thought ... Imagine in your head that each single click of the left mouse button will ring a bell. For those of us old enough to remember the good old days of trams and buses, then you might recall that the conductor would often give a 'ding-ding' in order to signal the driver to move off from a bus stop. Well the speed of the double clicking that you are trying to achieve is very similar to the speed of the conductor giving a first 'ding' followed by the second 'ding'. At longest we are aiming at a half second maximum for both clicks of the left button to be over with. The speed is quite important. If we don't do both clicks fast enough in succession, then the computer will think that we are trying to do a **click** action and then another **click** action, rather than a **double-click** action. As ever, two wrongs don't make a right!

I stated in the beginning of this section on exercises that the mouse can be a bit tricky to master. This double-clicking action is probably the trickiest of all. If you find later that you have trouble making it work, then you need to keep faith and probably come back to exercise again for more training. The main problem seems to be, in my experience, that there is an unintentional tendency to move the mouse body when people are trying to make the pair of clicks. It's as though they are concentrating too much on the clicking and forget to keep the body still.

We now define the term **'double-click'** to mean the same as the single click but to have this very rapid double press and release of the left mouse button instead. (Note – there isn't a common need for such a thing as a right double-click. Now at least there is a consolation!)

Practice this **double-click** over and over again in the expanse of the background of the Desktop. You can do no harm here, as long as you keep away from the icons. When you think you have got the hang of it, then we are ready to move to the next step.

Okay, now the next step. We shall now try to use this double-click to do a real task.

We shall now double-click the **My Computer** icon. Let us review exactly what this means. It means – first move your pointer to point over the My Computer icon, as in the next picture …

… and then click twice in rapid succession, as we have been practising, but do not move the mouse body when you are doing it, not even just a tiny bit! Then relax.

Go ahead and try it now.

Well, if you manage it successfully, then the **My Computer** window will open up again, just as before in the last exercise. If you didn't manage it successfully, then you are probably still staring at the My Computer icon, but with it now in the selected (highlighted) state.

If you failed to open up the window, have another go. Keep on having another go at the double-click, until you finally get the window opened up.

Okay. We will assume now that you have been successful (If you haven't, then go back to the practice session where you are practising on the expanse of the Desktop background).

What I want you to do now is simply close the window using the Close button with a click action (not the double-click, that is not a valid thing to do to a screen button). If you have forgotten which is the Close button, here is a picture of it again:

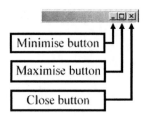

Fine. That's all we are going to do on this exercise. Try doing it over and over again; let's say twenty times. **Double-click** on the **My Computer** icon to open the window. Then close it with the **click** action.

When you have mastered the double-click on My Computer, try the same on My Documents and on the Recycle-bin.

Exercise 4 – Learning the mouse 'drag' action
This next exercise aims to show you how to move objects around on the monitor

screen, so that you can position them anywhere you like. We begin as in the other exercises with the computer powered on and the monitor displaying the **Desktop**. As we have said before, if at any stage the mouse body gets too close to the edge of the mat, then pick the body up completely, and re-position it in the centre.

First, I would like you to go ahead and click on the **My Computer** icon. The icon consequently becomes selected as a result of the click action.

Now I want you to position the pointer over the My Computer icon again, but this time I want you to press the left mouse button and keep it pressed – don't release it. With your finger keeping the button pressed, I want you to now slide the mouse body to the right, such that the pointer moves to the right also. Notice that a 'ghost image' of the icon appears to be moving with the pointer! Keep pressing and sliding, until the pointer reaches the approximate centre of the top of the screen. Now release the button. With the button released, now move the pointer down to position it in the middle of the screen.

Okay. Let's stop a while and analyse what happened on your screen. You should have noticed that the My Computer icon has now moved position towards the right and is now situated in the centre of the top of the screen, similar to the following picture:

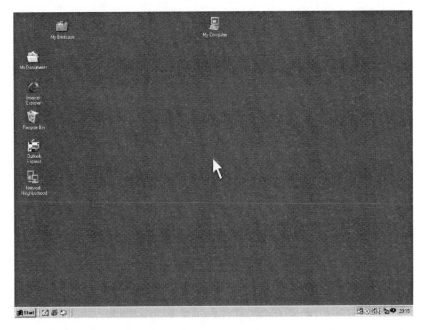

We call this type of mouse action a '**drag**' action. We say that you have dragged the My Computer icon from its original position to another new position. We use this drag action quite a bit in personal computing, not only to move objects about but also when we want to change the size of some of them. We shall cover the topic of re-sizing in Chapter 6.

If for any reason the My Computer icon has not moved position on your screen, then you have not kept the left mouse button pressed while you were sliding the mouse body into the top centre of the screen – try again until you do move it.

Did you notice that when you released the **button** and moved the **pointer** down into the middle of the screen, then the **My Computer** icon ceased moving? – Even though the pointer continued to move to a new position! The drag action only works while the left mouse button is kept pressed down and it stops the moment you release it. You can press the button a second time if you wish and effectively start another drag action, but the first one stopped the moment that the button was released.

When we began this exercise, I asked you to first click on the My Computer icon. This was not really needed as part of the drag action. The reason I asked you to do it was so that the icon would be selected (highlighted 'blue') before we began the drag action, and that you would not be confused if you accidentally let go of the left mouse button too early. You will always notice that an icon becomes selected (highlighted 'blue') after a drag action, but it doesn't have to be beforehand, as we shall now demonstrate.

First, click anywhere on the background of the Desktop, in order to remove the highlight from any of the icons. Now I want you to now reposition the pointer over the top of the My Computer icon but don't press the left mouse button just yet. OK, we note that the icon still is not highlighted. Now press and keep pressed the left mouse button. Now slide the mouse body to place the pointer up in the top left corner of the screen – back in fact to the original location of My Computer – and then release the left mouse button. We have just performed the drag action again, and we note that the icon is left in the highlighted state, even though it wasn't when we first started.

We can perform drag actions as much as we like to position any of the icons on the Desktop in almost any position we fancy. This is in fact one of the reasons why we use the term 'Desktop' to describe this general screen that we first see at the end of the power on process. We can treat this screen as though we were looking at the top of a desk, and we can place objects in many different places upon it, just like a real desktop.

Now try to reposition the 'My Documents' and the 'Recycle Bin' icons. Place them first anywhere over on the right hand side of the screen. When you have done this, then put them back again into their original positions. Don't worry too much if they are not exactly back as they were. However, a very good exercise in controlling the mouse is to see if you can line them up so that they are visually in a straight vertical column. You might notice if you attempt to do very small drag actions that icons appear a bit reluctant to move at all, for such small but genuine movements of the mouse pointer. It appears as though there is a minimum amount of pointer movement required, in order for the drag action to get started, which is in fact true. My tip for achieving small drag movements is to make a larger one first to get it started, then to come back a bit with the pointer to make the final tiny adjustment.

Before we leave the exercise on the drag action, I would like to describe and show you something else that often gets beginners confused when starting out learning about computers. However, you should only attempt to perform this next sequence of actions if you have fully mastered the drag action on icons first. If you are not yet confident about it, them by all means read the text, but maybe miss out performing the actions. Come back to it another time when you have more confidence in your skill. If you are okay now on the drag action, then don't be frightened to have a go.

We are going to learn that the long grey line (we call it a **bar** – in fact we call it the **Taskbar**) at the very bottom of the screen is itself an object that can be moved. I want you to be confident with the drag operation because we shall move it about a bit, and if you are not confident then you might have difficulty putting it back in its original place again. The reason why I am bothering to show you this, at all, is that beginners often inadvertently move it without realising, and they start to panic when they cannot put it back! Once it has been moved then it will stay in the new position, even if you power the computer down and power it back up again! If this ever happens to you, then you will have the knowledge from what comes next for resolving the problem.

Here we go.

Position the **pointer** so that it is roughly central in the middle of the long grey strip at the very bottom of the screen (that is, in the middle of the **Taskbar**) as in the next picture. Make sure that it is not on top of any icon type pictures (there are some at either end of the bar) and be careful to make sure that the tip of the pointer is actually pointing well inside the grey area of the bar and not just above it, or close to the edge. If you move the pointer slowly, you may notice that the pointer symbol actually changes as you cross over the top edge of the bar. Ignore this change and keep on moving it (the pointer will eventually change back into the normal arrow shape). The following picture illustrates whereabouts I want you to position it, and also shows that the pointer should still be showing its normal symbol:

Your own **Taskbar** may appear slightly different to the above so don't be concerned.

Now perform a **drag** action and re-position the pointer close to the right hand edge of the screen. Keep the drag action going until you notice that a grey rectangular image appears down the side, and then let the left mouse button go, to end the drag. The instant that you release the button the Taskbar appears to jump location, and now is a vertical bar (a bit thicker in appearance), stuck to the right hand edge of the monitor screen, as in the next picture:

If your monitor doesn't now have the grey Taskbar now down the right hand side, then you have made a mistake, and you will need to try again. (If by any chance the Taskbar now appears too fat along the bottom of the screen then read the note about it further down this page).

Okay. Now, with the pointer over the grey area of the Taskbar, as shown in the above picture, I want you to do another drag action and position the pointer close to the centre of the top of the screen until you see another grey rectangular outline appear. Now let go off the drag, and magically the Taskbar jumps location yet again, this time appearing at the very top of the monitor display.

And yet once again, with the pointer tip pointing inside the centre grey of the Taskbar, do a drag action and place the pointer now close to the left hand edge of the screen, until you see the grey rectangular outline appear. Let go of the drag and the Taskbar makes another jump of location.

Finally, repeat the process a fourth and final time to drag the Taskbar from the left side back down to the bottom of the screen.

We are now back where we started at the beginning of this exercise. That is, providing that you have put all the icons back in their original places!

There is an unlikely, but small chance that you might have increased the width of the standard Taskbar by mistake when you have been dragging it about. If it looks okay, then ignore what I am about to say. If it now appears twice as thick at the bottom than when you started, then you have most definitely have committed the mistake. To fix the problem, you need to move the pointer to the critical point we mentioned earlier on where you are *passing the very tip of the pointer slowly over the edge of the Taskbar* and it changes into a strange new 'double-headed arrow' symbol. As soon as it changes into this new symbol, then press the left mouse button as for a drag action and try drag the width of the Taskbar back to its normal thickness. Let go of the drag only when the position of the new symbol is at the point where you think the edge of the normal Taskbar should be. The mistake, if you made it, was caused by pressing the left mouse button too early when you started the drag action! You should wait until the tip of the pointer is well inside the grey area of the Taskbar and has returned to the normal pointer symbol before you press the button to start the drag action to move the Taskbar. In effect here, what you are doing is dragging the frame of the taskbar rather than the bar itself.

Although it is good fun to start re-arranging the Desktop in different ways, I would prefer that you keep things more or less as they were when we first started out in this chapter, simply because all the rest of the book will make the assumption that this is how your screen will appear to you. Be it on your own head if you don't and consequently get confused with further instructions! Once you have completed the book, then you are then at liberty to arrange the Desktop as you wish and to your own preference. However, you will normally find that keeping the Taskbar situated along the bottom of the screen is standard with most computer users, and turns out to be the most convenient.

We have reached the end now of our series of exercises using the mouse. I hope that you have enjoyed them and that your skill with the mouse has at least reached the point where you don't find it a complete and utter mystery!

Though I've said it before, I will say it again – for first-timers, the mouse can be tricky device to master. But it is well worth the effort getting to grips with. The mouse sometimes can be much faster than using the keyboard to do things. Other times, it is the reverse, and the keyboard can be quicker. If you want to be proficient at using the personal computer, then you really need to master both of these methods of human interaction with the computer.

The secret about successful use of the mouse lies with the amount of practice you put in. The more you practice, then the more skilful you will become. If you find yourself still a bit unsure about using it, then go over these exercises time and time again. There is no shame in taking your time to master the mouse. I have personally being using one for the last fifteen years and I still occasionally make a slip!

The last section in this chapter is for first timers who have tried their best, but are really struggling to use a mouse correctly. If your hands have seen a lot of life, then they may not be as supple as you would wish them to be! Don't despair, and don't let that put you off using a computer altogther. I will introduce another kind of mouse in the next section that you might find a much easier to use than the standard variety.

5.3   What to do if you don't like using the mouse

The original design of the standard mouse pointing-device was made more than twenty years ago, and has changed suprisingly little over this period. Some people find it fairly easy to use; but some do not.

At the start of this chapter, I placed a lot of emphasis on holding the mouse correctly. This is a very important consideration and paying attention to it may solve the difficulties experienced for many people. Sadly, there are others who, despite valiant efforts, cannot come to terms with using a standard mouse. This last section aims to offer a ray of hope for those who are still really struggling.

Here, I have included two alternative methods of coping without using a conventional mouse. The **Trackball** is a recommended alternative, and the keyboard **MouseKeys** is a suggestion for use as a last resort.

The 'Trackball' mouse device

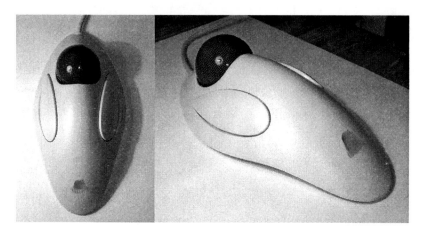

The above pictures show a newer design of mouse pointing-device called a **Trackball**. With this type of design, the mouse body is fixed and does not move at all. A red ball on top is free to spin in any direction, and movement of the screen pointer occurs as a result of rolling it with the underside of your fingers or thumb.

The mouse buttons are also fixed on the body so they can be operated without any danger of interfering with the movement action. This style of mouse should be of help to those of you who find it difficult to keep the pointer still when making the double-click action.

With this type of design, it is also easier to position the screen pointer very slowly and therefore more accurately. It should assist those who have difficulty with bending their fingers. However, some people find the slower pointer movement can also be a disadvantage because it requires more activity to make larger screen movements.

Fitting a Trackball can be as simple as plugging it into the processor unit in place of the conventional mouse lead.

The keyboard 'MouseKeys' for mouse actions

Another alternative to using a mouse is to make some changes to the computer's software settings, so that you can use the numeric keypad at the far right hand side of your keyboard in order to make mouse type movements and actions.

Only use this alternative approach if you really cannot use the conventional mouse, or a Trackball type alternative.

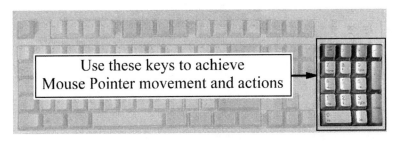

Use these keys to achieve
Mouse Pointer movement and actions

This alternative approach has both good and not-so-good implications. The good part is that all mouse actions now can be achieved by pressing keys instead of using the conventional mouse pointing-device. The not so good part is that making a mouse action like a click for example requires more complex sequences of key presses. We also lose some of the key functions that were previously available to us.

If you feel confident enough to make the required software setting changes yourself, then go ahead and I will lead you slowly through the steps to tell you how to do it. If you don't feel so confident, then maybe you can get help from a knowledgeable friend to do it for you. Any changes that you do make can be reversed later if you so choose.

To make the changes, we use a facility called '**Accessibility Options**', to be found inside a new window called **Control Panel**. The Control panel window is accessed from the My Computer window (we opened this window previously during our earlier exercises of section 2.1). I shall now show you how to do it step by step:

1. Begin at the **Desktop**. Press the **Windows Key** and see the **Start Menu** appear.

2. Then press the **S key** and see a subsidiary menu appear.
3. Now press the **C key** and you should then observe that the **Control Panel** window opens up.
4. Use the mouse to click on the **Accessibility Options** icon and thereby select it (it becomes highlighted).
5. Press the **ENTER key** and see the **Accessibility Properties** window open up (note – it changes its name slightly from Options to Properties!).
6. Use the mouse to click on the word '**Mouse**' as in the next picture:

7. Use the mouse to click on the '**Use MouseKeys**' checkbox as in the next picture, and make the tick appear (Note – to reverse the changes later, repeat the same steps but click again on this checkbox to make the tick disappear):

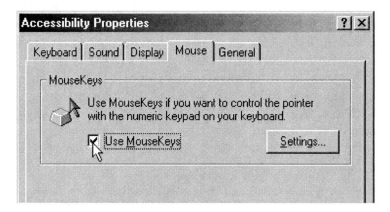

8. Use the mouse to click on the '**Apply**' button at the bottom, as in the next picture, and eventually after the hourglass pointer disappears, watch the wording change to a 'greyed out' appearance:

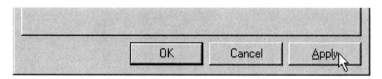

9. Use the mouse to click on the 'OK' button also shown in the last picture, and eventually after the hourglass pointer disappears, notice that the **Accessibility Properties** window closes completely.
10. Finally, close the Control Panel window by clicking on the 'X' button in the top right hand corner, as done in previous exercises.

You should now be back to the **Desktop**. In the bottom right hand corner of the monitor screen, you should see that a new symbol has appeared on the end of the grey Taskbar as in the next picture (the other icons may be different on your computer):

This symbol indicates that the **MouseKeys** facility is now in operation, and if you press any of the **numeric keypad** keys (numbers 1 to 9, except 5) you now will notice that they can move the screen pointer in various directions.

The following table describes the function of the the **numeric keypad** keys when the **MouseKeys** are active:

Key	Function
5	**Click**
+	**Double-click**
/	Select the **Left Mouse Button**
*	Select **both Mouse Buttons**
-	Select the **Right Mouse Button**
Ins	Lock the selected button
Del	Release the selected button
8	Move pointer upwards
2	Move pointer downwards
4	Move pointer left
6	Move pointer right
9	Move pointer diagonally upwards and right
3	Move pointer diagonally downwards and right
1	Move pointer diagonally downwards and left
7	Move pointer diagonally upwards and left

Here is how to use them:

- All number keys, except 5, move the pointer on the screen

- To **click** on an object, move the pointer tip over the object first, then press the '**/**' **key** to select the Left Mouse Button, then press the '**5**' **key** to make the click action.

- To **double-click** on an object, move the pointer tip over the object first, then press the '**/**' **key** to select the Left Mouse Button, then press the '**+**' **key** to make the double-click action.

- To **right-click** on an object, move the pointer tip over the object first, then press the '**-**' **key** to select the Right Mouse Button, then press the '**5**' **key** to make the click action.

- To **drag** an object, move the pointer tip over the object first, then press the '**/**' **key** to select the Left Mouse Button, then press the **Ins key** to lock the button, then move the pointer to where you intend to go, then press the **Del key** to end the drag action.

6

Windows, Games and Drawing Pictures

6.1 Working with a Window

Now that we have become used to typing with the keyboard and have started to use the mouse, the time has come to learn a bit more about windows in general. The knowledge that you gain from this section will then prepare you to use the computer for some interesting tasks, like playing games and drawing your own pictures and diagrams.

First we should discuss once more why a **window** exists at all.

You may remember from our discussion in section 3.2 that the master program controlling the whole computer is itself called 'Windows'. (Note that we use the plural form of the word and a capital letter when we use it as the name of the master program). In this book, I am using **Windows 98**, and it is this master program that provides the images on screen that we call the **Desktop**. When we want to do a particular job, such as write a letter, or make a drawing, we need to have a subsidiary program running, like **Notepad** for example. To create somewhere for that subsidiary program to run and operate, the master program creates a window. The subsidiary program always exists within the confines of that created window. This brings us to the first reason why a window may exist – it is as a place for a subsidiary program to run and operate.

There is also a second reason why a window might exist. In our exercise with the mouse in section 5.2, we learnt how to click on a **Desktop icon** and 'open it up' to display a window. For example, we clicked on the **My Computer** icon and it opened up into the My Computer window. Inside the My Computer window was a collection of other objects, which we didn't investigate further at the time. These objects were themselves icons and represented further features of the master Windows program. This gives us a second reason why a window may exist. If there is a need to group a number of objects together (for whatever reason), then we will often find them grouped together inside the frame of a window.

Another important illustration of this second use is the **My Documents** window which we met during the mouse exercises of the last chapter. My Documents is actually a folder of the type we discussed in section 3.1. You may remember that folders are objects that may be used for grouping files together (or possibly combinations of files and further sub-folders). When a folder is 'closed' it is shown as an icon, but if we 'open' the folder then we see a window containing a collection of files, or files and sub-folders. The My Documents folder is an important object because it is used as the standardised or **'default'** folder (default means the factory set option) for saving many files that we create when using the computer. For example, it was inside the My Documents folder where we saved the shopping list in section 4.2. We didn't have to choose this folder. The Notepad program automatically selected it as the suggested place to save the list.

So, in conclusion therefore, about why windows exist at all, we should now appreciate that there are two principle reasons for their existence:

- one is as a place for a *subsidiary program to run and operate*

- the second is as a method of *grouping other objects together* that may have something in common.

Now we shall discuss more detail about working with windows in general. We begin by examining a standard window and the associated controls, as shown in the picture opposite:

Starting at the top, the **Title Bar** is the blue bar at the top of the window. It actually has several purposes.

- The first obvious purpose is a place to show a 'title' for the window, which may be a reference to the name of a **program** running in the window (and possibly another **file** in use by it), or it could simply be the name of a **folder**.

- A second purpose is a place to locate the **Window Size controls**. You will always find these at the right hand side of the Title Bar in most every window you meet.

- A third purpose is a place to locate the **Control Menu icon** for the window. You will always find this at the extreme left hand side of the Title Bar. The Control Menu icon is a bit of a 'left-over' object from previous versions of Windows and not many people use this much these days for its original purpose.

- A fourth and very important purpose is as a 'handle' for us to grab and take hold of the window by, if we want to move it about on the screen. We do this by doing a drag type of mouse action on the plain area of Title Bar, as we shall see later when we perform some more exercises.

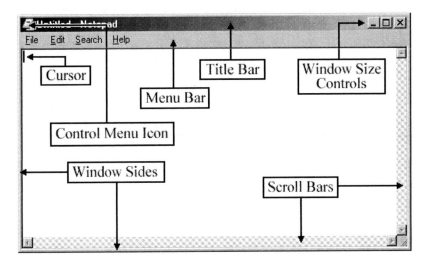

Enough about the Title Bar, let us now discuss the other controls.

The **Menu Bar** is the grey bar under the Title Bar, and contains a number of **drop-down menus**. There are four fairly standard ones shown here, but this can vary depending on circumstances. We have already met the **File drop-down menu** in chapter 4.

Some windows can show a **Cursor**, but many others will not. If a Cursor does exist, then it is created by a program that is running inside the window, and is generally associated with entry of key presses from the keyboard to create text. It shows where the letter or number will be 'typed' when the key is pressed.

Every **window** is bounded by **window sides** to form a frame. These window sides are themselves controls and in general are flexible and moveable items such that we can change the size of the window if we choose to. We do this again using a drag action with the mouse. (Occasionally you may meet windows where the sides are fixed and you cannot move them). The ability to change the size of a window is a useful feature that allows us to shape the window for best display of its contents. As we shall see later in the exercises, it also allows us to 'uncover' other objects that may have been covered up by the window when it was first opened.

The last controls labelled in the previous picture were two objects that are known as **scroll bars**. There are two types of scroll bar – **horizontal** ones that are to be found sometimes along the bottom window side, and **vertical** ones that are usually down the right hand window side. The purpose of these scroll bars is to provide us with a means to take a look around and view the inside of a window, so that we can make visible parts of the inner contents that might appear hidden when a window's displayed area is not a big enough to show everything. The small arrowhead symbols at either end of the scroll bars are buttons that we can click by using the mouse pointer. We use these in order to move the visible area of the window around. We will get to understand these better when we do some practical exercise work.

Okay. Now we have more detailed knowledge about windows and associated controls in general, let us do some exercises to illustrate what we have discussed.

Exercise 5 – Minimising, Maximising and Restoring a window

When we have a **window** 'open' on the **monitor** screen, there are three different ways in which we might see it. It can be normal, maximised, or minimised. This next exercise will illustrate these three different states.

From the **Desktop**, use the **mouse pointer** and click the **Start Button** on the left of the **Task Bar** as demonstrated in this next picture:

The **Start Menu** will then pop-up.

Slide the pointer upwards now to highlight in blue the **<u>R</u>un option** as in the following picture:

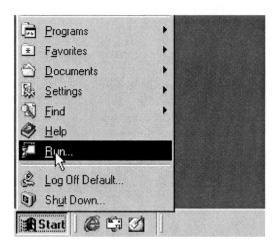

Now, with the pointer still on the Run option (it should still be highlighted), make a click.

The **Run** pop-up display will appear, as it did before when we wrote the shopping list. More than likely, the Open box will still be showing the word 'Notepad' from the last time we used it, but if for any reason it isn't then type it in again now using the keyboard keys. Now click on the OK button and you will see the Notepad program re-appear in its own window.

As an aside before we continue with the exercise, you have probably realised that we have effectively achieved just now using the mouse pointer the same job that we did before in section 4.1 using the keyboard keys. This is an important point to remember. It demonstrates that we can often do the same task in more than one way. Sometimes you can use the mouse pointer as the fastest method to do a task; sometimes it can be quicker to use the keyboard keys.

With **Notepad** now running, use the pointer and slide it over the **File menu option** as in the next picture. Notice how the option seems to change into a **button** once the pointer is actually over the area. Click on this button shape when you see it.

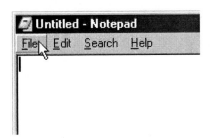

When you have clicked you will see the **File drop-down menu** appear. Slide the pointer down the menu to highlight the **Open option,** as in the following picture, and then click on it:

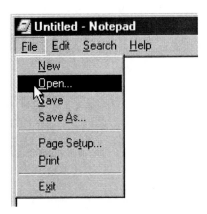

The **Open pop-up Menu** screen now shows itself. Now slide the pointer over the middle white box area to point to the icon for the file called "Shopping List Number 1", as in this next picture:

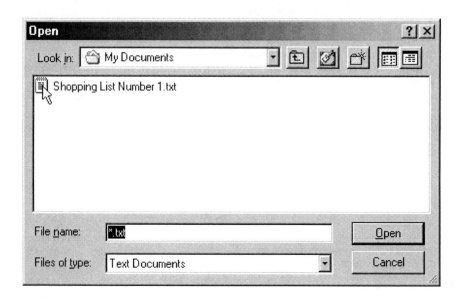

Your own monitor may show something slightly different if you have other files present so don't be concerned. Click when the pointer is over the area of the desired icon, and then the whole object (icon and its wording) becomes highlighted. Then move the pointer to click on the Open button. Suddenly, the 'Shopping List' file reappears in the Notepad window just as it was when we left it in chapter 4.

Okay. We are now in a position to demonstrate the three states that a window can be seen in – maximised, minimised and normal. We shall use the Window Size Controls to do this, so first let us remind ourselves what these three buttons look like and what the functions of them are:

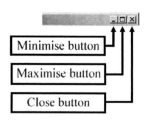

If the middle button as shown on your own monitor for these three controls does not look exactly like the last picture, then click on it and it should change to be the same. (Note – you will also notice that the window size changes as well when you do so!).

Okay. The state that the Notepad window is now in is the 'Normal' state. This state is the intermediate between the other two.

Now click on the left hand button – the **Minimise button**. Suddenly, the whole window disappears from view with a sort of 'shrinking' movement and all you see of it is its rectangular icon on the grey **Task Bar** at the very bottom of the monitor screen. The state that the Notepad window is now in is the 'Minimised' state. This state is very useful to see what is underneath a window. Our shopping list file is still open in the Notepad window but we cannot see it directly now.

If we have more than one window open on the Desktop, the Minimised state is a very useful to get a better view of the other windows without actually having to close the one that we have minimised.

Now slide the pointer over the rectangular icon that is on the grey Task Bar and click again, as in the next picture (note that you can lose a bit of the pointer's tail in order to make sure the tip is actually over the icon properly):

The result of your click should be that the Notepad window reappears in the Normal state. If this didn't happen, then the problem was that pointer tip was not properly over the rectangular icon.

Okay. Let's now try the third and last state. Click this time on the middle button – the Maximise button.

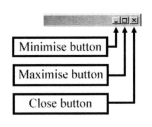

Now you will see the **Notepad window** suddenly expand to fill the whole screen. This is the **Maximised** state. Now have a look at the middle button again. You should see that it has changed its little picture to show two small squarish images – we call this button now the **Restore button**.

Finally, click on the new middle Restore button to get the Notepad window back to the Normal state.

We have now finished the exercise. If you wish you may leave the Notepad window open at this point and move straight to the next exercise. If you want to do the next exercise another time then you need to close the Notepad window ready for powering down. To close the Notepad Window, simply click on the Close button (shown in the last picture) and you will be back at the Desktop.

Exercise 6 – Resizing and moving a window

In this exercise, we will learn how to change the size of a window and to move it around on the monitor screen.

To begin the exercise, you will need to have the Notepad window open on the Desktop, and to have the 'Shopping List Number 1' file opened within the window so that you can read it. If you have just completed the previous exercise then your computer should be set up ready to commence; otherwise you should follow the early part of the instructions given in the last exercise to reach this same starting point.

Our first job is to reduce the height of the Notepad Window. We will do this by lifting up the bottom horizontal window side and moving its position upwards, whilst the rest of the window remains still.

Okay. Here we go. Position the mouse pointer very carefully, so that the tip of the pointer arrow is pointing roughly in the middle of the length of the bottom window side, and try place the tip actually upon it. You will observe that as soon as the pointer tip is anywhere over the image of the **window side** itself, then the pointer changes from the normal white arrow into a black vertical double-headed arrow, as seen in this next picture:

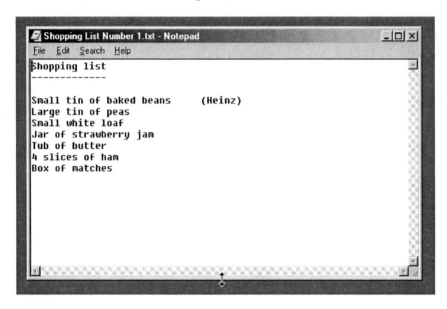

This black double-headed arrow is telling you that you are now correctly positioned if you want to attempt to move the window side, and the double head reminds you that you may move it in either of the two directions indicated. We achieve the move by using the drag action of the mouse that we learnt in chapter 5 (exercise 4), and in our case we shall be moving it upwards.

Now perform the drag (press the left mouse button and keep it pressed) of the window side in an upward direction until you have it positioned just above the last line of text 'Box of matches' in the shopping list, as shown in the picture opposite.

Notice that while the **drag** action is in progress, there is a 'ghost' image of the **window side** showing you where the side will be repositioned if you were to let go of the left mouse button. All the time that you keep your finger on the button then the drag action remains in progress, and you can use this fact to 'fine tune' the very precise spot where you will move the window side to.

With the 'ghost' image correctly positioned, now let go of the left mouse button to end the drag action. As soon as you have ended the drag, you now see that the window side has moved completely and that the window itself is smaller in height.

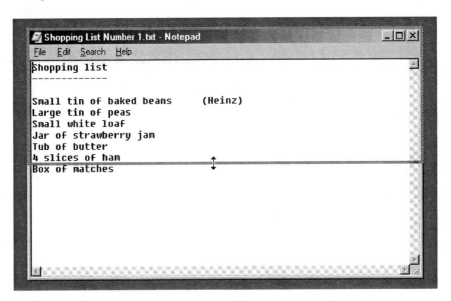

If you look carefully, you will notice that the **vertical scroll bar** down the right window side has modified its appearance slightly. Whereas before the arrow buttons of the scroll bar had a 'greyed out' appearance, they now have a solid black triangular arrow symbol shown on them. Notice also that in the strip of grey between the **arrow buttons** a new **button** has appeared! These changes mean that the visible area now shown by the window is only a part of the total content that exists to be seen. There is, in fact, an area of the window that is now not visible (Box of matches), and we shall investigate using the scroll bars how we might view it.

Position the mouse pointer over the new button that has appeared in the **vertical scroll bar** on the right, as shown in the next picture (remember the tip is the important part of the pointer):

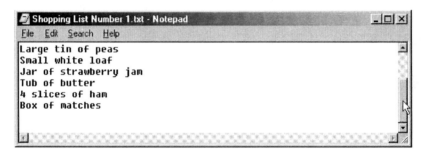

Now perform another **drag** action in a downward direction, so that this new button has moved down the length of the scroll bar as far as it can, as in the next picture:

End the **drag** by releasing the left mouse button. We now see that the visible area inside the window has changed. While we were dragging the new button it appeared as though the internal contents of the window were scrolling up the screen, just like the credits at the end of a TV movie! Now you can see why we call them scroll bars!

This 'new button' that we have dragged upon is actually called a **slider box** for fairly obvious reasons – it slides along the length of the scroll bar. A few interesting points to notice about it are these:

a. The length of the slider box represents the part of the window area that is currently visible in the window.

b. The total length of the scoll bar represents the total underlying window area that exists.

c. And the position of the slider box along the complete length of the scroll bar represents whereabouts in the total underlying area the visible part is currently showing.

Thus, we note from these points that in the last picture the currently visible area is just over half of that available to be seen, and also that we are currently viewing the lower half of the whole area.

We should also note from the last picture that the horizontal scroll bar along the bottom window side is still showing a 'greyed out' appearance and has no slider box. This tells us that there is no part of the width of the window area that is not currently visible. As we will shortly see, this too is about to change!

Now use the pointer to drag upon the middle part of the right window side. Be careful to point on the side itself and not the vertical scroll bar. Drag it leftward so that the 'ghost' image of the side is positioned between the words 'strawberry' and 'jam', as shown below:

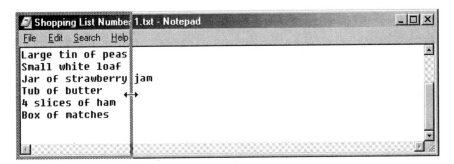

End the drag action and you will see the window side move to its new position. Now we also see that the horizontal scroll bar appearance has changed, as expected. It too has a slider bar. We can tell from looking at the position of this new slider box that we are currently viewing nearly half of the available width of the window and we are viewing the left-hand half.

Okay. Now we are looking at a re-sized Notepad window. Let us next examine how to move it to a new position on the Desktop.

Position the mouse pointer so that it is pointing somewhere central over the blue Title Bar, as in left picture below. Then perform a drag action towards the right, as shown in the right picture below:

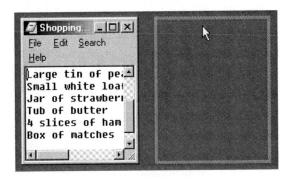

You will probably have noticed that, again, we can see a grey 'ghost' outline of the window during the drag, so that we have an idea where the new position of the window will be. End the drag action and you will see the window move completely from the original place to the new one.

Now try moving the Notepad window yourself to several new positions on the screen. Test how accurately you can position it by moving it over the top of the My Computer icon, such that the word 'My' is just visible to the left of the window but the word 'Computer' is covered up by it.

Now try moving the window off the right hand edge of the monitor screen. Notice when you end the drag that part of it is off the screen, but part is still on it. Try also moving the window off the bottom of the screen, below the grey Task Bar. Observe that nearly all of the window disappears, but there is still enough of the Title Bar visible so that you can get 'hold' of it with the pointer. Finally, bring it back into full view by moving it somewhere near the centre of the screen.

From the previous exercise, you learnt how to **maximise** and **minimise** a window. Try doing these actions now on the new re-sized Notepad window. Observe that when you restore the window back to the normal state, the computer always remembers the new size, not the old one.

Okay. You should by now have a fair skill of moving and repositioning a window. Just before we reach the end of this exercise, I want to say a few words about the little yellow messages that may have occasionally flashed up when positioning the pointer over the Title bar of the new size Notepad window. To see one of these again, move the pointer away from the window to anywhere on the Desktop background, then move the pointer back over the central part of the blue Title Bar, but don't attempt a drag or make a click.

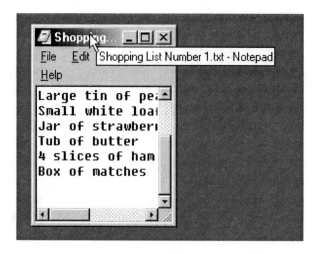

After a second or two, a little yellow message will flash up on the screen again, as shown in the previous picture.

These messages are called **Tool Tips** and the idea is to help you with information concerning the object or control that you are currently pointing at. They don't appear if you are quick in performing actions, but if you linger over an object or control, then they can appear after a second or two – but not always!

In the above picture, the reason why we see a Tool Tip is because we have shortened the width of the window to such an extent that not all of the title is visible on the Title Bar. The three small dots at the end of the word 'Shopping...' do in fact tell us that the title would be longer if there was enough room to display the all words. This technique of using three dots '...' to show that there are really more words if we could display them is used in other many other situations, so watch out and recognise them if and when you can. The words shown by the Tool Tip are in fact a complete expansion of the title in order that we might read it entirely. The Tool Tip remains visible until you perform an action, or move the pointer off the object.

As a final job in this current exercise, we shall slowly increase the size of the **Notepad window** back to something like the original size again.

I now want you to drag the **bottom window side** downward a bit, so that you can view a little more of the shopping list text again. Do this repeatedly, but just expose only a bit more of the window area each time you perform a drag. Eventually, you will see that the **slider box** in the **vertical scroll bar** disappears again, and the two arrow heads at either end of the scroll bar become 'greyed out' once more. When this has happened, then you should be able to see the left hand part of every line of text again in the window.

Now do the same with the **right window side**. Drag it bit by bit until the **slider box** in the **horizontal scroll bar** disappears from sight. Now we have uncovered the total area that exists within the window. This is the reason why both scroll bars have returned back to their original appearance as at the start of the exercise.

Okay. The Notepad window is now back to something like its original size, perhaps a little smaller. We have the skill to adjust it even further should we wish to. However, we have reached the end of this particular exercise, so I now want you to close the window using the close button and you should see only the Desktop once more on your monitor.

Exercise 7 – The Control Menu Icon

This next exercise is designed to illustrate the use of the **Control Menu icon**. This is a window control first introduced in earlier versions of the master Windows program and seems not much used these days.

This control is also sometimes referred to as the **System Menu** icon. It is to be found at the far left end of the **Title Bar**, just to the left of the title wording itself, as shown in this next picture:

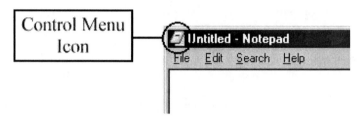

We begin the exercise at the **Desktop**. Open the **Notepad** window once more as we did for the start of Exercise 5, using the **Start button**, **Start Menu** and the **Run** options. With the word '**Notepad**' showing in the **Open box**, click on the **OK button**.

When the Notepad window opens, position the pointer over the **Control Menu icon** that we saw in the last picture. Now click on the icon to view the drop-down **Control Menu**, as shown below:

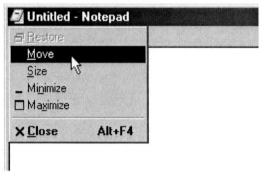

Before we click on any of the options, let us just have a quick look at this menu. We can see that it offers a number of functions that you may recognise. We have met all of these before, using other methods to achieve them.

The **Restore**, **Maximise** and **Minimise** functions are exactly the same as those provided by the three **Window Size Control buttons** located at the right hand end of the **Title bar**. Notice that the Restore function has a 'greyed out' appearance. This is because the window is currently in the normal state, so the function has no job to do. If the window was in either the maximised or minimised states, then these corresponding options would respectively be 'greyed out'.

The **Close option** too is the same as that provided by the '**X' button** at the top right corner of every window. There is an interesting reminder here of a keyboard combination that we met back in section 4.2, which is to press and hold the **Left ALT key** and then press the **F4 key**, then releasing both keys. You may remember that we used this previously at the very end of section 4.2 to close the Notepad window, before we started using the mouse. If you wish to use this keyboard combination in the future and forget exactly which keys you should use, then clicking on the Control Menu icon is a quick way to get a reminder!

We are not going to spend much more time on the Control Menu because it is rarely used by anyone these days. However, I will just show you the **Move option** in action because it is an interesting alternative to the drag technique on the Title Bar that we practised in the last exercise.

Position the **pointer** over the **Move option**, and then click. Instantly you will see the menu disappear and the Notepad window frame takes on a new look, similar to the 'ghost' images we saw in the last exercise.

Now leave the mouse pointer completely alone and use the group of four arrow keys on the right hand side of the keyboard to move the 'ghost' image around the screen – just the same as we did using the dragging of the Title Bar. These arrow keys are those shown in the next picture:

Re-position the window in a new spot of your own choosing. Now press the ENTER key. Instantly, the 'ghost' image disappears, and the window itself moves to the new location.

If you wish, you might like to try using the **Size** option from the **Control Menu** yourself. You will need to use the group of four arrow keys again to change the window size using only keyboard keys. I will leave you to explore this option. Remember to use the **ENTER key** as the 'command' key to finalise the action. What happens if you press the **ESC key** instead of the **ENTER key**?

To finish this exercise, position the pointer once again over the **Control Menu** icon at the far left of the **Title Bar** of the **Notepad** window and click to see the drop-down **Control Menu**. Slide the pointer down the options until you are over the **Close** option. Now click one final time to close the Notepad window and return to the Desktop.

There is one other function of the **Control Menu** icon that we should mention before we leave this subject. Experienced computer users often double-click on this icon as a fast method of closing a window. If you have mastered the art of the double-click you might like to try this for yourself by opening the

Notepad window yet again and then double-click the Control Menu icon to immediately close it again. If you are still struggling with the double-click, then perhaps not!

In conclusion of this last exercise, you might be asking yourself – What really is the point of providing the Control Menu, if all the functions can be achieved in other ways? The answer in truth is partly historical. As the master Windows program has developed over the years, new ways of doing things have evolved and have been added in. However, it is not always easy to drop features that some users have become used to and the tendency has been to leave the old methods available, so that the old 'die-hards' can still use these methods if they want to. For first-timers, there are some of the older functions that might be found to be quite useful – particularly as we have said before if you have trouble using the mouse.

We have now concluded all our exercises for this section on 'Working with windows'. In the next sections, we get to have some real fun!

6.2 Playing a game – Minesweeper

We have now reached one of the more interesting points in the book – learning how to play games! It has taken us a while to get to this stage, but I hope very quickly to show you that your efforts to date will be rewarded.

Playing games on computers is an excellent way to improve your skills and knowledge, so although we adopt a light-hearted approach to play them, there is a serious learning strategy underlying the action.

The game we are going to learn first is called 'Minesweeper'. The basic idea is that we will be presented with a playing board consisting of a number of squares that represent an area of territory. The squares are 'covered over' when we start the game, so that we cannot see what is underneath them. At the outset of the game, the Minesweeper program has hidden a number of 'explosive mines' throughout the territory that can blow us to pieces if we accidentally step on them. Here is what the opening board looks like.

As we progress through the game, we are invited to 'step' on any square that we choose by using a simple click of the mouse pointer. When we do this, its underlying content will be immediately revealed. If the square contains a mine then we are immediately blown to smithereens and the game comes to an abrupt end! If the square does not contain a mine, there may be one adjacent to it, and we will recognise this by a simple number displayed in the uncovered square from 1 to 8, showing us the total number of adjacent squares that have a mine on them.

Our skill – if we have any – is required to make deductions based upon the numbers displayed in order to predict where it is safe to tread next, and where it is not. We win the game only when all squares containing mines have been correctly identified by us. The Minesweeper program will time us while we play the game, so we can keep track of how fast we have been in making our decisions. Thus, we can play against others if we so choose by aiming for the shortest timing.

If a square should have no mines at all on any of the adjacent squares, then those adjacent squares will also be uncovered in the same move. We might see in one move, therefore, quite a number of squares being uncovered. Those squares which remain covered will either contain a mine, or be just one square away from one – so be very careful when you make the choice of which square to click on next!

If we deduce that an uncovered square contains a mine then we 'mark' the square accordingly. We make a 'mark' by performing a **right-click** action on it. There are two types of mark that we can make, one is a little red flag (to be used when we are certain from our deductions that the square contains a mine), and the other is a question mark (to be used if we are undecided but strongly suspect that it does). A little red flag appears when we first right-click a square. A question mark appears if we right-click it for a second time. We can also right-click a third time to remove a mark altogether.

Once we have marked all the correct squares with a little red flag, then the game will finish at that point. The counter shown in red at the left side of the 'smiley face' tells us how many mines there are altogether. The other red counter on the right of the 'smiley' face is the timer, and this starts automatically as soon as we make the first move.

To start you off playing, I will now take you through all the steps needed to get you underway.

The first job we need to do is to get the **MineSweeper** program started. We are going to do this using only the mouse pointer. Let me first say that you will need to take quite a bit of care now, until you get used to starting programs up this way. The method has a few traps to trip up the unwary! However, despite it being a little tricky, it is a good thing to learn how to do it because, generally speaking, most experienced computer users start all programs this way. So here we go ...

Begin at the **Desktop**. Use the mouse pointer to Click on the **Start Button** on the grey **Task Bar** at the bottom left corner of the screen. The **Start Menu** will then pop-up.

Slide the pointer up the Start Menu to point at the option called '**Programs**' which will then become highlighted. Keep the pointer steady over this option for a second or two, and then automatically another menu will pop-up along the right hand side.

Now, very carefully, slide the pointer directly sideways to the right, to slide it from the Start Menu into this new menu. If you do this correctly, the Programs option stays highlighted, even when you have moved over to the new menu. If you don't do it correctly, you will see something else become highlighted on the Start Menu and you will have to slide back left again to the Start Menu in order to re-establish the highlight on Programs.

If you make a mistake then it is probably because you are not sliding the pointer directly sideways. You should not make any vertical movement of the pointer whilst sliding sideways. You must also keep the pointer over the menu areas, don't let it stray off the edges.

Let me give you another tip before we go any further. If you get into a bit of a muddle whilst we go through this, you can use our old trick of pressing the ESC key in order to go backwards to reverse the showing of pop-up menus.

If you accidentally start up some other program by mistake (it might happen if you select the wrong options from these menus) then keep calm. Wait until that program has finished loading and starting, then close it with the Close button. If by chance another pop-up menu shows itself on starting the unintended program, then you might need to click on a Cancel button, or some other non-committing button (like a No button for example) before you are allowed to click on the Close button!

Now back to the main theme. If you have slid the pointer over onto the new menu correctly, then you will notice that one of the options on this new menu becomes highlighted. You should see something like this next picture on your monitor screen:

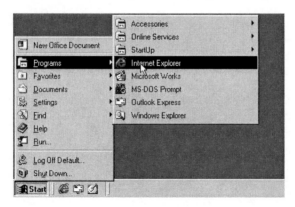

Your task now is to carefully move the pointer vertically upwards, keeping it over the new menu the whole time that you do so, until you reach the option called '**Accessories**', which should be near the top.

With Accessories highlighted, wait for a second or two and a third menu will pop-up to the right of the pointer. Slide the pointer directly sideways again to the right, and when the pointer is safely on this third menu then slide it downwards to highlight an option called '**Games**'.

> **Note – if you cannot identify an option called 'Games' following the Accessories option, then the games programs have not yet been installed on your computer. These are contained on the Windows 98 CD-ROM installation disk and you should enlist the help of a more experienced user to go through the installation procedure.**

With Games highlighted, wait for another second or two and a fourth menu will pop-up to the right of the pointer. Slide the pointer directly sideways again to the right, and when the pointer is safely on this fourth menu then slide it downwards to highlight the option called '**Minesweeper**'.

Now with your pointer over the highlighted option Minesweeper, make a click on it. Suddenly, all the menus disappear and after a moment or two, the Minesweeper program will load itself and then start up by displaying the opening window.

Keep the Minesweeper program window ready to use, but don't begin to play it just yet. In the next part of this section we will discuss the method for playing, and after reading it you will be in a better position to try it out for yourself.

Okay. There we have it. You have now learnt the technique of how to open nearly every program that you will ever use on your computer using only the mouse! In this case it was the Minesweeper program but any other program you choose to use can be opened in exactly the same manner.

Minesweeper

We will now just run through the starting moves to play the game, so that you get a better idea of how to play it. Once you are underway, then I will leave you to have a game by yourself on your own.

We begin with the left picture overleaf where we choose a square at random to click on as our first move. Notice that the red counter to the left of the 'smiley' face shows '10' which is the total number of mines that we have to locate to win the game:

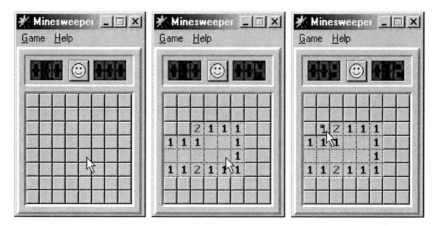

When we click on a square, then that square is uncovered. If it has a number on it then the move stops at that point. If the square does not have a number on it, then in the same move, all the neighbouring squares are uncovered. This continues until all squares on the perimeter of the move have a number on them.

The above centre picture now shows us what the board looks like after we have made the first click. The square that the pointer is over reveals that is has no mine, nor is it adjacent to one, so the uncovered square has no number and is just plain. The red counter on the right of the 'smiley' face shows that '4 seconds' have now elapsed since we began.

In the same move as our first click, all the surrounding squares were uncovered and a few more besides. The move ended showing a perimeter of squares, each of which had a number showing.

Let us now use a simple coding system to specify and discuss individual squares. We will use a column/row coding such that '3c4r' means 'the square which is in the 3rd column from the left and the 4th row down from the top'.

If we examine the square 3c4r, we notice that it has only one uncovered square next to it in its top left corner. We also notice that 3c4r has a number value of '1'. Using our great powers of deduction, we can fairly safely assume therefore that this uncovered square must have a mine underneath it!

We now mark the mine by a right-click on the uncovered square of 2c3r. The result of this operation is illustrated in the right-hand picture.

Now, having established that square 2c3r contains a mine, we can make another deduction concerning square 1c3r to its immediate left. This square cannot contain a mine, or else the square immediately below it (1c4r) would have to show a number value of '2', and it doesn't! The fact that 1c4r only has a number value of '1' means that of the two squares above it (1c3r and 2c3r) only one of them has a mine. Well, we have already marked 2c3r with certainty, therefore our deduction must be correct.

We can now safely click on square 1c3r, and this is shown in the left of the next group of pictures:

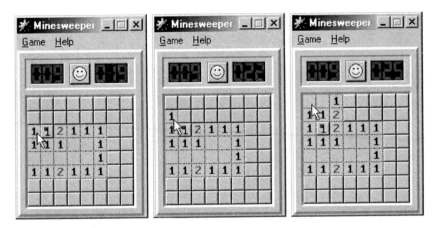

Now that square in turn also tells us something important. Its number value is also '1' and that has to be as a result of the uncovered squared 2c3r to its right with the little red flag on it! Therefore another deduction can be made that square 1c2r has no mine, so we click on this one, as in the above centre picture.

From that last click on square 1c2r, we see that it also has a number value of '1'. This tells us that square 1c1r cannot have a mine under it either! When we click on 1c1r we notice that quite a few more squares are now automatically uncovered.

And so the game goes on...

I will now leave you to try the Minesweeper program out for yourself. You should have the starting board all ready to go on the Desktop. Try it out now and see how you get on. If you get blown up by a mine and want to restart another game, then simply click on the 'smiley' face button and the game resets itself.

When you have had enough of playing Minesweeper, then come back to this text and read the last part of this section. Keep the Minesweeper window open, so that you are ready for the final part.

Okay. Before we conclude this section on 'Playing a game', I would now like to go over some of the other features you can explore with the Minesweeper program window that you will often find in other programs too.

By now you should be used to positioning the pointer before you click on something, so the time has come to shorten the wording of our instructions. From hereon, when I ask you to 'click on' something, I really mean position the pointer first and then make a click action. Similarly, with 'double-click on' and 'right-click on'. Do remember though, it is the tip of the pointer that must be on top of the object we are referring to, when you press the mouse buttons.

Under the **Title Bar**, we see the **Menu Bar** consisting of just two options – '**Game**' and '**Help**'. We will have a look at both of these to see what they contain. **Click** first on **Game**, and see the drop-down menu appear as shown below:

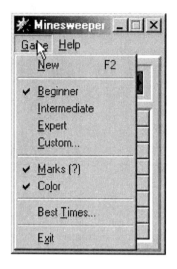

The first option **New** is something that many programs put top of the first list. It usually refers to a new session of whatever it is that the program does. In our case here, it will reset the window so that we have a new game.

The next options actually change the complexity of the game. Notice that **Beginner** has a tick in front of it. To see how this works, I want you to click on **Intermediate**.

As soon as you do this, then the menu disappears and the Minesweeper window changes its shape, as seen below.

Now we have a game that is considerably more complex to play. Not only are there more squares to play with, there are also more mines to discover – 40 in all! Click again on **Game** but this time select the **Custom** option.

Now we get a new pop-up window, as shown in the picture opposite.

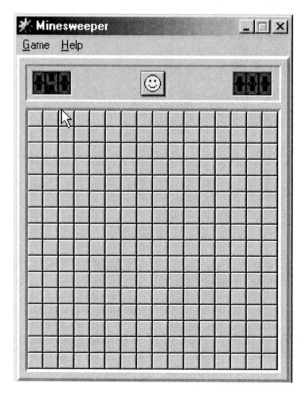

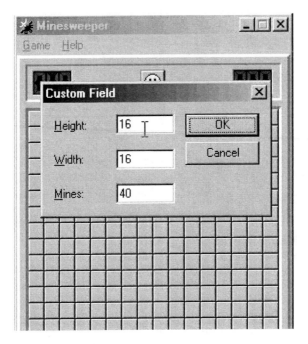

The pop-up window is called a **dialog box**. It allows us to have a form of 'dialog' where we can change several things at once. In the example here, we can change three parameters – **Height, Width** and **Mines**. When we are happy with the values of the parameters, we click on the **OK button** to put the changes into effect.

To make changes to any of these three parameters, we can type new values directly into the **boxes**. Notice in the last picture that the **pointer** has again changed its symbol. This is because it is pointing over the white part of the Height box. If we now click on the white box, then a cursor will appear inside it, and we can then use any of the keys on the keyboard to modify the value – including the **DEL key** or the **Backspace key** if we want to rub typing out.

Modify the values shown on your own screen, using the white boxes, and entering values of your own choice. The value limits are 24, 30 and 667 respectively. If you try entering higher values then the program will actually use the maximum limit. Click on OK when you have finished.

You should now see a customised version of the Minesweeper window appear.

Later on you can play about with the game, but I now want you to change the complexity back to Beginner. Do this by clicking again on the **Game** menu and then choosing the **Beginner** option with another click.

Okay. We should now be back with the simplified version of the program.

The final point I want you to look at is the **Help menu**. Click this menu from the **Menu Bar** and you should see something like the following:

Click on **About Minesweeper** and you will get another pop-up window that tells you details about the program creators and other items. This 'About' option is something else that you will often find included on the Help menu of many other programs. Click on OK to return to the main window again.

Finally click on the **Help menu** and select **Help Topics**. This style of pop-up window is also very commonly found in other programs. I will leave the various items in this window for you to explore on your own. You can move the pointer over many of the objects that you see and click on them to discover what they do.

Try the different 'tabs' out by clicking on the words **Index** and **Search**, and then back to **Contents**. The great thing about the Help window is that you cannot do any 'damage' to the main program when you use it, so feel free to try experimenting on your own. Just remember the **Close button** in the top right hand corner, when you want to finish using the Help facilities.

That now concludes this section on 'Playing a game'. Have fun playing Minesweeper at your leisure, and close it using the Close button when you are finished. There are more good games for you to try out as you please – Solitaire in particular is a firm favourite with many users.

To start these others, you only need to select them from the **Games** menu in just the same way that we started Minesweeper at the beginning of this section.

If you need assistance with the rules for playing other games, you should use the **Help Topics** option from the **Help menu** that you will see on the Menu bar of these other program windows.

In the next and final section of this chapter, we will learn how to use a program to draw and save our own drawings and pictures.

6.3 Drawing pictures with 'Paint'

In chapter 4, we learnt how to do a simple job of writing a note. Now we are going to learn how to do another simple job of making a drawing. The task is to make a map for friends to show them the precise whereabouts of an imaginary new house. To make this map we shall use a program already on your computer called 'Paint'. When we have finished, we will save the drawing to the Hard Drive for permanent storage. For those first-timers with a printer, we shall show

how this can be printed out, and then we will close down the program. Finally, we shall show how to re-open the same drawing at a later time, make a small modification to it and then how to save it again.

We begin from the **Desktop**.

In the last section, we learnt how to start the Minesweeper program using only the mouse. The method we used employed a series of **pop-up menus** first activated with a click of the **Start button**. We shall now use the same technique to open and run the **Paint program**, but we won't describe each step in the same level of detail. If you have any difficulties using this technique then go back to the last section and read once more the tips we gave there to assist you in performing the task correctly.

Okay. Click now on the **Start button** at the bottom left corner of the screen on the grey **Task Bar**. The **Start Menu** will then pop-up.

Slide the pointer up the Start Menu to point at the Programs option. Wait a second or two for the next menu to pop-up on the right hand side. Now carefully slide the pointer directly sideways to the right onto the new menu, and then slide the pointer over the Accessories option.

With Accessories highlighted, wait for a second or two and a third menu will pop-up on the right hand side. Carefully slide the pointer directly sideways onto this one. Now slide the pointer downwards to highlight the option called '**Paint**'. Finally, click on the **Paint option** to start the program running.

When the Paint program window starts running, its size will most likely be in the 'normal' state. If so, then make it a maximised window by clicking on the **Maximise button**, which is the central one of the three in the top right hand corner of the window, at the right hand end of the **Title Bar**. Now the program will take up the whole of the screen. The next picture illustrates what the **Paint program window** will look like when maximised.

Note – This picture has been taken from a 17 inch monitor screen that is configured to display in a manner known as 'Display Resolution 1024 by 768'. As first-timers, we won't go into the detail of exactly what this means at the moment; we will just say that it refers to the amount of fine detail that can be shown. Your own display may be different from this and therefore you may observe the Paint program slightly differently on your own monitor screen. Don't be concerned about it. The general principles will still apply.

When the Paint program first begins, we see a large white area on the screen that represents 'paper' that we can draw upon. Our first job is to resize this paper so that we know what size our final drawing will be.

Notice that in common with other windows, there is a grey Menu Bar near the top of the screen, directly underneath the blue Title Bar. Click on the word Image and select the Attributes... option. You now see a pop-up dialog box like that in the next picture:

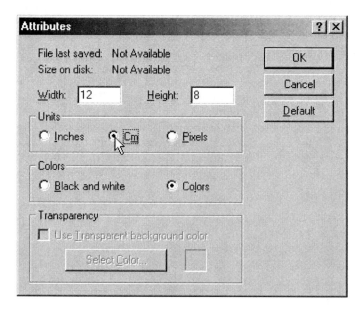

Click first on the **Cm** (centimetre) option as shown in the picture, then click on the **Width white textbox** so that a cursor appears. Type using the keyboard keys to alter the value to '12' (remembering that the **DEL** and **BackSpace** keys allow you to rub out). Then click on the **Height white textbox** and alter that value to '8'. Now click on the **OK button**.

The **Attributes** dialog box disappears, and the 'paper' is re-sized to the new values. If you go back to the Attributes dialog box at a later time you will discover that the actual size accepted by the computer is set slightly different to the values you typed in. This is because the smallest dot we can make on the paper is fixed in its size by the computer settings, and there has to be an exact whole number of these tiny dots on the paper overall. The computer adjusts the values automatically to get the nearest ones to those we typed in, but chooses values that don't have a fractional number of tiny dots. (This can mean that the values end up fractional sometimes!).

By the way, the name we give to the size of the smallest dot we can make on the paper is a **pixel**. You might have noticed in the Attributes dialog box that we can size the paper in units of either **inches**, **centimetres**, or **pixels**. Later on, we will be able to see what a pixel actually looks like when we use the **magnifying glass tool**.

Okay. Now we have our paper correctly sized and we are ready to start work.

The next thing we will do is make an adjustment to the appearance of the paper image on the screen so that we can work more comfortably with it. Click on the icon of the **Magnifying glass** in the set of **tools** as shown alongside:

Now position the pointer down below the tools and click on the '**2x**' wording to make it highlighted. As soon as you have done this, then the paper appearance will change in viewing size, and will appear double that which is was previously. If the paper is now too big to fit on your screen, then you will see **scroll bars** become visible along the bottom and the right edges. (Whether the paper appears too big or not depends on the actual monitor you are using, and what the 'display resolution' has been set at). This new magnification does not affect the true size of the paper, only the appearance of it on your monitor screen.

You should now decide which magnification is the best for you to work with. The preferred one should be that which gives you the biggest appearance of the paper on the screen, but without the scroll bars showing. Make your own choice now using the **Magnifying Glass tool**, and select from between '**1x**' and '**8x**' to get the best view.

Okay. We are now ready to start to do some actual drawing.

When the **Paint program** first starts running, you might notice that the 'default' choice of tool is the **Pencil tool**. You can see this because its icon appears first selected in the toolbox. As soon as you move the mouse pointer anywhere over the 'paper' area, then the pointer symbol changes to an image of a pencil.

For the map we are goint to make, we will begin drawing using the **Line tool**. Select this now by clicking on its icon as shown in the next picture:

Notice that when this **Line tool** is selected, we have five options presented underneath the toolbox that allow us to make choices of line thickness by clicking on the appropriate one. The above picture shows the thinnest line as selected (highlighted). For the moment, we will leave the option set to this top choice, which gives us a line thickness of **one pixel**. (A pixel, remember, is the smallest dot we can make on the paper).

Now position the mouse pointer somewhere in the bottom left hand area of the 'paper', say about a quarter of the distance in from the left paper edge and about a quarter of the distance up from the bottom paper edge. Notice that the pointer symbol has now changed into cross-wires with a tiny circle at the centre. The position where you place the pointer will be the starting point for a line that we are now going to draw horizontally across the paper towards the right.

We draw a line by using a **drag** action of the mouse. With the pointer at the starting point, press the **left mouse button** to start the drag. Keep the button pressed while you slide the mouse body across to the right, and move the pointer somewhere over to the right hand side of the paper, say about a quarter of the distance in from the right paper edge. *Don't let the drag end just yet.* Now, gently adjust the pointer position, either up or down as required, until the line that we are drawing is absolutely straight and horizontally flat across the paper. There should not be any jagged steps, anywhere along the length of the line if you can avoid them. Don't let the drag end until you are happy with the final position. With care, you can make quite fine adjustments.

Now, carefully, let the drag end by letting the left mouse button release!

If you have been successful, then you should now be able to move the pointer around on the paper area, and the line that you have drawn is now fixed in the desired position, looking something like this:

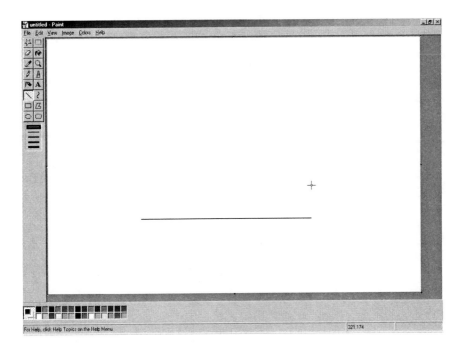

Okay. We should now discuss what to do if we make a mistake.

To undo the last action that you have made with any tool, you can, at any time, click on **Edit** from the **Menu Bar** and select the **Undo** option. If you are happy with the line you have drawn, then you can move on to the next task. If you want to go back and try again, then use this Undo feature and have another go.

> **A tip you might like to consider is to press and hold the SHIFT key down with one hand, at the same time that you are dragging on the mouse with the other. This will constrain the drawing of the line and make it easier to get it perfectly horizontal! Try it and see! You can always undo any unwanted lines.**

Now we are going to draw another line about 1 cm above the last one. We could use the **Line tool** again, but I want to show you another very useful method for making a copy of something that you have already drawn. Click on the Select tool as shown in the next picture:

This tool is rather special. It is used to create a small area anywhere on the paper that is outlined by four 'dashed' lines (as illustrated by the icon's image). This outlined area is called a selection and anything inside it can be copied to a memory device within the master Windows program called the **clipboard**.

The **clipboard** is a very unusual and clever feature of the master Windows program, and we shall learn more about it in later chapters. It is like a hidden place internal to the computer where we can store copies of things taken from our working area on the paper. We can do this most any time we want to, but we can only store one copy at a time. We can also copy things in the reverse direction, that is, from the clipboard back onto our paper. When we perform a reverse copy, we use the jargon 'paste'. We say that the contents of the **clipboard** are **pasted back** into our work. This creates an additional part to the drawing on the paper that we can move about and place anywhere we please.

Let us try this out practically so that it becomes clearer what we are talking about.

With the **selection tool** itself selected (as in the last picture) move the pointer now to the area left and above the line we have drawn. Then start a drag action and reposition the pointer to the right of the line and just below it. The next picture illustrates what we are trying to achieve:

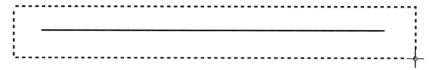

Now end the drag action. From the **Menu Bar**, click on **<u>E</u>dit** and then click on **<u>C</u>opy**.

This last click has now made a copy of all the drawing contained within the area of the dashed line, and has placed it inside the memory device we call the clipboard.

Before we paste the copy back onto the paper, I want you now to click on the lowest icon that you can see underneath the toolbox and highlight it blue, as shown below:

Choosing this lower icon changes the way in which our copy will look when we come to do the paste. If you study the last picture closely, the diagrams on the icons are trying to show that the lower one offers a transparent background to the image when we paste it, but with the upper one, the background will not be transparent. You might like to explore the differences between these two yourself at a later date.

Now point back with the pointer to the **Menu Bar**. Click on **<u>E</u>dit** and then click on **<u>P</u>aste**. Suddenly a new image appears in the top left corner of the paper, which is an exact copy of the original line surrounded by another dashed frame. We can move this dashed frame area to any part of the paper that we choose. We do this by re-positioning the pointer anywhere inside the frame, and making a drag action on it.

Perform a drag now on the frame, and place the new copy of the line above the original so that you can see both of them. Leave a space between the lines of about a centimetre as in the next picture, so that we have room to put a street name, and then end the drag:

⬦

Notice that the pointer symbol changed shape into a 'four headed arrows' symbol when we place it inside the frame. The frame itself disappears temporarily while we are performing a drag and returns again when we end it. If the new position of the second line is not quite how you would like it, you can do another drag (making sure the pointer is inside the frame) and make fine adjustments to its final placement.

When you are happy with the final position, then we need to lock it permanently in its new place. We do this by a simple click anywhere on the paper outside of the frame.

The dashed line of the frame then disappears permanently.

Okay. Now we have drawn the Main Street! The next job is to start drawing a side street going up the paper. To do this we will go back to using the **Line tool**. Click now on the Line tool and position the cross-wires in the middle of the top line (somewhere just left of centre) and actually on the black of the line itself. Now start the drag action and slide the pointer vertically upwards, ending the drag about a quarter way in from the top edge. You can use the tip I gave you before if you want to. To make a perfectly vertical line, hold the SHIFT key down with one hand while you make the drag on the mouse with the other.

Now make a second vertical line, about a centimetre to the right of the one that you have just done. The choice is yours how you do it. Either use the Line tool again, or you can try a copy and paste action using the clipboard once more. If you do use the clipboard, then copy a bit of the 'junction' where the last vertical line meets the upper horizontal line, when you use the Select tool. You will find that when you paste it back onto the paper that it can be manipulated such that it overlaps directly on the horizontal line and forms a neat second 'junction'. This is an advantage of the fact that we have a 'transparent background' when we clicked on the icon shown in the picture one before the last.

Your drawing should now look something like this:

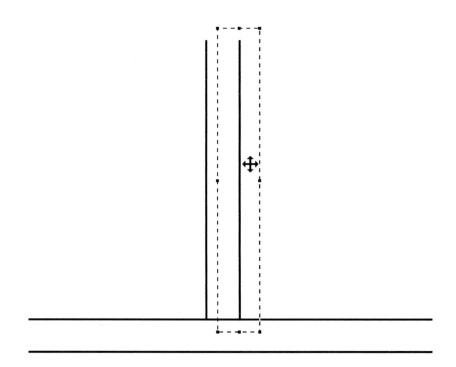

The next thing we need to do is to clean up the junction and remove the line across the bottom of the street we have just drawn. To do this we will use the Eraser tool. Click now on this tool as shown in the next picture:

With the Eraser tool selected, you will now see underneath the toolbox a range of different sizes for the tool. We can leave the option set at the default, but if you need very fine control then you might like to pick a different one. The choice is yours.
The **Eraser tool** changes the pointer symbol into a square. Now place the pointer over the line across the junction and click to rub a piece of it out, as in the next picture:

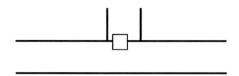

If you move the pointer out of the way after the click then you can see the part that you have rubbed out. Carefully position the Eraser again to rub a bit more out and click again. Repeat until you have the line across the junction completely removed. Remember, if you make a mistake you can use the Undo facility found on the Edit menu to go back one step and have another go.

A good tip to remember about using the Eraser is that you can first increase the magnification of the paper if you want using the Magnifying Glass, and then perform your rubbing out. When you increase the magnification, you may find that the drawing image is very large and most of it has disappeared off the edge of the visible area of the paper. In this situation, you should use the **scroll bars** to scroll back and forth and find the part of the drawing that you are interested in. When you have finished the rub out, then you can revert back to the original magnification and carry on where you left off.

You can also use the Eraser tool in a drag type of action if you wish. During the time that the drag is in progress, the Eraser will be rubbing out continuously. This can be of great help if you have quite a bit of rubbing out to do, like a whole line for example.

Okay. Now we have a completed side street off the main street of our drawing. The next job is to add a few houses. We will use the **Rectangle tool** to do this. Select this tool as shown in the next picture:

The options now shown underneath the toolbox represent the different ways that a rectangle can be drawn. We shall use the default option shown highlighted above which is an outline form of rectangle.

The Rectangle tool is used in a similar manner to the Selection tool. First position the pointer at the spot where you want the top left-hand corner to be, and then use a drag action to re-position the pointer to the spot where you want the bottom right-hand corner to be. As soon as the drag action is ended, then the outlined rectangle will be finished and become part of the drawing.

If you change your mind about the rectangle while you have the drag in progress, you can do it, but you have to be a little smart! The way to change your mind and not draw a rectangle is to keep the drag in progress (that is, keep your finger pressing down the left mouse button) and very sneakily use your second longest finger to make a right-click (press and release). This effectively stops the drag, and stops the drawing action.

For our drawing, you can add rectangles to represent houses or other buildings in any way that you choose. I will leave it up to you how many you actually add to your drawing, but I suggest at least six. Go ahead now and make these along the side of the side street. You might even add one rectangle on to the edge of another to make a more realistic illustration of a building that isn't a simple shape. When you have done, your drawing should now look something like the picture overleaf.

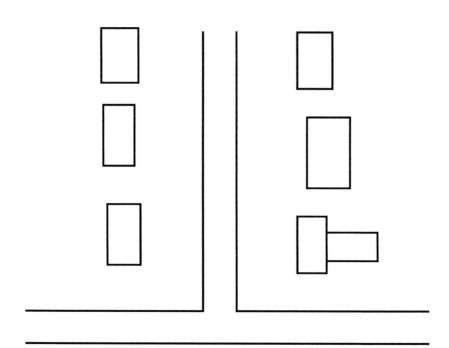

The next job is to attach some names to the streets. To do this we will use the **Text tool**. Now let me say a word of caution before you try to select the Text tool. You must have the paper magnification set to 'x1' before you can use it. If you try to select it without putting the magnification back to 'x1', then you will hear a strange 'exclamation sound' from your computer speakers, and the tool itself will refuse to allow you to select it (it won't appear as though it has been pressed, like the other tools have so far).

The Paint program designers have chosen to make you choose the 'x1' magnification first so that you elect the correct '**font**' before you start creating text size (if the word **font** is new to you it means shape or style of the printing typeface). This is quite important when printing the drawing out on a printer. If you get the wrong font size, then the printed copy might look very different when it is finally printed out.

So, now make sure the magnification of your paper is back to 'x1' by clicking on the **Magnifying Glass** tool and adjusting the highlighted option under the toolbox accordingly. Then click the **Text tool** button, which has the letter 'A' as an icon on it. You should check also that when the Text tool has accepted your request to press it that the lower of the two icons under the toolbox is highlighted (as we did before when we performed a paste action), *so that the background is transparent.*

Now we shall discuss technique for using the Text tool. When I use the tool personally, I always create the text first in some spare space on the drawing, well away from any other lines or images, and away from where I will finally position it. I make sure that I am satisfied that my text is complete and says what I want it to, and is as big as I think it should be. Only when I am satisfied about its appearance do I then move it into its correct and final position. To do the placement, I use the **Select tool** to create a dashed box around it. This 'grabs' hold of the text, and then I carefully and very precisely slide it into place with a drag action. The reason I go to these elaborate lengths is that it is only when you can see all the text (from end to end) can you decide how to get it centrally in the place where you want to put it. If you don't do this and try drawing it immediately in its final place (guessing where the text should start off from), then invariably you get it wrong and want to move it over a bit. But when the text is located close to other lines and images, it becomes difficult to separate things out to select only the words with the Select tool, without disturbing the surrounding lines.

Let me show you what I mean...

The Text tool is selected. We now place the pointer anywhere to the left on the paper but under the drawing we have done so far, leaving a bit of space between the chosen spot and the underside of the long 'Main Street' line. Perform a drag action to draw out a long thin rectangle formed by the dashed line that appears. Make this rectangle about the same thickness as the 'Main Street' and about half its length, as shown in the picture below (use a rough estimate, the exact dimensions are not really important):

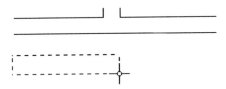

Now let the drag action end. You should then see that a **'flashing cursor'** appears inside the dashed rectangle.

Note – The sides of the rectangle itself have now become 'moveable' sides. If you want to change the shape of the rectangle, you can position the pointer precisely over the 'dots' in the sides then the pointer becomes double-headed and you can drag and change the shape (this is the same 'moveable' type of side that we have met before for exercise 6, section 6.1, moving a window's sides). When you have finished, to get the 'cursor' back, just click inside the rectangle.

At this point, you now have the option of deciding the size and type of font you want to use. We shall use the 'default' which is known as 'MS Sans Serif, size 8'. If you wish to change the font, you can click on View from the Menu bar and select Text Toolbar. Then you can change things as you wish. The '**B**', '*I*' and '**u**' buttons in the Text toolbar can be pressed for 'Bold', 'Italic' or 'Underlining' respectively. Close the Text Toolbar when you have finished using its own little Close button.

The 'flashing cursor' inside the dashed rectangle may stop and disappear if you click or make some other action after first making the rectangle with the Text tool. To get it back again, just click anywhere inside the dashed rectangle.

Okay. Now we are ready to type in some text. With the flashing cursor visible, go ahead and type in the words 'Main Street' using the keyboard. Once more, the DEL and BackSpace Keys are available if you make typing mistakes and want to edit the text. If you make a complete 'dog's dinner' of the whole thing, you can press the ESC Key and all the text and rectangle will instantly be removed, ready to start again!

When you have the text finished, click anywhere on the paper background outside of the dashed rectangle and the text will become part of your drawing.

Now we wish to move and carefully position the text symmetrically in the middle of the 'Main Street' lines. You can do this either at 'x1' paper magnification, or if you want to – and I recommend it – you can change the magnification back to where you had it before you selected the Text tool.

Okay. We are ready to reposition the text. Choose the **Select tool** (the one in the top right hand corner, with the dashed rectangle icon on it). Recheck that the Select tool is using the 'transparent background' option (as we did before), and then position the pointer just to the left and above the text. Drag downwards and to the right, such that the selection rectangle completely surrounds the text 'Main Street' but nothing else. Now position the pointer inside the selection rectangle – I usually do this somewhere inside on the right, so that the pointer symbol is not obscuring my view of the text. Then use a drag to position the text in the middle of the 'Main Street' lines. To finish off, click anywhere on the paper background outside of the selection rectangle, and your repositioning will be completed.

If you have followed all of this carefully, your drawing should now look something like this (If not, remember you can use the Undo facility to have another go!):

Main Street

Now we want to name the side street. The name we shall use in our example will be 'Chestnut Avenue'. Repeat the text production actions over a second time, using this new name as the text, up to the point where you have the selection rectangle surrounding the text and you are ready to move the text into final position. Remember that in order to use the Text tool, the paper magnification must be set at 'x1' or you are not allowed to use it.

Now with the second piece of text surrounded by the selection rectangle – before you start to move it – click on the Menu Bar and select 'Image' and then 'Flip/Rotate'. A pop-up dialog box will then appear. Click on 'Rotate by angle' and '270°' as shown in the next picture:

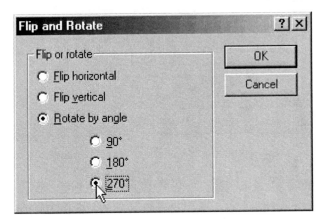

The selection rectangle now will become rotated onto its left side. Now you can make the final positioning movement with a drag action, to place the second text in between the 'Side Street' lines, as in the next picture:

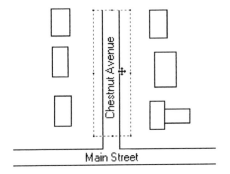

The drawing now is really looking good and taking shape. We will only make a few more additions to finish it off. The first of these is to show you how to use the Colour (or Color) selection palette. (You say 'Tom-mar-toe', I say 'Tom-may-toe!' Remember that this program was written in America, where they have abandoned proper spelling!).

Now position the pointer over the Red color box of the Color Palette and click on it. The next picture shows things just after a click has been done:

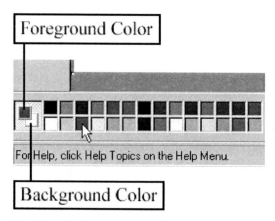

You may notice that the **Foreground Color** has changed following the click from Black to Red. (If you ever need to change the **Background Color** you use a right-click instead of a click). Now select the **Color Fill** tool:

 Position the pointer over the top right-hand building, in the white area that is the centre of the outlined rectangle, and make a click. Instantly, the centre is filled with Red. By the way, for future reference, the active part of the new pointer symbol for the Color Fill tool is the 'tip of the paint' outside of the can!

Now click on the Black Color box of the Color Palette and the Foreground Color reverts back to Black.

Okay. We are almost done with our drawing! This final part is just to demonstrate how to use the free-hand **Pencil tool**, if you ever need it.

Before I demonstrate the Pencil tool, I want you to add a third bit of text just to the right of the building we have coloured Red, saying 'We live here', using the same principles for adding text we have described previously.

Then choose the Pencil tool:

 To use this tool, you simply make a drag action. All of the time that you move the pointer with the left mouse button pressed, then a pencil mark is drawn on the paper.

The color used for the pencil mark is the Foreground Color as shown by the left-hand side of the Color Palette. Use the Pencil tool to make a free-hand sketch of an 'arrow', with its 'tail' starting under the third bit of text and curved around so that the 'head' is pointing towards the building, as shown in the next picture:

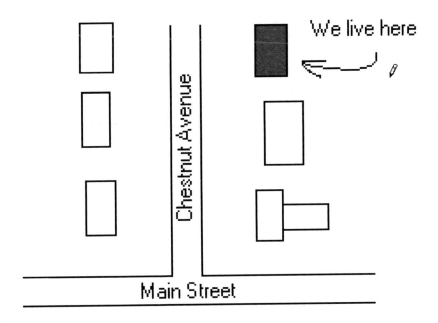

This last job with test how your skill with the mouse is coming along! The Undo facility might come in very handy here!

Okay. We have reached the end of the drawing. Now we need to save our work and give it a suitable Title.

From the **Menu Bar**, select '**File**' and then '**Save As...**'. The '**Save As**' **dialog box** will then pop-up. Type your name for the drawing in the '**File name**' **textbox** as shown in this next picture:

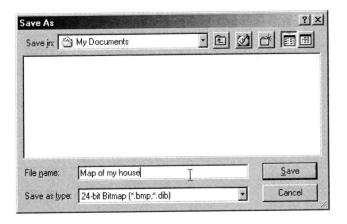

Notice that the **'Save as type' textbox** will automatically select '24-bit Bitmap' as the type for the file. Again, the folder automatically selected is the **My Documents** folder.

> **An interesting learning point from the above picture is that the dialog box is not showing you the text file in this folder named 'Shopping List Number 1', which we created before, in chapter 4. It is in fact still there, but the reason why you cannot now see it is to do with the 'Save as type' textbox. Because this is set to '24-bit Bitmap' it only shows files that are known as 'bmp' type files. It does not show any other type of file. The 'Shopping List Number 1' file is of type 'txt' and that is the reason why it is not being shown. We shall learn more about file types in chapter 8.**

When you have named the new file for our drawing, click on the **OK button** to finally save it to the Hard Drive.

Before we finally close the Paint program, if you have a printer attached to your computer you might like to print it out. The Paint program is typical of many other programs in that you will usually find the **Print...** option available on the **File drop-down menu.**

However, you might want to consider just exactly how it will appear on the paper before you make a printed copy. There are two other options available on the File menu that you should investigate. These are **Print Preview** and **Page Setup...** You may need to navigate back and forth between these latter two to get the best results.

First, click on **File** and then on **Page Setup...** and check that the paper size is correct. A4 is the common size for most general printers these days, and you should remember that A4 is 21 cm wide and 29.7cm in height when considered in **Portrait** style (the longest side vertical). The margin settings will also affect the final print out and the view that we see when we use the previewing facility. You may need to come back and adjust these later.

One of the points about printing in general that you should always consider is 'Will your drawings and paintings fit on the printer paper – taking into account the actual image size and the margin settings in use?'. The full image size of the drawing we made was set by us at the outset to be 12cm by 8 cm, when we set the Attributes option. This size is the size of the white area we have up to now been calling 'paper' on the screen. Don't confuse this screen 'paper' with the real paper in our printer. The screen 'paper' was an imaginary size and we could make it any size we pleased (within limits) when we began. It was chosen for convenience and to give us a starting area on the screen in which to make our drawing. For printing, you should think of this as now as being 'cut out' if you like from the screen and electronically stuck onto the real paper in the printer.

This is where the margins come in. The margins are effectively a border on the *physical* paper guaranteed to be kept clear. Our image will then begin after the top margin and after the left margin, and appear pushed up against these. The other two margins, that is – the bottom margin and right margin – only come into play if our image is too big. For example, if there isn't enough room on our physical paper to fit both the left and right margins in as well as the full width of our screen 'paper' image, then the screen 'paper' image will be electronically chopped short. We would then find that we get two pieces of paper printed out on the printer instead of one, with the second piece containing the right-hand bit of what was 'chopped' off.

If this ever happens to you with other drawings, you should remember the discussion we have had here! Particularly if you get a blank second paper coming out of the printer! Always add up the size of the margins to the size of the screen 'paper' image, and check that the total is less than the size of the physical paper.

Now have a look at **Print Preview** by clicking first on the **File** menu and then on this option. It will give you some idea how it will finally look when it comes out on real paper. If there is a problem with image width plus margin widths being greater than physical paper width, then you will see it in the preview images. You might then consider switching to the **Landscape** option in **Page Setup...**, which will give you width at the expense of height.

When you are happy with the settings, make your print of the drawing by choosing the **Print** option from **File** menu. Sit back and admire your handiwork as it comes chugging out of the printer!

Now close the Paint program by clicking on the close button in the top right-hand corner of the window.

If at some future point you would like to edit the drawing we have just made, you can do this fairly easily. We will now describe two alternative ways that you might attempt to start this.

- The first way is as follows. Start the **Paint program** running (using the procedure we discussed at the beginning of this section) and then from the **Menu Bar**, select 'File' and then 'Open' and use the dialog box that pops up. Click with the pointer on the icon in the large white box for the file in question – 'Map of my house' – and then click the **Open button**.

- The second way is even quicker. Start the **Paint program** running. From the **Menu Bar**, select 'File', and then take the selection further down the drop down menu that says '1. Map of my house'.

This alternative method uses a feature that you will often find used by many other programs. The last four files that have been used with the program are 'remembered' and kept as options numbered 1 to 4 on the File drop-down menu, with the most recent being number 1. As you create a new file, then the oldest file is 'forgotten' each time and the newer file enters the list as number 1, pushing the others down in the stack.

This now concludes Chapter 6. I hope you have enjoyed learning about windows and the exercises on how to manipulate them. Playing Games can be good fun too, and quite relaxing when you have been working hard on the computer for a number of hours.

Finally, I hope you found the long section on using the Paint program a useful and enjoyable exercise. It has actually taught you quite a bit about the general use of programs, as well as giving you a simple-to-use program that is also very powerful. Many people grossly underestimate the power of this program that comes as standard with the master Windows program.

Later, in chapter 9, we learn to use a more powerful type of word processing program called 'Wordpad' (more powerful that is than the simple Notepad program), and we shall learn how to write text documents and mix into them pictures previously created with the Paint program.

7

The Desktop

7.1 More about the Desktop

In Chapter 2, we introduced the screen display known as the Desktop, which is the display we are left with when we first switch on the computer. We then went on to learn about using the keyboard and the mouse, and how to use simple programs like Notepad, Minesweeper and Paint. The time has now come for us to return to the subject of the Desktop and discuss this in greater depth. When we have completed this stage, your knowledge and understanding will have reached a suitable level where you can begin exploring the computer on your own, and not need so much guidance at every step and turn.

The top illustration opposite shows the main items to be found on the Desktop:

The Desktop Background

The **Desktop background** is the most basic area where objects are placed that we want to work with. There are three common types of object that we find here – **windows, icons** (including shortcuts), and the **Task Bar**. Occasionally we see other objects, but in truth, they are variations of types of window in different guises.

The Desktop background is a kind of 'neutral place' where we can position the mouse pointer with safety. If we click or double-click on the background, then nothing serious happens, other than the focus of attention will change away from other objects. You may remember we discussed the idea of things having the 'focus' in section 5.2, exercise 2. We shall be saying more on this topic later in this section.

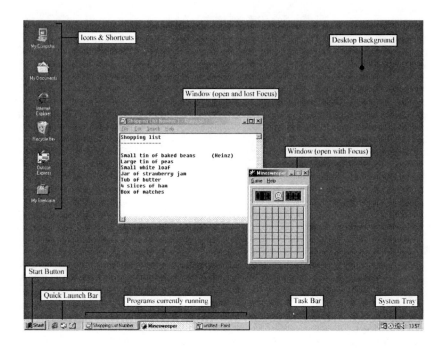

If we right-click on the Desktop background then we see something happen. Try this yourself now and you should see a pop-up menu appear like the next picture:

This action of **right-clicking** on things is a very useful trick to remember and you may like to try this yourself when you come across other objects in due course. It usually reveals a pop-up **menu** that gives you options specifically about the object in question. You don't necessarily have to take any of the options if you don't want to, and you can safely clear the menu by simply pressing the **ESC** key if you only want to read it.

Not every object that you right-click upon will show you such a menu. For those that do they usually provide for quicker ways of achieving tasks, which can be done in other ways, but possibly requiring more steps. For example, the third option in the above menu will line up all the icons present on the Desktop neatly in perfectly straight rows and columns. You could do this yourself by a drag action on each icon in turn, but this would take a lot more effort. It is much easier to use the option from this menu.

Rather than spend time now covering the detail of all options on this last menu, I will leave them for you to explore at your leisure. However, there are a few points worth mentioning before we move on. The **Active Desktop** option is one that first-timers would be wise to leave alone for the time being. The reason is that it can substantially change the way that the whole Desktop appears and behaves. This could throw you into confusion because the discussions we have in this book may no longer strictly apply. The **Refresh** option does not appear to do anything. What it actually does is to make sure that the display you are currently viewing on screen is in agreement with the computer's own internal memory of what should be being displayed (occasionally it can get out of step). The **Properties** option is an interesting one that you might see for other objects as well. It can show you valuable information about the object that you are concerned with. In this instance, it brings up the **Display Properties** window that has many features for changing the Desktop appearance. Again, be careful with it because you can make changes that you might wish you hadn't, and have great trouble undoing them! One last comment – if you change something using a menu option and then want to go back to how it was before, this can sometimes be done by finding the same option and activating it a second time. Options where this works can be spotted when they show a 'tick' symbol on the menu. The act of selecting it a second time will remove the 'tick' symbol and de-activate the option.

When you are ready to remove the above pop-up menu, either click again on the Desktop background, or press the ESC key.

One additional helpful feature of the Desktop background is that if you click on it and then press the **F1** key, you will get a pop-up **Help** window that gives assistance with all matters connected with the master Windows program itself. This Help window is similar in how it works to that of the Minesweeper program, which we discussed in section 6.2. Try this out now for yourself. Have a general look around it by clicking in turn on the tabs marked **Contents, Index** and **Search**. The book icons can be both opened and closed by a click action. When you have finished browsing around, close it using the Close button in the top right-hand corner. Don't forget how to use this Help window in the future. If you get stuck with a problem it can provide a handy source of information that is always readily available, even when the computer manuals have long been lost to the cupboards!

Icons and Shortcuts

Icons are small picture-like objects that provide a method of linking quickly with some underlying program, folder or other item. We saw this linking mechanism at work in practice during the mouse exercises, when we 'opened' the My Computer icon. It provided a link to quickly reach and display the My Computer window. The images displayed on icons usually relate in some way to the underlying functions, and software designers are very inventive with the images that they come up with for their programs.

There are two types of icon that we witness on the Desktop.

- The first type is a system icon and these are created for us by the computer system itself.

- The second type is called a shortcut, which we are allowed to create ourselves (though there are some shortcuts also created by the system).

You can spot the difference between the two types because shortcuts are the only ones to have a tiny black arrow shown on them in a small white box to be found in their bottom left-hand corner.

Examples of system icons are **My Computer**, the **Recycle Bin**, **Network Neighbourhood** and such like. These icons are permanent and you cannot delete these from the Desktop even if you accidentally try to.

Shortcuts on the otherhand, being objects that we can create for ourselves, can be deleted from the Desktop; and we shall be performing some exercises in the next section that do both of these tasks.

The Task Bar

We have breifly mentioned the Task Bar a number of times in previous chapters. In Exercise 3, section 5.2, we showed that it could be moved from its normal location to different edges of the Desktop background. Now I want to discuss the detail of the various components that you will find on the Task Bar.

The **Start button** you already how to use from Exercise 5, section 6.1. The Start Button is the most general way to start any program running. All programs installed on the computer can be started by using the Start Button and its associated pop-up menus.

Just to the right of the Start button is the **Quick Launch bar**, which is shown again in the next picture:

 Its function is self-descriptive and it usually contains a few icons that provide quick links to launch commonly used programs. The **Quick Launch bar** takes advantage of the fact that the **Task Bar** is visible all the time, even when other program windows are maximised to cover the whole screen. You can therefore always see and use these icons to load and run the linked programs without having to close the window you are working in. To activate any of the icons you only need make a click action, not a double-click.

In the last picture, the first icon is a link to **Internet Explorer** (to access the Internet), and the second icon is a link to **Outlook Express** (to access Electronic Mail). These programs are covered in detail in two further books in the 'First Time' series of Computer Books, due to be published later.

The third icon shown in the last picture is a very interesting and useful one.

It isn't used with a program as such. The icon represents the **Desktop** itself (the picture is a blotting pad, pen and paper, as you might find on real desktops!) and it provides an ultra fast method of minimising all the windows that you might have open at any moment, so that you get just the Desktop displayed on the screen. Effectively, it is like a 'switch'. You click on the icon once to go straight to the Desktop, and you click on it again, when you are ready, to go back to what you were doing and where you were previously.

There is one last point I want to mention about the Quick Launch bar before we leave it. If you study the last picture closely, you will notice a small, vertical greyish line at the far left-hand side of the bar. This line is meant to represent a small 'handle' that you can 'grab hold of' with the mouse pointer. When you position the pointer over this 'handle' then the pointer symbol will change to a double-headed arrow. With this new symbol showing, you can then perform a drag action and move the Quick Launch bar to a new position on the Task Bar by sliding it along. You can even drag it off the Task Bar altogether if you want to, onto the Desktop background where it then becomes a new type of window. However, I don't recommend that you experiment with this now because once you have moved it, it stays moved until you put it back again – even if you switch the computer off and back on again. I mention it here because one day you may do this by accident, and panic when you can't get things back to appear how they were!

If you do accidently move the Quick Launch bar then you should remind yourself that it has this 'handle'. By juggling with it and dragging it about, you can get things back to appear 'normal' again on the Desktop. If you move the Quick Launch bar off the Task Bar altogether, where it becomes a window, then you need to remember to place the pointer over the Title Bar to then drag it around the screen and get it back on the Task Bar!

Moving along the **Task Bar**, we see to the right of the **Quick Launch bar** three long rectangular boxes with the names of programs that we currently have running. They are actually sat upon yet another bar that is technically called the **Task Manager bar**. The following picture shows this more clearly:

We recognise that this is a bar because again we can see at the far left-hand side another 'handle' (you may come across other bars in the future and you will recognise them also by this same feature). Like the Quick Launch bar, this one too can be moved about, but only along the Task Bar itself, not onto the Desktop background.

Every program that is running will have its own box on the **Task Manager bar**. These boxes are actually buttons that you can click on with the mouse pointer. When you click on one button then it appears pressed down (like the one for Minesweeper in the centre of the last picture) and any others will pop back up again, to appear not pressed.

The button that appears pressed corresponds to the program that currently has the focus of attention. This means that if you press any keys on the keyboard then it is this program that receives and responds to them and not any of the others. If you look back at the picture of the Desktop at the start of this section, you can see also that the Minesweeper program window is the only window with its Title Bar coloured blue (showing dark grey in this image), also indicating that this is the window that currently has the focus. The window for the Notepad program has its Title Bar coloured pale grey. This means that it does not have the focus, which agrees with the state of its corresponding box on the Task Manager bar. Only one program can have the focus at any one time.

Notice also from the picture of the Desktop that we have three boxes on the Task Manager bar but can only see two windows open. This is because one of the programs running – the Paint program – is in the minimised state. If we were to click on the box with the wording "untitled – Paint" then this would press its button and switch the focus away from Minesweeper and give it to Paint. We say that the Minesweeper program has then lost the focus. As soon as a minimised program receives the focus then this forces it into either a normal or maximised state, whichever state it was last in before it was minimised, so that a window appears on the Desktop capable of receiving the focus.

The final item to discuss on the **Task Bar** is the **System Tray** located at the far right hand end. The following picture shows the System Tray in detail:

The System Tray contains a variable number of icons depending on the software that has previously been installed on your computer. At minimum, you will see the **System Clock** at the far right.

These icons are special reference objects that provide some services in relation to the software that they are associated with. Let us see how we use them.

If you position the mouse pointer over each of the icons in turn and wait for a second or two (don't press any of the mouse buttons yet), then a small yellow pop-up textbox called a **Tool Tip** will appear, giving you some information relating to the icon. Try this out for yourself on your own computer. Position the pointer over the System Clock. When the Tool Tip appears, it will show you the current System Date. Now try the other icons you have in the System Tray to see what information they are able to tell you.

In addition to showing the Tool Tip text, you can use the icons to get quick access to various services depending on the functions that the software supplier has made available to computer users. You activate this access by either a click, or more often, a right-click of the mouse. Try a **right-click** yourself on the **System Clock**. You should get a pop-up menu looking something like the next picture:

On your own monitor screen, you may see some of the options in the menu 'greyed out', depending on whether you have a window open on the Desktop or not. Remember that when options are 'greyed out' they are no longer active at that particular moment in time, and this is usually because of another factor. For example, if you try this right-click on the System Clock from the Desktop but with no window open, then all of the functions on the menu that relate specifically to windows are 'greyed out'. As soon as you open a window on the Desktop and try this again, you will see that they are no longer 'greyed out' and hence active and available to you.

Whenever you want to remove any of these pop-up menus, either press the **ESC key** or click somewhere else.

We will now explore just one of the options from the last menu to give you some idea about the type of services that these icons in the System Tray provide. The others I shall leave for you to experiment with at your leisure.

With the menu from right-clicking on the System Clock showing (last picture), click on the option for 'Adjust Date/Time'. This results in a dialog box popping up as shown in this next picture:

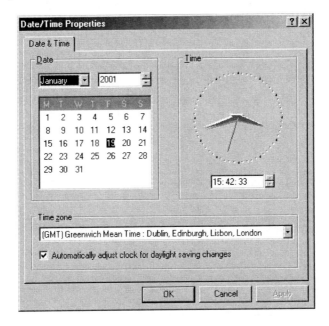

Now you have the facility to quickly make an adjustment to the **System Date & Time** by clicking on various objects in the dialog box. Your settings are probably correct so you may not want to disturb them. This won't happen unless you make changes and then click on either the **Apply** or the **OK** buttons. If you want to experiment without permanent effect, then you can providing you click on the Cancel button to exit from this dialog box.

This dialog box has some interesting controls on it that we have not met before. Notice that all controls are 'grouped' together in some way by a line outline that has a title for the group. The object in the top left corner of the **Date group** of controls is a drop-down list box and is currently highlighted showing the month of 'January'. If you click on the button just to the right of the word 'January' (it has a down pointing arrow symbol), you will see a list appear containing all the months. Should you need to change the month then you position the pointer over the appropriate item in the list and click again. This new month will then appear displayed in the control. Also, the Apply button will then change from the 'greyed out' condition to allow you to put the change permanently into effect if you want to.

Either click on the **Cancel button**, or press the **ESC key** to exit the dialog box without making any permanent changes to the computer's settings.

We have now completed our individual discussion of the objects that you find on the Desktop background. To summarise, we know that on the background there are basically **windows, icons & shortcuts**, and the **Task Bar**. We have discussed the various items that you can see on the Task Bar and have some idea of what they do.

Before we end this section on the Desktop, I want to talk again about windows in general and running programs. In doing so, I want to bind this together with information that we have already covered in previous chapters, so that you have a good understanding about the nature of the computer in an overall sense, and can relate this to what you can see on the screen when you study the Desktop.

Let us review what we now know by making a series of statements...

Statement 1 The computer is controlled at the top level by the master Windows program that automatically starts running when we first switch the power on. The master Windows program I have been using to illustrate this book is Windows 98, written by the manufacturer 'Microsoft'. It is the master Windows program that creates all the things that we see on the Desktop.

Statement 2 To perform specific tasks, like creating a written note with **Notepad**, or playing a game like **Minesweeper**, or making a drawing or picture with **Paint**, we need to have secondary **programs** running. These secondary programs are allowed to run only within the framework of that which we call a **window**. Each separate program will run in its own window.

Statement 3 We can have more than one program running at once if we wish.

Statement 4 The most general way to start a secondary program running is to **click** on the **Start Button** (at the far left-hand side of the **Task Bar**) and then the **Start Menu** will appear. We then slide the mouse pointer up this menu to the 'Programs' option and wait for another menu to pop-up alongside. We then slide the pointer horizontally across onto this new menu and then make another choice of option from here. We keep following the chain of menus until we finally reach the option for the secondary program itself, and then we click on it to get it running. A good tip to note is that we have not reached the final option for the secondary program if you spot a small black arrowhead on the right side of the option, pointing sideways. This black arrowhead means that there is yet another pop-up menu to come.

Statement 5 If we purchase new programs and have them installed, then they will become new options from these menus.

Statement 6 If we want to stop using the computer and power it down, then we should close all running programs first using their **Close buttons**, and then carry out the **Shutdown** procedure. To do this procedure, we click on the **Start Button** and choose the **Shutdown** option. We follow this through into another pop-up dialog box and ensure that the Shutdown option is highlighted here also, and then click on the OK button. We know that this is the only correct way to stop using the computer. *We should never attempt to simply turn the mains power off*.

Statement 7 If we start a secondary program running like **Notepad** then we will see a rectangular button appear on the **Task Bar**, as well as a window on the **Desktop background**. We can maximise the window to fill the whole screen area, or have it in the normal state, or even possibly minimise it where there is no window visible on the Desktop. There will always be visible a rectangular button shown on the Task Bar containing the program name, while that program is running.

Statement 8 When we have more than one secondary **program** running, we will see several rectangular buttons on the **Task Bar**, each displaying the name of the program it is associated with. If any of these appears in a 'pressed down' condition, then that is the program that currently has the **focus** of attention, and any actions we then make such as key presses will be directed to just that program (unless the key presses are special ones).

Statement 9 We can switch between one of several programs that might be running by clicking on the appropriate **rectangular button** on the **Task Bar**. If a program should be in the **minimised** state, then it will change to show a window on the **Desktop background** in either the **normal** or **maximised** states. Any program that we switch to will automatically be given the focus of attention.

Statement 10 If we want to stop the running of a program, we normally click on the **Close button** in the top right-hand corner of a window. There may be one or two things that also need to be done before the window finally closes, such as saving any changes that we might have made to data files that we have been using with the program. If we forget to save changes to a data file and attempt to close a program, then the program usually reminds us of this fact.

We have now studied the Desktop in as much detail as a first-timer really needs to know. In the next section we are going to do some practical work with the Desktop. You should find this good fun as well as being useful in getting your computer organised in the way you want it to be.

7.2 Exercises with Desktop shortcuts and folders

When you first purchase a new personal computer, the icons and shortcuts that you see on the Desktop, and the folders you find on the Hard Drive, will be more or less as they were left when the master Windows program was first installed on the computer. We will call this the 'basic layout' of the computer.

The exercises that we are now going to study will show you how you can change this basic layout by adding **shortcuts** of your own to the Desktop, and how to add new folders of your own to the Hard Drive. You can then alter the basic layout of the Desktop on your own computer so that it better suits you, for the way you want to work.

Adding new shortcuts to the Desktop is a particularly good idea for starting programs running that you use very frequently. It saves time because you don't have to go through all those menus associated with the Start Button. If we also create new **folders** on the Desktop then you can get fast access to these too; and you can make different folders for different projects, so that you can save related working files together in the same place.

Exercise 8 – Creating a shortcut to the Paint program
We begin this exercise at the **Desktop** with no other programs running.

With the mouse pointer positioned anywhere over the **Desktop background**, make a **right-click** to bring up the related **pop-up menu**. Then slide the pointer down the menu to the **New option** and wait a second for the next menu to show. When this appears, move the pointer sideways and then select the **Shortcut option** with a click as shown in the first picture:

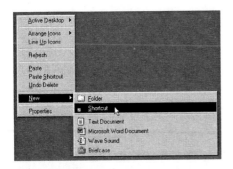

Following the click, a new **pop-up dialog box** will appear, as in the second picture:

We will now use the **Browse button** shown to select the correct wording that is needed in the **Command Line**. If we knew the correct wording already, then we could simply type this in directly.

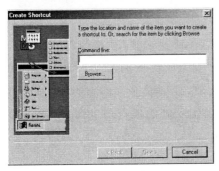

However, as first-timers, we don't know it so we use the Browse button to search for the program file we want. When we find it, Browse will fill it in for us automatically. This correct wording is known as the **full pathname** for the **program file**. We shall learn more about pathnames in Chapter 8.

Click on the **Browse button**. The **Browse dialog box** then appears as in the next picture. Don't be concerned if your own version of this appears slightly different. This will be because the folders on your Hard Drive are not the same. Now locate the **Program Files** icon as shown in the picture and click on it to highlight it. (If you have many folders, you may need to use the scroll box control in order to see the icon within the display area). Now click on the Open button:

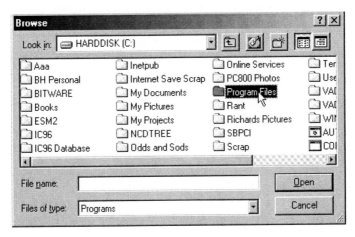

When the **Program Files** folder opens, another similar display of **folder icons** will show itself. You then need to do the same procedure again on the **Accessories** icon, that is, click on it first to highlight it, then click on the **Open button** to open it to the next level.

When you have opened the **Accessories** icon, you will see it appear in the **Look in** box (just under the blue Title Bar), as shown in the next picture:

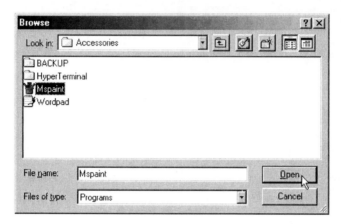

The final browsing actions are to click first on the icon for **Mspaint** to highlight it, and then click on the **Open Button**. (If you see something that says Mspaint.exe instead, don't worry, click on it just the same).

Okay. When you have clicked on Open, the **Browse Dialog box** will disappear, and the correct wording that we require will now be showing highlighted in the **Command Line**, as can be seen in the next picture:

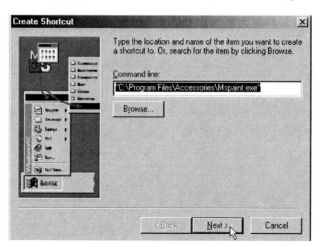

Notice that although we know this program by the name 'Paint', the actual file is called 'Mspaint'. An important point to learn here is that when you are specifying the name of an actual file, it is very important to be precise. (If you haven't guessed it yet, the 'Ms' bit stands for 'Microsoft'). Notice also that the last part of the actual name of the file is '.exe'. This bit is usually hidden when we see files shown in the dialog boxes (we could alter some settings if we want to so that they are shown). It is known as the extension to the filename. Again, we shall learn more about exact filenames and extensions in Chapter 8.

Okay. Now click on the **Next Button** (as shown in the last picture).

The final dialog box that appears will have a **Finish Button** showing on it. Click on it and the dialog box will disappear to reveal a new **shortcut** appearing on the **Desktop** looking like this:

Notice in this picture that we can see a small black arrow in a white square box in the bottom left corner of the paint pot image. You may remember from the last section that this confirms that this is a shortcut and not a system icon. You can now do a drag action on this icon and position it wherever you want on the Desktop background. My own preference is to place shortcuts I have made myself over on the right-hand side of the screen, so that I know I can delete them in the future without disturbing any from the original basic layout. Go ahead and reposition the one on your own computer to suit yourself.

The last part of our exercise will be to rename this shortcut to give it a name that we would like it to have, rather than the automatic one that the system gives it. We shall call it **'Paint'** instead of **'Mspaint'**. This ability to rename shortcuts can prove very useful for tidying things up to suit the way we want to work. You can do it for all the icons and shortcuts that you see on the Desktop (including new folders that you create). However, I would advise you to do this only on objects that you create yourself and to leave the system icons alone.

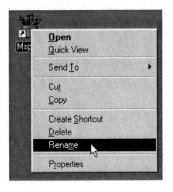

We will now do this renaming trick. Position the mouse pointer over the centre of the shortcut we have just created and right-click. A pop-up menu will appear. Slide the pointer down the menu and click on the **Rename** option, as shown to the left:

Okay. After the click, the menu disappears and now we see that the wording of the name of the shortcut becomes highlighted, as in the next picture:

If you can cast your mind back to section 4.1, you may remember that whenever we see some text that is highlighted in reverse video in a textbox – as we do in the above picture – then the very next keyboard 'letter' key we press will first delete all the existing text and then replace it with the letter we have just typed.

Okay. Type the upper case letter 'P' by pressing first pressing and holding the **left SHIFT key** and then pressing the **P key**, remove all fingers when done. Follow this typing with the letter keys for 'aint' and then press the **ENTER key**. There we should have it. The name of the shortcut has been changed to **'Paint'** as we see in our final picture:

Notice that the shortcut has the focus on the Desktop after we have renamed it.

Okay. We have completed the exercise of creating the shortcut to the Paint program. Before we leave it we ought to test that it works properly. In doing so, I want to show you another novel way to start a program running.

With the mouse pointer positioned over the centre of the **Paint shortcut**, make a right-click action. From the **pop-up menu** that appears, click on the **Open option**. Suddenly, the Paint program starts running and the Paint window opens up!

Neat trick don't you think? Close it in the normal way, and we are ready for the next exercise.

Exercise 9 – Deleting a shortcut to the Paint program

The last exercise created a shortcut on the Desktop. Now we will learn how to remove one. In comparison, this exercise is going to appear rediculously short!

We begin again from the **Desktop**. Position the mouse pointer over the centre of the **Paint** shortcut and make a **right-click** action. From the **pop-up menu** that appears, slide the pointer down and click on the **Delete** option.

When the '**Confirm File Delete**' message box appears (it is checking to see if you really intend to get rid of it), click on the **Yes** button. And there you have it – it has gone!

Well not quite. It has actually gone into a temporary folder internal to the computer called the **Recycle Bin**. In exercise 13 we shall learn how to recover it, and place it once again on the Desktop.

Exercise 10 – Creating a new folder on the Desktop

We begin at the **Desktop**. Position the pointer anywhere over the Desktop background and make a **right-click**. We then see the same **pop-up menu** as we did at the start of exercise 8.

Slide the pointer down to the **New** option and wait a second for the next menu to show. Now move it sideways and click on the **Folder** option, as in this next picture:

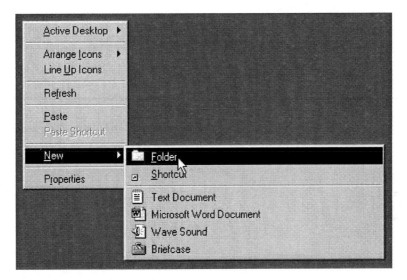

The menus will then disappear and we see a new icon appear on the Desktop, as shown in the following picture:

We can see here that the **name textbox** has already high-lighted the words 'New Folder' ready for us to type in the new name for this folder. Using the keyboard, now type the words 'Project Folder' and then press the ENTER key. That's all there is to it! We now have created a new folder on the Hard Drive and created a shortcut to it on the Desktop, all in one go!

However, before we leave this exercise, we ought to discuss just how we might go about using this new folder to save new work inside it.

Up to now, whenever we wanted to save work in either **Notepad** or **Paint**, we would use the **Save As...** option from the **File menu**. This option when selected would show a **Save As dialog box** looking like this next picture:

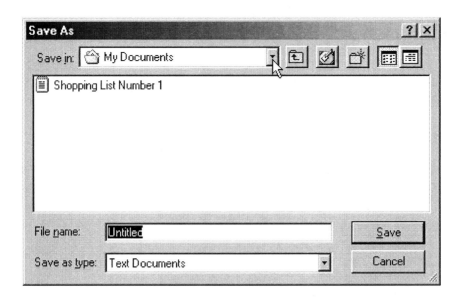

What we see in this picture, in the large central white area, is the current content of the folder called My Documents. We know this because the white box above it, labelled 'Save in:', contains the wording 'My Documents', and is also showing the yellow icon of a folder. The folder content is the text file called 'Shopping List Number 1' that we created earlier.

Now this upper white box has a grey button on its right-hand side with a black down-pointing arrow. It is known as a **list box**, and we have seen this type of object before in section 7.1 when we were talking about changing the **System Date & Time**. Previously the object was showing the month of 'January', and when we clicked on its button we saw a complete list of all months so that we could choose one.

The **'Save in:' list box** does a similar job. If we should click on the button then a list of other items would be displayed, as in the picture opposite.

The items displayed are alternative places that we can choose to save work files. At the bottom of the list we can see our new Project Folder.

We would then click on our **Project Folder** and see the list disappear, showing our new **folder** as the current folder in the **'Save in:' box**. Now the large central white area would be blank because our folder has nothing in it yet. Finally, we would click in the lower **'File name:' box** and edit the wording to show the name we want to give to the work file we are trying to save. Then we would click on the **Save button** to actually save the work file in the new folder.

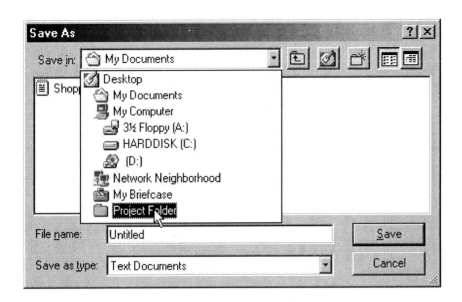

A similar situation occurs in reverse when we want to retrieve a work file from the new folder to do more work upon it, or maybe print it out. This time we would use the **Open dialog box** from the **File menu**. We would again have to change the default entry in the **Look in: list box** from '**My Documents**' to show '**Project Folder**'. Then we would see the file we wanted to open.

We will now conclude this exercise by giving you a task to do on your own. Using the knowledge that I have just given you, I want you to start **Notepad** running and re-open the 'Shopping List Number 1' file. Re-read section 4.3 if you become lost in attempting to do this.

When you have it open within the **Notepad** program, I want you to save it just as it is, but to the new '**Project Folder**' folder. Close down the Notepad program when you have it saved in the new location, so that you are back to the Desktop.

Now, as the final test to see if you have done this correctly, I want you to open the shortcut on the **Desktop** (by whichever method you prefer: double-click or right-click and then choose Open, etc.) so that you can see the **Project Folder window**. Your screen should show something like this next picture:

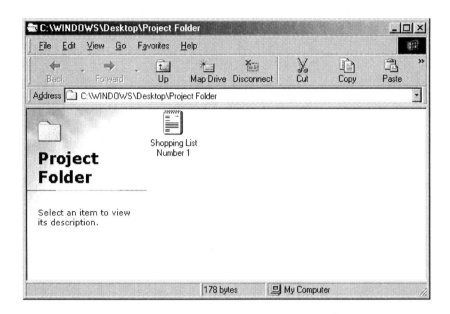

If you have done this correctly, then you are well on the road to using the computer by yourself with a fair degree of competence. If you haven't done this correctly, then you have made a simple mistake somewhere and you should go back and carefully check the steps you took. Have another try. The most likely mistake is that you used '**Save**' and not '**Save As...**' from the File menu.

One final comment – have a good look at the last picture and study the upper white box labelled 'Address'. This shows the actual structure of our new folder in the grand hierarchy of the Hard Disk itself. We shall learn exactly what this text means in Chapter 8.

Exercise 11 – Creating a new folder within a folder

We begin at the **Desktop**. Position the pointer over the icon called **Project Folder** and **right-click**. From the **pop-up menu**, click on the **Open** option.

Now position the pointer anywhere in the large white area inside the window, but not too close to the file that we saved here in the last exercise. Make a right-click action again. From the pop-up menu choose **New**, and wait a second for the next menu, then click on **Folder**.

Following the click, the menus disappear and we see a new icon appear in the window with the name textbox highlighted, ready for us to type in the name we wish to give to the folder. Using the keyboard, type the words 'Project X' and then press the ENTER key.

That's all there is to it. In a few simple steps, we have created a **folder** within the **Project Folder** called '**Project X**'.

If you so wished, you could proceed further and create more folders for 'Project Y', 'Project Z' and so on. You are then effectively creating what is known as a **folder structure**. One practical reason why you might want to do this on your own computer later on is to organise and group your work files in some logical fashion. This makes it easier to find them at a later date, and also easier if you ever want to delete them. By organising your work logically, you will have more confidence in months and years to come that you know why files were originally made and what purpose they serve.

To round off the exercise, we will now neatly line up the **icons** within **Project Folder**. Here is a very simple way to do it. Close the **Project Folder** window using the **Close** button. Now re-open it again with a **right-click** on the **Project Folder icon**, and then click on **Open**. Now we see that the icons in the folder are neatly arranged.

Before we leave this exercise, I want to discuss one more point.

With the **Project Folder window** still open, position the mouse pointer over the **icon** for Project X and **right-click**. Then click on the **Open option** from the **pop-up menu**, so that you now have the **Project X window** open. Your screen should look something like this next picture:

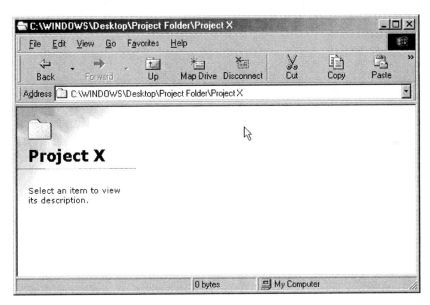

Now look closely at the upper white box labelled '**Address**'. Compare this with the Address from exercise 10, which was 'C:\WINDOWS\Desktop\ Project Folder'. Can you see a pattern emerging here?

As we 'nest' one Folder inside another, then the new Address becomes that of the 'parent' folder, with the new folder name tagged on the end and separated by a symbol that we call a 'back-slash' ('\'). This symbol is to be found on your keyboard at the bottom left-hand side, just to the left of the Z key. The meaning of an Address is something that we will discuss further in Chapter 8, where we get to understand more about files and folders on the Hard Drive.

While we are on the subject of the back-slash symbol, here is another tip. In personal computing, there is yet another slash symbol called 'forward slash' ('/') that can be found on the keyboard on the right-hand side, just to the right of the Full Stop key. Many people get the two slash symbols confused and cannot remember which is called which. Here is an idea to help you remember. Imagine you are an ant crawling along the line of the address from left to right, in the same way that your eye reads the line from left to right. As you crawl along and meet the slash symbol, if it is a back-slash ('\') then it could fall backwards and hit you on the head (because it slopes that way)! If it is a forward slash ('/') then it would fall forwards and you would be okay! ... Well, the idea is only an aide-memoire!

Exercise 12 – Deleting a new folder from the Desktop

We begin from **Desktop**. Position the mouse pointer over the **icon** for **Project Folder** and make a **click** action.

You should now see that the icon has become highlighted, as in the next picture. This is quite important. Do check that it is.

Now using the keyboard, press the **Delete** key. (If you have forgotten its whereabouts, it is in the group of six keys, just to the right of the ENTER key. Section 4.1 will show you a diagram.).

A confirmation message box will now appear. Type the **Y key** to say 'Yes' to the delete. (We can click here on the **Yes button** instead, but I thought I would remind you that you can often use either the keyboard or the mouse in many circumstances).

As soon as you have pressed the **Y key**, then the message disappears and the icon for Project Folder is removed completely from the Desktop.

The importance of making sure that the **Project Folder icon** was highlighted before you pressed the **Delete** key goes back to the idea of objects having the 'focus'. I want to stress this point quite forcefully to you. You need to be extra careful when deleting any item, be it a folder, a file or anything else. *Always remember that the object with the focus gets any key presses.* If you make sure you can see which object has the focus before you make the deletion, then you have greater confidence that you are doing the right thing and not making a mistake.

This concludes the exercise on deleting a folder from the Desktop.

Exercise 13 – Restoring a deleted item using the Recycle Bin

We begin from the **Desktop**. Position the pointer over the icon of the **Recycle Bin**, as shown in the next picture:

Now **right-click** and wait for the **pop-up menu**. Click on the **Open** option. The **Recycle Bin window** will now open up. We want to restore the **Paint shortcut** object back to the Desktop, but leave the **Project Folder icon** deleted. Position the pointer over the Paint shortcut and then right-click. A pop-up menu will appear, as in the following picture:

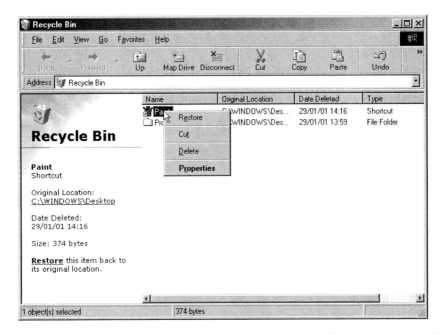

Click on the **Restore** option. After a seond or two, the **Paint shortcut** will disappear from within the **Recycle Bin window**. Now close the Recycle Bin window using the **Close** button in the top right-hand corner.

When the Recycle Bin window has closed, you will then see the full Desktop once more, and somewhere you should see that the Paint shortcut has re-appeared.

The actual position on the Desktop that the Paint shortcut returns to will most likely be different from the original one before it was deleted in exercise 9. If you have many icons showing on the Desktop, you will need to search around a bit to find it.

Okay. There we have it. The deleted shortcut is back on the Desktop. This concludes exercise 13.

Exercise 14 – Emptying the Recycle Bin

We begin from the **Desktop**. Before we start, have a look at the **icon** for the **Recycle Bin**. Notice that the icon picture shows that there appears to be some paper inside the bin!

Now position the pointer over the **Recycle Bin icon** and **right-click**. A **pop-up menu** appears as shown in the next picture:

Click on the **Empty Recycle Bin** option. A confirmation message box will now appear. Click on the **Yes** button and the message will disappear. Then when you see the full Desktop again, click anywhere on the background to take the focus away from the Recycle Bin icon.

Now look at the Recycle Bin icon again. It will show an icon picture where it no longer has paper inside it but appears empty, as in the next picture!

The Recycle Bin is now completely empty. The Project Folder icon cannot now be restored, as we did previously with the Paint shortcut in exercise 13. All the contents of that folder have also been permanently removed from the computer, including the Project X folder and so on.

If you care to open the Recycle Bin window again (right-click over the icon, and select the Open option) you will see that it is completely bare. Close the window if you do open it to return to the Desktop.

This concludes our exercise on emptying the Recycle Bin. But is it really true that these objects have been removed absolutely from the Hard Drive of the computer?

The answer to that is not entirely. Let me explain why not ...

In the early days of personal computers, machines operated at a much slower speed than they do today. They were particularly slow in terms of writing and reading data to and from files stored on storage disks. The consequence of being very slow meant that designers were always looking for ways of speeding up operations.

Designers eventually came up with a very fast idea for deleting files. Instead of removing all data from the disk (which can be a lengthy process on big files), they rely upon the simple technique of placing a small 'marker' on the file, to indicate that it is no longer valid. All the former storage space that was used by the file is now free for other files to use, if and when needed, but the old data is not explicitly removed.

The only time that such data is genuinely destroyed is if either a new file overwrites all of the old data, or if the disk is put through an operation known as 'Hard Formatting' (which overwrites everything). There is an operation called 'Quick' or 'Soft Formatting' but that doesn't destroy data.

So, by using specialist software programs, it is possible for someone to recover parts of data from storage that have been used previously by files that are now considered deleted.

You should therefore take great care if you store information on your personal computer that is of a sensitive business nature. You may think by sending it to the Recycle Bin, and then emptying it, that a file and data have been removed. In truth, parts of the file may still exist for others to snoop upon by specialist means. This is particularly true if you sell or dispose of a computer to a third party.

If you want to absolutely delete files and their data from personal computers, you can purchase specialist programs written to do this very job, but that is getting into discussions a bit too deep for 'first-timers'.

7.3   The many ways of starting programs

One of the interesting features of the modern personal computer is that no matter what the task is that you need to do, there are usually several ways to achieve the same end result. Indeed, for even just the simple job of opening a folder shortcut on the Desktop, we have already found three ways to do this. We can either:

- **double-click** on the **icon**
- **right-click** on the **icon**, then click on **Open** from the menu
- **click** on the **icon**, then press the **ENTER key**.

The same is true of methods for starting programs running, and in this section, I want to explore these alternative methods so that you are not confused when you see them in operation. You can also then choose the method that is best and easiest for you.

We have already used three methods of starting programs in previous chapters. Let us quickly review these:

The 'Run' Method
In chapter 4, we wanted to get started quickly writing a note, so we pressed the

key known as the **Windows key** on the keyboard. Here again is where the key is located:

We pressed the **Windows key** and this then caused the **Start Menu** to pop-up in the bottom left corner of the screen. From this menu, we pressed the **R key** to select the **Run** option, and the **Run dialog box** appeared. Then we typed the word 'Notepad' in the **Open textbox** and pressed the **ENTER key**.

The Notepad program then started running.

You can use this method for other programs too by typing the correct program name and then pressing the ENTER key. There is also a **Browse button** that you can use to seek out a program if you forget the name. This button works in exactly the same way as that we used in Exercise 8, section 7.1.

The 'Start Button' method (most generalised method)

In chapter 6, we started both the **Minesweeper** and the **Paint** programs using this second method.

We first clicked on the **Start Button** at the left side of the **Task Bar**.

From the **Start Menu** that popped up, we selected the **Programs** option, and waited for the next menu to automatically appear. We then used the other **pop-up menus** in succession until we saw an option displaying the program name we required. Finally, we clicked on it to get the program started.

This method is easy to use once you have mastered the control of the mouse pointer, and you can comfortably slide it across the series of pop-up menus that appear. It is by far the most generalised and common method of starting up programs.

The 'Desktop Shortcut' method

We used this third method in Exercise 8, section 7.1. It involved first creating a **shortcut** left permanently on the **Desktop** background. Our exercise example made a shortcut for the **Paint** program, as shown in this next picture:

Once we had made such a shortcut, it was simplicity itself to start the underlying program running by opening it with a **right-click** action and then choosing the **Open** option from the **pop-up menu**. Normally we would only create such a Desktop shortcut for those programs that we use very frequently.

This completes our quick review of the three methods covered so far for starting a program running.

Now I want to introduce you to a ***new idea*** for working with a computer, which takes quite a different approach to how we have done things so far.

For all the work we have done to date – that is: writing notes, playing games and drawing pictures – we have first started the appropriate **program** running, and then created a new **data file**, or opened and edited an existing one, to contain and save the work we are producing.

The new idea for working turns the process of starting a program on its head. If we first locate a data file that we have previously created, we can then attempt to 'open' it, and this action will automatically start up the appropriate program needed to work with it.

This idea works because the master **Windows program** knows certain things about the data file just by looking at it! (Clever things are computers!). One of the things that it knows is something called the '**type**'. We shall learn more about file types in chapter 8.

From knowing the **file type**, the master Windows program can make an association between the file and the program that first produced it. So if it knows (by association), which program needs to be used with it, then why not go find the program and start it running! That is just precisely what it does.

Okay. The proof of the pudding is in the eating. Let us now try out this new idea by practising with an exercise.

Exercise 15 – Opening a data file to automatically start a program

We begin, as ever, at the **Desktop**. Now normally, I would ask you to do something like …

...Position the mouse pointer over the icon for My Documents and make a right-click action. From the pop-up menu, click on the Open option...

But we have done all of this several times now in previous exercises. The time has come for us to shorten this request into something a little snappier! Here we go … Right-click on My Documents, and then click on Open …

Now that wasn't quite so bad, was it? OK, now go ahead and try doing it. You should then see the My Documents window open up on the Desktop.

Now right-click on 'Shopping List Number 1' and click on Open.

If all was well, you will now see the Notepad program window open up on the Desktop, and it already is displaying the data file 'Shopping List Number 1'. Are you impressed?

This concludes exercise 15. However, wait just a minute before you close the program down again. While we have the data file open, I want to show you where you can find out its type.

From the **Notepad Menu Bar,** click on **File** and then click on '**Save As...**'.

The **Save As... dialog box** will then pop-up, as shown in the next picture:

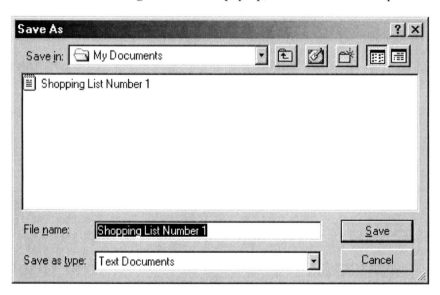

Look closely at the bottom list box labelled 'Save as type:' and you can see that the type is set to 'Text Documents'. It is here where the type is determined.

We shall learn in chapter 8 that 'Text Documents' are files that have a coded type known as '.txt'. The three letters of 'txt' are actually part of the real name of the file, but the master Windows program normally hides this from us, when it displays the name.

If you care to repeat exercise 15, but open the data file called 'Map of my house' instead, and bring up the equivalent Save As... dialog box, you will then discover the type is '24-bit Bitmap'. These files have '.bmp' as the three letter coded type.

However, we are getting a little ahead of ourselves now, so we will stop at this point. Press the **ESC key** to close the Save As dialog box without actually saving anything.

Now close the **Notepad window** using the **Close button** to return to the **Desktop**. The exercise is now concluded.

To end this section, it is worth briefly just chatting a while about the merits of the different methods we now have for starting programs running.

The method you use yourself for starting programs really is one of preference. As you have just seen, the last method of opening the data file is very fast indeed. It saves you quite a bit of effort with the pointer and reduces the total amount of clicking necessary with the other three methods. However, you do need to have a data file already in existence, so it is only really of use for editing work that you have started beforehand.

There is a potential drawback as well with the method of opening a data file. The idea only works because there is an association between the data file and its parent program. If that association is disturbed for some reason or other, then it will obviously no longer work. The reasons why an association might become disturbed can vary from an error or file corruption occuring on the Hard Drive, to installing new software that overwrites an earlier association with a new one of its own. These things shouldn't happen but sometimes they do.

The Run method requires you to know the *exact name* of the program that you want to run. It can be useful for programs like Notepad and Calc (a calculator) that are easy to remember, and can be quite fast if your hands are already using the keyboard. You can activate it entirely with only key presses, so you don't need to switch over and pick up the mouse. However, in general you won't necessarily know the exact name of a program. We witnessed, for example, that even the Paint program is really named 'Mspaint'.

Using the Start Button is the most common and generalised method, but you need to have good control over the pointer. Sometimes 'first-timers' do not realise that their lack of control often causes them to start up programs they did not intend to. This can be confusing if you think you have started one program only to suddenly see the opening displays from another!

If you use one or two programs very often, then it makes sense to put a shortcut to those programs on the Desktop background. Then it is there ready and waiting for you every time you switch on the computer.

Now we have reached the end of chapter 7. In the chapter 8 we learn more about how files are actually stored and how we can manipulate them.

8

Files, Folders and Drives

8.1 Why we should learn about files and file management

In chapter 3, we learnt that computer programs and data files are both forms of software, and that software is information that is written and stored as codes on the surface of disks. We also know that the codes for these forms of software are contained in files (as the smallest unit of storage), and files in turn can be grouped together within folders. Our understanding therefore of what software is and how it is stored on the personal computer is beginning to build quite well.

However, to be really confident in our use of the personal computer, we need to be sure that we can work safely with files and folders. There will be times when we may need to move files from one folder to another. There will be times when we may need to make duplicate copies of files. Where and when necessary, there will also be times when we need to (heavens above) delete files altogether!

For first-timers, it is this aspect of using a personal computer that fills most of us with utter dread! We are always frightened that we might inadvertently do something silly that will cause our souls to be damned to purgatory for a very long time! By far the worst situation is if we have to use a computer in our workplace. It isn't so bad making mistakes in the comfort and protection of our own home, but making a complete fool of ourselves in front of our workmates is not something to be enjoyed.

One of the secrets of proficiency and confidence with a personal computer lies in a having good understanding of the way that the storage mechanism works. When you know one hundred per cent that you have made and secured a good copy of a data file to fall back on, then you don't feel so vulnerable if you make a simple mistake. You can, if all else fails, simply replace the changed file with a copy of the original, and pretend the mistake never happened at all.

Towards this end, we will now begin to discuss the file system and general storage structure in more detail. In the course of our discussions, I hope too that we will unravel the mysteries of the different 'types' of file, and how this can affect the views we are given by the computer of files inside folders. We will end the chapter with a few more exercises, which should improve your skills at managing and manipulating files, and thereby build your self-confidence.

8.2   Computer Files

What exactly constitutes a file?

Our answer to this question will of necessity be simplified, to avoid the deep technical detail that would only cloud the issue. But our answer nevertheless will be accurate in its fundamental nature. Don't be put off by a few bits of jargon that I might have to introduce. It is only the idea that I want you to remember.

To begin to understand a file, we must first know a little bit about the codes inside them that contain the true information.

Computers have for many years settled upon a unit for making up codes called a **Byte** (pronounced "bite"). Now others may tell you that codes are written in a form of mathematics called the binary system of ones and zeroes. I could do that, but I am not going to. I will tell you – perfectly legitimately – that individual codes may be considered as ordinary decimal numbers, starting at zero (0) and counting up to two hundred and fifty five (255). A Byte can therefore be any single whole number in the range 0 to 255, inclusive.

An interesting natural question that arises is "How are these numbers held and stored on magnetic disks?" The answer is that they are stored in small compartments as a magnetic pattern created by the wizardry of the electronics of the disk mechanism itself. When a new disk is first manufactured it is completely blank, and these compartments have to be magnetically created on the surface of the disk in order to hold the code numbers. This process is called **formatting**, and the supplier normally formats the Hard Drive when the computer is first prepared for use.

Now we don't need to know the intricate detail of what a specific code means. Even if we tried to explain it, the meaning changes from one circumstance to another. All you really need to know is that either a program file, or a data file, begins with the first code – a number between 0 and 255 – and ends with the last one. In between, all that exists is a series of further codes one immediately after the other. The series of codes is just a long chain of numbers.

We can now begin to build a picture of a basic file. The following diagram attempts to make that illustration:

A typical small file:

84	104	101	32	67	97	116	32	115	97	116

First   Last
Byte   Byte

This is what constitutes a file. In our example, the first byte has the code 84, the second byte has the code 104, and so on up to the last byte which has the code 116.

Every file you will ever meet, be it the most complex program file, or the most simple data file (and vice versa), would look just the same if you could see it – but with different numbers, obviously!

The total length of a file can vary considerably. **Program files** tend to be quite large, so to help us work with large numbers we use special 'prefix' terms to make things easier to manage. There are three common prefix terms you may meet – **Kilo** (meaning a thousand), **Mega** (meaning a million), and **Giga** (meaning a thousand million). For example, you will often hear of files being **'KiloBytes'** (KB) in length, **RAM memory** being **'MegaBytes'** (MB) in total size, and Hard Drive sizes quoted in **'GigaBytes'** (GB). Strictly speaking, these prefix terms are slightly larger than the normal decimal meanings by a few per cent. A megabyte, for example, is actually 1,048,576 bytes, rather than 1,000,000.

Now just to consider what we have discussed about the constitution of a file, ask yourself this next question. We know **program files** are different kinds of software from **data files**, so if they all look internally just like the last picture, 'How can the computer and ourselves distinguish between them?' The answer is to be found in the way we name the file, and in the introduction of the idea of files as having a **'type'**.

In the dawn of the personal computer age, way back in the early nineteen eighties, this question was settled by giving every file a specially structured name consisting of eleven letters. You were not allowed to have more than eleven letters, and anything longer was considered illegal. The first eight letters could be (with a few small restrictions) almost anything you like. The last three letters were specially reserved to show the type of a file.

Let me give a few examples of types, which are in use today:

Last 3 letters	**Meaning in terms of type**
TXT	A data file containing text as you might type from a keyboard
EXE	A program file containing instruction codes for the processor
BMP	A data file containing a picture in the form of individual pixels
DLL	A supplementary program file containing further instructions
DOC	A data file containing a document for use with MS WORD
XLS	A data file containing a spreadsheet for use with MS EXCEL
MDB	A data file containg a database for use with MS ACCESS

Now in displaying the name of a file, it became a convention to separate the first eight letters of a filename from the last three by a dot symbol ('.'). We therefore might refer to a file by the name 'MYFILE.EXE'. This tells us first and foremost that it is a program executable file (remember from section 3.1 that executing a program means the same thing as running a program).

> **Note – we have been talking about 'letters' for filenames up to now. This is not strictly accurate. We should use the more complex and all-encompassing term of 'characters' meaning letters, or numbers and certain symbols. I will continue to take the liberty of using the word 'letters' because it is friendlier to use. But you know I really mean characters!**

With the introduction of the master **Windows program** in its later versions, the restrictions on the way we name files have been relaxed. We can now use both upper case and lower case letters (or even mixed combinations), and the length of the name can be much greater than just eight first letters (the complete length in total can now be up to 255, and can include spaces). However, we still retain the convention of keeping the last three letters for use as an indicator of type. We have a bit of jargon for these last three letters. We call it the **file extension**.

> **Note – you might have spotted in the table of three-letter type coding that I have used upper case letters exclusively. This is how it used to appear years ago. No distinction was ever made between upper and lower case, and even if you typed lower case, the display would be converted automatically to upper case. In earlier chapters, we have often referred to this topic of using lower case letters. It was the relaxation in the rules from later versions of the master Windows program that meant we could (and still can) use either. The computer will not mind one way or the other and will treat them both in the same way. The only difference now is that lower case will be displayed as lower case.**

There is another use for the **extension** of a file that we should mention, and that is to tell the master Windows program which icon symbol to use when the file is being displayed in a dialog box. If you look back at some of the pictures of dialog boxes in chapter 7 this will be evident.

All in all, you might now begin to appreciate that it is a risky business to interfere with the extension given to a file. Normally, the program that first creates a data file determines the coding it will use for the extension and it is wise for first-timers to leave this well alone. Now, remembering that the dot symbol ('.') is used to separate the user's name for a file from the extension, it makes sense to take great care about using the dot symbol as part of the user's name. If you are not careful, you may find that your desired name for a file accidentally overides the type that a program wants to give to your file.

Okay. That brings us to the end of our discussion about files. I hope that you now have a better appreciation of what they are and some of the features surrounding their names. In the coming sections we will talk about **drives** and **folders**, and how it all hangs together in the organisation of the permanent storage devices of the **Hard Drive** and **Floppy Disks**.

8.3   Disk Drives and Folders

We learnt in chapter 3 that the main permanent storage device for the computer is known as the **Hard Drive**. It contains a rigid spinning magnetic disk, hermetically sealed in a strong metal casing.

The origin of the term 'drive' goes back to the early years of large commercial computers. Storage devices in those days were machines in their own right, and housed in their own special cabinets. The term 'drive' then became synonymous with a separate mass storage mechanism, where removable magnetic disks could be 'mounted' on a drive unit.

Then came the development of the personal computer; the first designs catered only for removable **Floppy Disks** of limited storage capacity. These disks were very 'floppy' indeed, being a thin round sheet of coated plastic, protected by a slightly thicker plastic envelope. Their reliability was not so good and they could easily be physically damaged. Consequently, it was important to make at least one copy of your work, and such copies were then locked away in a safe place.

> **Note – Today's Floppy Disks have better reliability, are slighty smaller, and have a more rigid plastic envelope. However, they can still be easily damaged by stray magnetic fields (from items like screwdrivers for example).**

To copy files from one Floppy Disk to another, personal computers were fitted with two **Floppy Drive** mechanisms. The first one was called the '**A**' **drive** and the second was called the '**B**' **drive**. Later, when technology had reduced the size of rigid magnetic disk units, one of these could also be fitted inside the personal computer casing. It was then designated the '**C**' **drive**, and often referred to as the '**Hard**' **drive**. Increased demand for even more storage would result in a fitting a second such unit, and not surprisingly this became known as the '**D**' **drive**.

Today, technology has produced a Hard Drive storage capacity that is really quite impressive. One single disk unit now holds far more than a whole array of former disk drive cabinets. It is so large that many manufacturers now divide it up into two or more '**partitions**' and treat these as though they were separate drive units. Thus, we often meet personal computers that have a '**C**' and a '**D**'

drive contained within one physical disk drive unit.

The next form of storage that we meet in personal computing is the **CD-ROM**. We know from their use in music that generally these are **'read only'** disks, where the information content is pre-determined at the time of manufacture. If a personal computer already has 'C' and 'D' drive letters allocated for magnetic storage, then the CD-ROM drive will become the **'E' drive**, and so on.

Fairly recently, **CD-R** (recordable) drive units have been introduced. These use CD-R disks that can be written onto by users just the once, and read as many times as a normal CD-ROM. There are also **CD-RW** drive units that use different disks (CD-RW disks) and these can be written to many times. These disks though tend to be a bit more expensive than CD-R counterparts.

Now from the computer user's point of view, we refer to a particular disk drive (be it **Floppy Disk**, **Hard Drive** or **CD-ROM**) by its associated drive letter. We also have a convention for specifying drive letters when we wish to use them in our work with software. The normal practice is to use a double symbol approach. The first symbol is the drive letter and the second symbol is the 'colon' (':'). When the master Windows program comes across a colon preceded by an alphabetic letter, it knows that we are referring to a drive, and that this letter is the drive letter for the particular drive that we want to specify.

For example, we would write drive specifiers in our work as follows:

A: or B: Meaning either of two **Floppy Disk drives**
C: Meaning the first of the **Hard Drive** partitions

Let us now discuss how mass storage is organised. We will talk about the Hard Drive in particular, but the principles in general will be equally applicable to both Floppy Disk and to CD-ROM. We are going to avoid the deep technical detail of how a Hard Drive is physically structured. Instead, we will form a simpler conceptual picture of the organisation that will be of more practical use to us.

We begin by introducing a top-level folder called the **Root Folder** (an older name for the same thing is **Root Directory**, which you may still come across). This is the starting point whenever the processor unit searches to find any file. You may like to think of the Root Folder as being all of the storage space, as one massive folder.

Now the **Root Folder** can either contain **files** directly inside it; or it can contain other folders, sometimes known as **sub-folders**. Each sub-folder can likewise contain files or even more sub-folders. Our conceptual picture of the inside of the Hard Drive therefore is an inverted 'tree', looking something like this next picture:

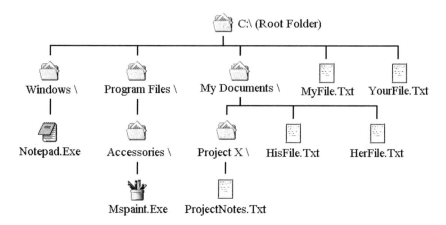

This picture is only a simplified example. The structure of the Hard Drive on your own computer will be much more complex than this, having many more files and folders. However, it does give you a good illustration of the general idea. Keep this picture in mind when you are working with your own computer, and you will have a better understanding of how things are arranged.

Reviewing the example in our last picture, we see that the **Root Folder** contains three **sub-folders** (one called '**Windows**', one called '**Program Files**', and another called '**My Documents**') as well as two **text files** ('**MyFile**' and '**YourFile**'). In the **Program Files** folder, we find the **Accessories** folder, and in the Accessories folder, we find the **Mspaint** program.

Notice also in the last picture that we see a '\' symbol (the back-slash symbol) after the end of a folder name. This is not strictly part of the name but is used as a convention to separate the folder name from the items inside it, when we come to refer to the structure in any written reference. For example, if we want make a written reference to the the file Mspaint.Exe within the Hard Drive structure, we would write is as follows:

C:\Program Files\Accessories\Mspaint.Exe

The above reference is called the **full pathname** of the file, and we have met this before in exercise 8, section 7.2.

If we meet a reference written in this way, we would interpret it as meaning that ... the file Mspaint.Exe is to be found in the folder called Accessories. The Accessories folder is in turn to be found in a folder called Program Files, which itself in turn to be found in the Root Folder of drive C: (which is the Hard Drive).

Okay. We now have an understanding of folders and files on the Hard Drive. I stated earlier that the principles were also applicable to Floppy Disks and CD-ROMs. Whilst this is certainly true, there is though a major difference between

CD-ROMs and the other two. Whereas with the Hard Drive and Floppy Disks, we can both write and read to these storage devices, with the CD-ROM it is generally a read-only storage device (CD-R and CD-RW are exceptions, but these devices are beyond the scope of this book for first-timers). In terms of managing and manipulating files therefore, it is generally only the Hard Drive and Floppy Disks where we have the ability to do this.

In section 8.6, we will try some practical exercises for managing and manipulating files. However, first we should learn a little more about Floppy disks and CD-ROMs, and we now do this in sections 8.4 and 8.5 respectively.

8.4   Floppy Disks

The Floppy Disk is a very convenient and portable form of storage. A typical modern 3½ in. disk and its key features are shown in this next picture:

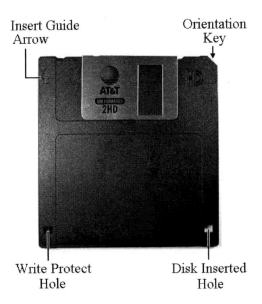

The **Insert Guide Arrow** imprinted in the top left corner of the black plastic jacket shows the direction in which the disk should be inserted into a Floppy Disk drive. This face should also normally be uppermost when inserting the disk. Hold the disk at the bottom of the jacket (as we see it in the picture) when you are inserting it.

The **Orientation Key** is the cut-away corner in the top right corner of the picture, and this prevents the disk from being inserted in the drive the wrong way round. If you are pushing a disk into a drive and find it only goes halfway in before it comes to a stop, then it will be this 'keying' mechanism that is operating and preventing it from going in further. You should then turn the disk over and try inserting it again.

The **Disk Inserted Hole** is for use only by the computer itself and it informs the drive mechanism when the disk is correctly seated, or when the disk is removed.

The **Write Protect Hole** is normally covered over with a tiny piece of black plastic on the underside that can slide back and forth with a mechanical 'click'. When the hole is covered (as in the picture) then you can both write and read files upon the disk. If you want to prevent any further writing to the disk, then slide the tiny piece of black plastic away from the hole so that the hole is clear and shows right through (just like the Disk Inserted Hole). You can then read the files on the disk, but you cannot write to it (until you cover the hole once again). This feature is very useful if you make backup copies of files and want to prevent any further possibility of deleting or changing the backup copy. By uncovering the hole, you prevent yourself from accidentally changing or destroying your backup copy.

The storage capacity size of a modern 3½ in. disk is 1.44 Megabytes when it has been formatted. (You may see on a box of these that they are 2 megabytes when in the unformatted state. This figure is of no practical value to you). The disks are also known as 'High Density' disks, to distinguish them from earlier types. Consequently, you may see them advertised as '2HD' type disks.

A typical Floppy Disk drive mechanism is shown in the next picture:

Hinged Door

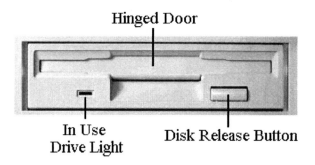

In Use Drive Light   **Disk Release Button**

To insert a disk into the drive, push it against the hinged door and then continue to insert it all the way until the **Disk Release Button** pops out. Only when this button has finally popped out have you pushed it far enough in. The disk normally drops down slightly to seat itself when it is correctly home.

The **In Use Drive Light** will illuminate when the magnetic read/write 'head' is reading or writing to the disk. It is a golden rule that you should never attempt to remove a disk when this light is on.

To remove a disk from the drive, push the **Disk Release Button** inwards and the disk will eject itself partly from the drive. When you can take hold of the disk jacket with your fingers, you can safely extract it by gripping it and pulling it out.

In section 8.6 we will conduct some exercises to show you how Floppy Disks can be correctly used.

8.5 CD-ROMS

The next picture shows a typical CD-ROM drive unit to be found in a modern personal computer:

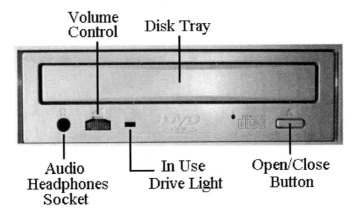

The **Open/Close Button** on the lower right-hand side is the method by which the **Disk Tray** can be both opened for a **CD-ROM disk** to be inserted, and then closed again ready for the disk ro be read by the computer. The button normally employs a push-push style of operation (push once to open, push again to close).

Occasionally when you use the Open/Close Button you may think that it is slow to respond. You need to be patient because if the computer has been reading a CD-ROM disk; it may have a few internal tasks to complete before it will open the Tray and let you remove it. There can be a delay of several seconds.

The Disk Tray itself is electronically controlled. You should never attempt to open the Tray using mechanical force, or you will damage the drive mechanism.

The **In Use Drive Light** indicates when the drive is being accessed by the processor unit. It often illuminates when the Tray is closed (either with a CD-ROM disk inserted or not). This is the computer testing for the presence of a disk. You may also hear strange 'whirring' noises coming from modern drives. This is caused by the motor speed accelarating to very high rates in order to give faster data transfers.

In addition to its normal use as a computer data device, most drives can also be used to play **Audio CDs**, and a headphones socket is usually provided to give users a choice for personal listening in privacy. The volume control is functional only when headphones are in use. If your computer is fitted with multimedia capability, then you can also listen to Audio CDs through the attached speaker system.

More recently, some specialist CD-ROM drives can also be use to replay **DVD disks** (Digital Versatile Disk). The drive shown in the above picture indicates that it has this capability by the marking in the centre of the case, just under the Disk Tray. DVD disks can store both video and audio, and many movies are now being sold for private viewing using this medium. Additionally, some computer software is being offered on DVD disk, taking advantage of the fact that the very high density of storage for this new medium means that large quantities of files, previously taking several CD-ROMs, can now be accomodated on just one DVD.

The next picture shows how a CD-ROM should be inserted into a Drive Tray. The printed label side of the CD-ROM disk is always uppermost:

When handling CD-ROMS, take care not to touch the underside that contains the data tracks. These tracks show a sparkling rainbow of colors when reflecting light, indicating their extremely fine structure. Touching this surface will most likely leave fingerprint smears that affect the true reading of data, and this is very bad practice.

Always keep CD-ROMs in their protective cases when not inside the drive. Use the edges of the disks, or the hole in the centre, to get a physical grip of the disk as you transfer it to and from the drive. Disks are released from their protective cases by pressing the central plastic retainer down with the finger of one hand, whilst taking a grip of the disk edges with the thumb and finger of the other hand.

When you first insert a CD-ROM into a Disk Tray and then close the it, an automatic signal is sent to the processor unit to tell the master Windows program to read the disk immediately, and update internal information concerning the drive.

Most commercial CD-ROM disks also have a special program file in the Root Folder that is designed to run automatically, after it has been inserted into a drive. This '**Auto-Run**' program will pop-up a new program window on the monitor screen, and normally give you instructions about using the disk.

If you want to insert a CD-ROM into a drive, but stop the 'Auto Run' program from actually running, then press and hold either SHIFT key down (the left or the right key) before inserting it, and keep it held down until all activity of the In Use Drive Light has ceased. This activity can take a minute or two. If you release the SHIFT key too soon, then the 'Auto Run' program will run.

8.6   Exercises in managing and manipulating files

In this chapter, we have learnt the basics about files, folders and drives. Now we will perform a few exercises to reinforce this knowledge, and learn a few tips that will come in handy with our general work using the computer.

To carry out these exercises, we will continue using the shorter style of giving instructions, which we introduced in exercise 15.

Exercise 16 – Making a copy of a file to a new 'File Copies' folder
We begin at the **Desktop**. **Right-click** on the **My Computer icon** and then click on **Open**. You should now see the **My Computer window** open up, looking similar to the next picture:

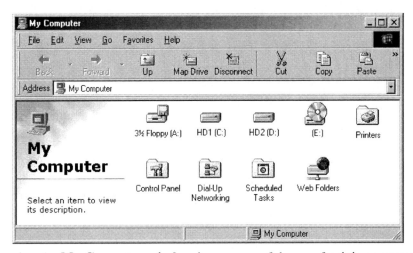

Opening the **My Computer window** is a very useful way of gaining access to icons representing the various drives that we talked about in the previous sections. In this picture we see the **Floppy Disk drive** labelled as '**3½ Floppy**

(A:)', and then two grey box icons labelled **'HD1 (C:)'** and **'HD2 (D:)'** that appear as two Hard Drives. (Your computer may only have the C: hard drive icon, followed by the CD-ROM icon as D:.)

> **Note – we cannot tell from this picture if these Hard Drives are physically two separate devices, or one large device that has been partitioned into two parts. In general, it doesn't really matter from the user point of view. The only time it may be important is if the physical device develops a fault and we lose the contents. If they are one device then you may lose both C: and D: contents together. This is one reason why if you make a backup of your important work, it needs to be to some form of removable storage that can be taken off the computer completely and stored away in a safe place.**

We can next see the icon for the **CD-ROM drive**, simply labelled as **'(E:)'** followed by a series of specialised folders. When a CD-ROM disk is present in the drive, we can usually see its title as the icon label, and sometimes the icon will change to show an image that is relevant to the content of the disk.

In this exercise, we will make a copy of the **'Shopping List Number 1'** file, from the **My Documents** folder to a new folder on the **C: drive** that we will rename as **'File Copies'**. Our first task is then to create the new folder, ready for making a copy of the file inside it.

Okay. **Right-click** on the **Hard Drive (C:) icon** and then click on **Open** (your drive C: may have a different label so I will not refer to it as 'HD1'). You will then see the **Drive C: window** and a series of folders, looking something like the next picture.

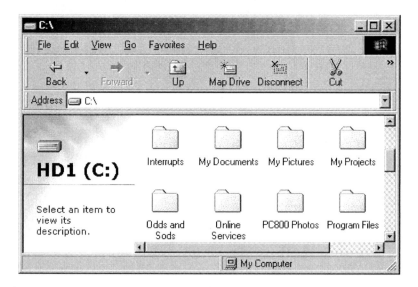

Don't be concerned if you have many more folders than the picture. If you do, then you may need to use the scroll bars to make hidden parts of it visible inside the frame. Notice on the blue Title Bar that the window name is 'C:\'. The back-slash symbol is indicating that we are looking at the Root Folder, as we discussed in section 8.3.

From the **Menu Bar** (at the top), click on **File**, then click on **New**, and then click on **Folder**. You then should see a new folder appear inside the **C:\ window** looking like the next picture:

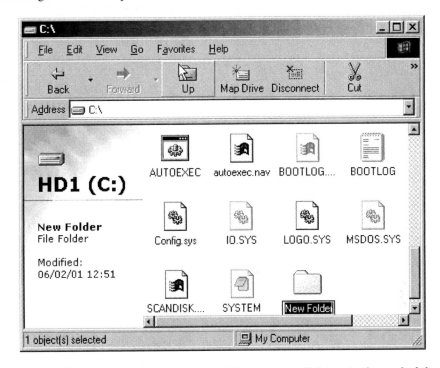

Note – You may have to use the scroll bars to scroll down to the end of the list of folders, in order to see the new folder. A good tip is to maximise the window size with the centre button in the top right corner, then you have a much broader view.

Also, if you have trouble on your first attempt at creating the new folder, you may think that it has not worked when in truth it did. If you make further attempts, don't be surprised if you eventually see two or more 'new folders'. In the next exercise, I will show you how to delete any folders that you may wish to remove.

We see that the default folder name is now highlighted blue, ready to replace it with our own name. (If you lose the highlight for any reason, you can get it back quite simply: click once on the name – wait for a second – then click on it again, and the highlight should return).

Using the keyboard, go ahead and type the new name '**File Copies**'. Then press the **ENTER key** to finalise it. We then see that the folder name changes accordingly.

Okay. We now have our new folder, correctly named and ready to take the copy of the file we wish to make. Our new folder is in the Root Folder of Hard Drive C:

Now, from inside the same **C:\ window** (note – not this time from the Desktop), find the **icon** for the **My Documents folder**. You may have to use the scroll bars in order to bring it into view. When you can see it, right-click on it to select it, and then click on Open.

We now have the **My Documents window** open, and we should be able to see both the '**Shopping List Number 1**' file and the '**Map of my house**' file, which we created in previous exercises.

Now click on 'Shopping List Number 1' to select and highlight the icon. Then move the mouse pointer up to the **Copy button**, which is located on the bar towards the top of the window at the right, just under the **Menu Bar**. This new bar is called a **Tool Bar**. As soon as the pointer moves over the word '**Copy**', it changes the appearance to look more like a button, as shown in the next picture:

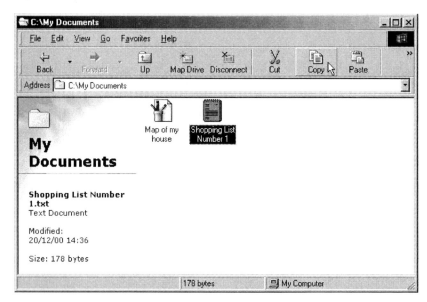

Click on the **Copy** button. This action has now placed a complete copy of the file we have highlighted onto the special object called the **clipboard**. You may remember the clipboard from our work with the Paint program in section 6.3. This is a special memory device within the master Windows program.

Now click on the **Up button**, which is also located on the grey Tool Bar further along to the left. This action takes us quickly back to the **C:\ window**. The meaning of 'up' here lies in the conceptual picture that we have of the inverted 'tree' structure of all the folders and files on the Hard Drive, which we discussed in section 8.3 (have another look at this section if you need to refresh your mind with a mental picture of this 'tree' structure).

Okay. We are now back looking inside the C:\ window.

From inside the **C:\ window**, find the icon for the new folder that we made called '**File Copies**'. You may have to use the scroll bars again in order to bring it into view. When you can see it, **right-click** on it first to select it, and then click on **Open**.

Okay. Now we are inside the **File Copies window**. Using the grey **Tool Bar** again, click this time on the **Paste** button. In a few seconds, we see a new icon appear to show us that a copy of the file '**Shopping List Number 1**' is now contained in our new **File Copies** folder.

Close the **File Copies window** in the normal way using the '**X**' button in the top right-hand corner and also the other open windows. This brings us back to the Desktop and concludes exercise 16.

Exercise 17 – Deleting either files or folders

In this exercise, we will learn how to delete either a file from within a folder, or how to delete the whole folder itself.

Before we begin the exercise itself, I want you to check that the **Recycle Bin** is empty. You can check this visually by simply looking at its icon on the Desktop. If it shows an 'empty' image then move straight to the start of the exercise. If it is showing an image with 'paper' in the bin, then it needs emptying before we begin the exercise. Do this by right-clicking on the Recycle Bin icon and then click on 'Empty Recycle Bin'. When you get the confirmation message, click on 'Yes'. Now the bin will be empty.

We now begin the exercise at the **Desktop**.

Right-click on the **My Computer** icon and then click on **Open**.

Right-click on the **C: drive icon** and then click on **Open**.

Right-click on the **File Copies folder** icon and then click on **Open**. (Use the scroll bars if you cannot see it at first).

Okay. We should now have the **File Copies window** open, and we should see the copy that we made in the last exercise of the file named 'Shopping List Number 1'.

Click on '**Shopping List Number 1**' to select and highlight it.

Now, on the keyboard, press the **DEL key** (located in the group of six keys just to the right of the ENTER key). When the confirmation message appears, click on the '**Yes**' **button**. We now witness that the icon disappears from the window.

Note – an alternative to using the DEL key is to right-click on the file's icon, and click on the 'Delete' option from the pop-up menu.

Okay. The file has now been deleted. Now we will delete the folder itself. If we had chosen to delete the folder first, then the file would automatically have gone too, because its parent folder would no long exist. However, I am doing things the long way around to show you how to delete each type of object in turn.

Okay. We are still looking at the **File Copies window**.

Click on the **Up button** from the **Tool Bar** within the window. This takes us back to the **C:\ window**.

Click once on the **File Copies folder icon** to select and highlight it.

Now press the **DEL key** again, and click '**Yes**' to the confirmation message. We witness that the **File Copies folder icon** disappears from the window.

Okay. Now we have deleted the **parent folder** as well as the **file**. Close the C:\ window using the usual '**X**' button.

If you care to open up the **C:\ window** again (I will leave you to work out the instructions here for yourself), you will see that all the folders appear in alphabetical order, but the **File Copies folder** is now no longer displayed.

Before we finish this exercise, we shall need to restore both folder and file from the Recycle Bin, ready for exercise 18.

If you have any windows open on the Desktop then close them now.

From the **Desktop, right-click** on the **Recycle Bin icon** and then **click** on **Open**. You will then see the two objects shown, which we deleted.

Right-click on the lower item for '**Shopping List Number 1**' and then click on '**Restore**'. After a few seconds, the item will disappear from the list, leaving just the item for the folder.

Now close the **Recycle Bin window**, open up the **C:\ window** once more, and you should see that the folder has re-appeared in amongst all the other folders. **Right-click** and open it just to prove that the file itself has also returned in the correct place.

It is an interesting point to note that in order to restore the file, the folder also had to automatically be restored. If it had not done so, then there would be no parent folder for the file to go back to! (Clever things are computers!).

Close any open windows to get back to the Desktop.

Now here is an interesting little point. If you are very observant, you will see that the Recycle Bin still has something inside it, yet both the file and its parent folder have been restored to the Hard Drive. The item left in it is from the second delete action that we made of the folder. Even though the parent folder was automatically restored (so that there was somewhere to put the file back inside) the shortcut object to just the folder – produced by our second act of deletion – was treated as a separate object inside the Recycle Bin. (Perhaps computers are not always as clever as they would like to be!).

I will leave it to you to clean out the Recycle Bin by yourself.

We have now concluded exercise 17.

Note – if you made several ' new folders' by mistake in exercise 16, you might now wish to go back and delete them – now that you know how to. It is always good practice to keep your computer storage in a 'clean' condition!

Exercise 18 – Formatting a Floppy Disk

Formatting is the process, which we discussed briefly in section 8.2, of creating the 'compartments' on a magnetic disk used to store byte codes. All newly manufactured disks need to go through this process before they can be used.

The formatting process can be repeated as many times throughout the life of a disk as is necessary; but every time it is done then all previously held coded information is lost. As a first-timer, therefore, you need to treat the subject of formatting with a great deal of respect. If you are careless, you can do a lot of damage that you will not be able to undo.

It is very rare that a Hard Drive needs to be formatted. Your supplier has already done this for you during the initial preparation of the computer. That should be sufficient for the lifetime of the drive. However, if you do have any problems in this area then you should leave well alone and consult an expert. *You have now been warned – so don't even think about it!*

However, formatting a Floppy Disk is something that first-timers should learn how to do. Again, you do need to be very careful. The question you must always ask yourself is 'Can I afford to destroy and lose the information content of the Floppy Disk I am about to format?' If you are not one hundred per cent sure, then you should put the disk to one side and use another.

Okay. With these warnings ever present in your mind, let us proceed to learn how it is done.

We begin at the **Desktop**. Find a 3½ in. High Density Floppy Disk that either has never been used before (it doesn't matter if it is already formatted or not), or a second hand one where you don't mind destroying the content.

First check that the **Write Protect Hole** is covered by the small plastic slide (if not then slide it to cover the hole) and then insert the disk fully into the **Floppy Drive** of your computer (see section 8.4 for more detail on how to insert the disk). You should see the **Disk Release Button** pop out when the disk is correctly inserted in the drive.

Right-click on the **My Computer** icon and then click on open.

Right-click on the icon labelled '3½ **Floppy (A:)**'. Then click on **Format**.

You should then see a **Format dialog box**, as shown in the next picture:

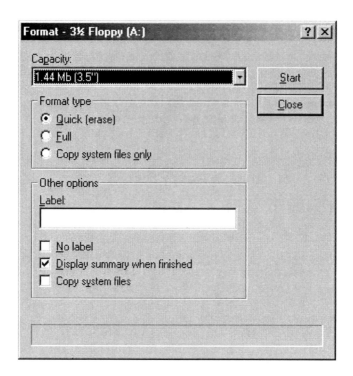

For this exercise, we will leave all the options as they appear in the default conditions shown. However, if you choose to give a name to the disk that you are about to format, you should type it in the Label box. You are restricted to using only eleven letters (I should really say characters – meaning letters, or numbers, or certain symbols).

Click on the **Start button.**

The options on the **dialog box** will then become 'greyed out' and you will see a form of 'progress bar' appear at the bottom of the dialog box. You also see that the **In Use Drive Light** has come on. The disk is now being fomatted.

When the format is complete, you will then see a **Summary box** appear, as in the picture opposite:

This summary box shows, among other things, how many **byte codes** can be stored upon the disk before it becomes full.

Wait for the **In Use Drive Light** to go out, and then click on the **Close button** to remove the **Summary box**. Now click on the **Close button** to remove the **Format dialog box.**

Only when you are sure that the **Floppy Drive 'In Use' Light** is out, push the **Disk Release Button** inwards to release the Floppy Disk, and remove it from the drive with your fingers. You will now be able to use the floppy for

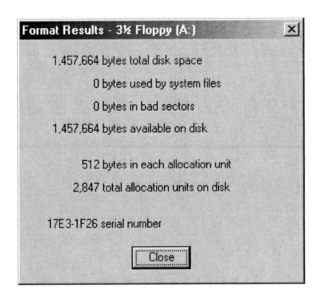

whatever purpose you choose, without any further formatting, either now or later on.

We have now concluded exercise 18.

Exercise 19 – Copying a file and folder to a Floppy Disk

For this exercise, you will need the blank formatted Floppy Disk that we created in exercise 18.

We begin at the **Desktop**.

Check that the **Write Protect Hole** is still covered by the small plastic slide and then insert the disk fully into the **Floppy Drive** of your computer. You should see the Disk Release Button pop out when the disk is correctly inserted in the drive.

Right-click on the **My Computer** icon and then click on **Open**.

Right-click on the **C: drive icon** and then click on **Open**.

Right-click on the **File Copies folder icon** (use the scroll bars if necessary to bring it into view), and then click on **Copy**.

Okay. We are still looking at the **C:** window.

Click on the **Up button** from the **Tool Bar** within the window. This takes us back to the **My Computer** window.

Right-click on the icon labelled '**3½ Floppy (A:)**', then click on **Open**.

Position the mouse pointer anywhere in the large white area inside the window and make a **right-click**. Then **click** on **Paste** from the **pop-up menu**.

Wait for a few seconds, and you should then see (very briefly) a **Copying...** **progress box**, indicating that file copying is taking place. This progress box will

189

automatically disappear when the copying is finished, and you will then see a new icon of the **File Copies folder** appear inside the **A:\ window**.

If you now **right-click** on this new **File Copies folder icon**, and then click on **Open**, you will see that a copy of the 'Shopping List Number 1' file has automatically been put in the folder. This illustrates an important point that by copying a folder to a new location (in this case to the Floppy Disk Root Folder), not only is the folder itself copied – but all its contents are as well! If there had been several other files in the folder, and maybe further sub-folders too, then absolutely everything in the 'tree structure' underneath that folder would have been copied at the same time!

Now close the File Copies window using the usual '**X**' button as normal, and you will be back at the Desktop.

Finally, check that the **Floppy Drive 'In Use' Light** is not lit (this is just a safety precaution that you should get into the habit of doing), push the Disk Release Button inwards to release the Floppy Disk, and then remove it from the drive with your fingers.

The last action after writing to a Floppy Disk is usually to write out a label indicating its content (and a good idea is to put the date/time on it as well) and then carefully stick the label onto the disk jacket. Labels for all your disks are normally included in the box when you purchase them. Now store the disk in a safe place.

We have now concluded exercise 19.

8.7   The need for making backup copies of your work

To end this chapter, I would like to conclude with some words of advice for your future work with the computer.

In this chapter we have learnt quite a bit about files and folders. We now have a reasonable understanding of what they are, and how they are structured on the Hard Drive. We can make new folders, make copies of files, and generally manipulate these in a way that suits our own purposes. To get the best out of your personal computer, you should now use this knowledge to your own advantage. In particular, there are hidden dangers ahead that you need to be aware of and take steps to safeguard against.

As your own tasks with the computer begin to build, the work files that you create will become more and more important to you. You can quite easily spend many hours using the computer, and produce a lot of hard work that you come to rely and depend upon. If you suddenly find one day, that some or all of these files become damaged, or can no longer be used for whatever reason, then your sense of frustration and anger at losing them will be very acute.

First-timers are very impressed by the power that exists within a modern personal computer. What they also need to appreciate is that it is not infallible. Hard Drives and other forms of file storage can, and often do, break down. For some reason or other, magnetic storage seems to be particularly delicate, and you therefore need to regularly make what we term '**backup**' copies, of the serious work that you do. Most importantly, it will be of no use making backup copies of folders and files – from one area of the Hard Drive to another – if the Hard Drive itself comes to grief! You should always therefore consider making backup copies to Floppy Disk and then storing these disks in a safe place for future emergency retrieval.

This idea of making backup copies of your work also extends to protecting yourself against changes that you yourself might make to files. It is not always a failure of the computers's hardware that can raise your blood pressure! Many is the time that I have started to edit some important work, only to be disappointed that my changes have not measured up to the quality I had wished. If you have a recent backup copy of your work prior to the changes, it is quite easy to cut and paste the best bits back into the working file, and thereby undo any damage that you might have inflicted on your work.

Another modern 'man-trap' that awaits you is the advent of the scourge known as the computer virus. The full treatment of this subject is way beyond the scope of this book, but it is worth mentioning this topic in passing, because this is yet another threat to the safety of your files.

A **computer virus** is essentially a new string of byte codes that can get added clandestinely to your normal files and thereby modify them in way that you certainly did not intend. They are particularly nasty inventions when added to program files. When you start to run an 'infected' program file, the new string of byte codes becomes a small piece of new program that gets an opportunity to do its nasty work, which can be almost anything that the computer is capable of doing. This may range from something petty that is simply annoying, to something extremely malicious that may cause irreparable damage to all your software.

Computer viruses can only get inside your computer if you perform actions that allow them to. However, it is not always obvious – particularly to the first-timer – what these actions are. You are therefore strongly advised to run special **virus checking software** on your computer at all times, so that you minimise the risk of a virus reaking havoc.

One method of introducing a virus into your computer is to use a Floppy Disk, either loaned or given to you by another person. If any file on the disk contains a virus, then at the speed of lightning, the act of reading or copying that file can introduce the virus to your own machine. If you employ virus-checking software to examine the disk before any other action takes place, then you can determine if there is a risk, and avoid the consequences. You must also avoid putting your Floppy Disks into some one else's computer, and then coming back and inserting them into your own. That effectively is just as bad as using some one else's disks. If you do employ virus-checking software, you must regularly update it to guard against the many thousands of new viruses that are created almost every day.

If you ever need to deal with a computer virus, you would be well advised to seek the help of an expert to get rid of it. It is at those times as well that you begin to fully appreciate the value of making backup copies of your work. At the worst extreme, you may find that you need drastic action such as re-installing the master Windows program, and if you do so, you may need to copy back all the work that you did prior to getting the virus infection. You can obviously only do that if you made them in the first place!

This now brings us to the end of this chapter. In the next one, we will learn how to use a more professional word-processing program for creating that special look to our letters and documents.

9

Writing Letters and Documents with Wordpad

9.1　Using Wordpad for word processing

In chapter 4, we began our experience of working with a computer by introducing the **Notepad** program, and using it to write ourselves a short list that we called 'Shopping List Number 1'. Notepad is a very simple program to use, and because of its relatively small file size, it is very quick to load and start running. Despite its simplicity, it is still a very handy program to work with, and many experienced computer users employ it frequently for smaller tasks.

When we want to produce documents with a very professional appearance, we find that Notepad has a number of shortcomings. One of these in particular is that the lettering is limited to only one style and size. This has a very serious effect on the visual impression of our printed pages. Yet another problem with Notepad is the difficulty of adding any lines, shapes or pictures into documents. A third problem is the restricted size of document that it can work with. The total document size is limited to 64 Kilobytes, which practically means about ten thousand words.

To overcome these restrictions, we need a new kind of program called a '**word processing**' program. Word processing is the art of storing and organising language by electronic means, and the personal computer is ideally suited to this function. The program we will work with in this chapter is called '**Wordpad**'. It is more complex than Notepad, but far simpler than some of the more expensive word processing programs that you will see advertised, which have now reached unbelievable levels of sophistication.

To get Wordpad loaded and running – click on the **Start Button**, then click on **Programs**, click on **Accessories**, and finally click on **Wordpad**. You should then see the Wordpad window open, looking like the next picture:

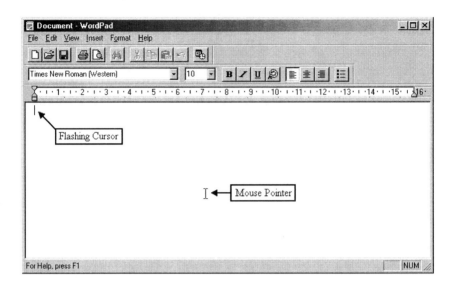

In the top left corner of the large white area, you can see a flashing cursor just as we did with Notepad. If you also position the mouse pointer in this area, you will see that the pointer symbol changes from the arrow symbol to a new vertical bar type image, again as we saw it change with Notepad.

One of the big differences we now see with Wordpad is that there are many new **buttons** appearing on two new **bars** underneath the **Menu Bar**. All of these buttons are alternative methods of achieving functions that you will also find repeated in the **drop down menus** from the Menu Bar. The buttons provide us with a faster method of activating these functions, but not every menu function is replicated on a button, so you may still have need to use the menus on occasion.

The two new bars are known as the **Tool Bar**, shown again here:

and the **Format Bar** shown here:

These bars can either be visible on screen or not. They are visible by default when you first open the **window**. If you wish them not to be visible, then you can use the drop down **View menu**, from the **Menu Bar**, and click on the appropriate option. The 'tick' mark of these options toggles between visible and non-visible for each click that you make.

There are also two other new features in Wordpad that you do not see in Notepad. These are the **Ruler**:

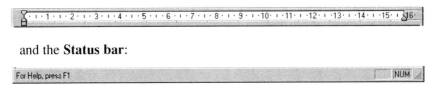

and the **Status bar**:

These too can be made visible or not visible from options on the drop down View menu.

The **ruler** is calibrated in centimetres as the default setting, but you can change this to other measurement units if you prefer. To do this, use the View menu, and click on Options... then click again on the Options Tab. You then have a choice of four different units to select from by clicking on them.

The **Status Bar** at the very bottom of the Wordpad window normally displays a short message to the left side, giving information relevant to the action that you are making at any given time. To the right side are two small boxes that show you if the **Numlock** or **Capslock** keys are active. The **Numlock key** refers to the numeric keypad at the far right of the keyboard. When active, it means that the central numeric keypad keys will type numerals. When not active, it means that these same keys will act as function keys according to the symbols upon them. This dual-purpose capability is a legacy from early days of computer development. These days, the symbolic functions are now available from separate keys on the keyboard. The **Capslock key** is found on the far left of the keyboard, just above the Left SHIFT key, and its job is to force all the alphabetic keys to type in upper case ('Capital') lettering.

Rather than take you through each and every function of Wordpad, which would take us considerable time (and probably bore you to insanity!), I propose to take you through a series of exercises that will show you:

- how to construct a business type letter, neatly presented and laid out in a traditional way
- how to make a poster advertising an item for sale
- how to embed diagrams into a letter to a friend.

These exercises should cover most of the normal functions that you will need for writing letters and simple documents.

If you want to learn more in depth about using the features in Wordpad, then you should click on **Help** from the **Menu Bar**, choose **Help Topics**, then click on the **Contents Tab**. The various topics shown are opened and closed by further clicks. I do recommend that you have a look at them because they are very short and easily read.

9.2   Writing letters with Wordpad

Our first exercise in writing letters is to produce the first draft. Then we shall move on to learn about editing. Finally, we will preview the letter to see its general appearance, and then print it out.

Exercise 20 – Drafting a business reply letter

To illustrate a typical example of working with Wordpad, we will now generate an imaginary business reply letter.

We begin with the **Wordpad window** opened on the Desktop from the last section. Maximise the size of the window to take full advantage of the size of your screen, using the central button in the very top right-hand corner of the window, immediately to the left of the Close button.

The appearance of lettering in a document is known in computing jargon as the '**Font**'. Our first task is to choose the Font style and the **Font size** that we wish to use for the business letter. If you look at the two drop down **List boxes** on the **Format Bar** you will see something like the next picture:

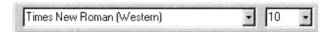

The larger, left one is used to select **Font style** and the smaller right one is to select **Font size**.

We will use the default Font style setting of '**Times New Roman (Western)**', but will change the Font size to '**12**'. Click on the **down arrow** of the **Font size list box** (currently showing '10') and this produces the list of all possible sizes. Then click again to select '**12**' as shown in the next picture:

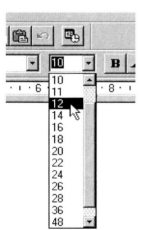

The value in the list box now changes to '12', and the drop down list disappears.

Now using the keyboard, press the **TAB key** once. The TAB key has an unusual symbol on it, and is located as shown in the following picture:

When you have pressed the **TAB key** once, I want you to look at the position of the cursor, as shown in this next picture:

You can now see that it has moved right to just underneath a small grey mark on the lower edge of the Ruler, at slightly over the 1¼ cm position. These small grey marks are the default Tab stops, and every time you press the TAB key it will move one more Tab stop along the Ruler.

Now press the TAB key several more times, until the cursor has reached the eighth stop, almost directly underneath the 10 cm position on the Ruler. Then we type '6 Chestnut Ave' and press the **ENTER key**. The cursor returns to the start of the second line.

Now press the TAB key a number of times again, to position the cursor at the same stop under the 10 cm position, and under the previous line of typing. Then type 'Readington' and press the ENTER key.

Continue your typing until you have the same text as shown in this next picture:

When you have typed in the last digit of the telephone number, press the ENTER key to return to the start of the next line, then press it once more to create a blank line. Now press the TAB key a number of times again to position the cursor back at the eighth stop, at the same 10 cm position.

Using the mouse pointer, click on the **Date/Time button**, as in the next picture:

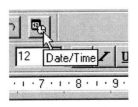

You will then be shown a list box from where you can select the date/time (as held internally by the computer) in one of several **formats** (format is new jargon for 'arrangement', and this word is used quite a lot in computing). Choose the date/month/year format as shown in the following picture, and click on OK:

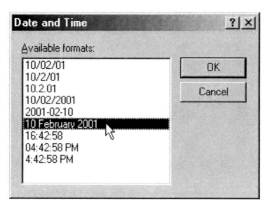

The list box then disappears, and you see this date/time format automatically appear in the text of the letter that we are writing, under the telephone number. Now press the **ENTER key** to return to beginning of the next line.

Our next task, having written our own address details, is to write the name and address details of the person to whom the letter is to be sent. I will leave you now to enter these yourself, as shown in the next picture:

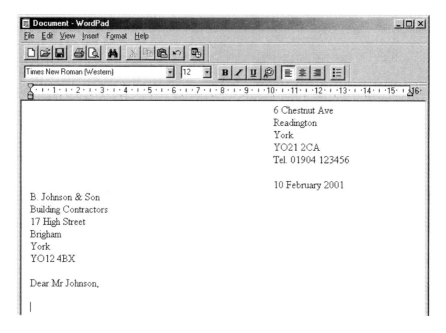

Add an extra blank line with the ENTER key at the end, after 'Mr Johnson', so that the cursor is ready for the Subject Reference Title coming next.

Now, before we proceed any further, we will save our work so far to the Hard Drive, in case anything goes wrong later. If a power cut or any other accident happens, we can then restart from this stage later if we have to, and not have to type it all in again.

Note – this habit of saving your work at regular intervals is a must if you are to avoid major frustration! Incidents can happen at any time, and you cannot predict when that will be. I have known people spend the whole of a morning typing away without saving once, only to lose the complete lot when a cleaner pulled out a wall power plug to plug in the vacuum cleaner! The air was very blue on that occasion! And it was not all the fault of the cleaner.

To save the work so far, press the **Save Button** as shown in the next picture:

This then brings up the **Save As dialog box**, which we have met several times before in previous chapters.

In the **Save As dialog box**, use the default folder of '**My Documents**'. Notice that the default for 'Save As type' is set to 'Word for Windows 6.0'. Now enter the '**File name**' as 'Accept Johnson Estimate', then click the **Save button**. The Save As dialog box then disappears, and we are ready to do some more typing.

Okay. We are now going to enter a Subject Title Reference line for our letter, so that as soon as the recipient reads it, they are able to see what the subject of the letter is about. To make this stand out, we will use both '**Bold**' and '**Underline**' Font type.

On the **Format Bar**, click on the each of the two buttons for these Font types so that they both appear 'pushed down', as shown in the following picture:

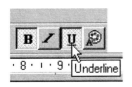

Now from the keyboard, type the line 'Re: Acceptance of your estimate dated 5th February 2001', and notice that as you type it, the actual text on the screen appears in 'Bold' and 'Underline' Font type. Finish the line by pressing the ENTER key. Now go back to the two buttons shown in the last picture, and click on each of them again, so that they appear as though they are not 'pushed down'. We do this so that any further typing we make is using the 'Regular' Font type once more.

Now press the ENTER key to create a blank line in between the Subject Title reference and the body of the letter we are about to enter.

Okay. We are ready to enter the paragraphs of the main body of the letter.

Note – For information, the '£' symbol is created by pressing and holding the Left SHIFT key and then pressing the '3' key of the number keys on the top row. Don't use the '3' key on the numeric keypad at the right-hand side.

Now I want you to enter all the rest of the text as it is shown in the next picture. After entering each paragraph, click the **Save Button** to update the copy of your work on the Hard Drive, just as we did before. You will now notice that each time you now click the Save button, the Save As dialog box does not appear; but the Hard Disk file called 'Accept B Johnson Estimate' is automatically updated immediately.

You can see that this automatic update happens if you watch the indicator lights on the processor unit front panel. The Disk Activity indicator light will briefly illuminate as the information is written back to the Hard Drive. If you are very sharp eyed, you may also see some wording changes on the Status Bar at the very bottom of the window.

Here is the text for you to enter:

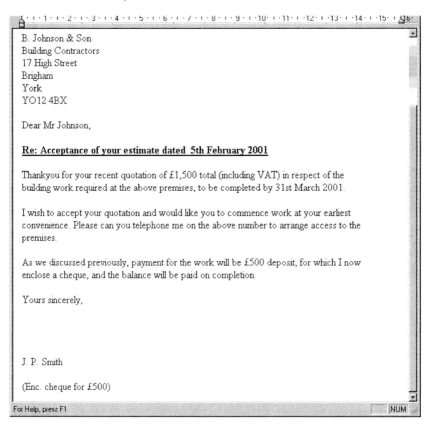

B. Johnson & Son
Building Contractors
17 High Street
Brigham
York
YO12 4BX

Dear Mr Johnson,

Re: Acceptance of your estimate dated 5th February 2001

Thankyou for your recent quotation of £1,500 total (including VAT) in respect of the building work required at the above premises, to be completed by 31st March 2001.

I wish to accept your quotation and would like you to commence work at your earliest convenience. Please can you telephone me on the above number to arrange access to the premises.

As we discussed previously, payment for the work will be £500 deposit, for which I now enclose a cheque, and the balance will be paid on completion.

Yours sincerely,

J. P. Smith

(Enc. cheque for £500)

For Help, press F1   NUM

Note – For information, there are 4 blank lines after 'Yours sincerely' to allow space for a signature, just above the printed sender's name.

When you have entered the last line of '(Enc. cheque for £500)', press the ENTER key one final time, to bring the cursor onto a new line at the bottom. This makes sure that the last line ends with an invisible 'carriage return' instruction, in the same way as every other line. It is good practice to do this, particularly because some printers will not eject a printed page until the last line of text is definitely known to have finished.

Make a final click on the **Save Button** to complete the first draft.

Now close the Wordpad window using the '**X**' button as we normal do. This concludes exercise 20.

Exercise 21 – Two 'modes' of typing (Inserting or Overtyping)

In this next exercise, we are going to uncover one of the great mysteries that often catch out first-timers when they begin to use a word processor! We will not make any permanent changes to our draft letter. *I therefore do not want you to press the Save button at any time during the exercise.*

When the Wordpad window is first opened, the **default 'mode'** of operation is known as '**Inserting**'. This simply means that when you enter new text on a line, it is inserted at the point where the cursor currently is, and pushing any existing text (to the right of it) further along the line, but not removing it.

If you press the Insert key once on the keyboard, you then change the mode of operation from 'Inserting' to 'Overtyping'. Here is the Insert key:

Overtyping mode means that when you enter new text on a line, it replaces any existing text (to the right of it) by actually removing it on a 'letter-by-letter' basis (I should really say character by character – to mean letters, numbers and symbols – but I made my apology in the last chapter!). For each new letter that you type, then one old letter immediately to the right of it disappears – it is 'overtyped'.

Now the mystery that often catches out first-timers is that they sometimes press the Insert key accidentally by mistake. They rarely realise that they have done it. Then they may see curious things begin to happen on screen and get very confused.

Should you ever find yourself in the **Overtyping mode** and want to go back to **Inserting mode**, you do this by simply pressing the Insert key once again. The Insert key operates a 'toggle' form of action, to alternate from one mode to the other.

In this next exercise, we will illustrate the difference between the two modes of operation, and thereby clear up any confusion. We will not make any permanent alterations to the letter. We will simply discard all the changes when we have finished.

Okay. Let's us now start the exercise and witness the difference.

We begin at the **Desktop**.

Click on the **Start Button**, then click on **Programs**, click on **Accessories**, and finally click on **Wordpad**. You should then see the **Wordpad window** open.

From the **Menu Bar**, click on **File**, and then click on '**1 Accept Johnson Estimate**'.

The document that we created and saved in the last exercise now appears in the window, with the flashing cursor positioned in the top left hand corner of the text area.

This technique of loading the last document was briefly mentioned before, at the end of chapter 6 when we used the Paint program. In Wordpad too, the last four documents are always listed (in reverse order) as options 1 to 4 on the File menu (as they often are with other programs).

The default mode of operation is **Inserting mode**, which we are currently in. Press the **Insert key** once, to deliberately change it to the Overtyping mode.

Okay. Now press the 'A' key once, and observe what happens on the top line. Your screen should look something like the next picture:

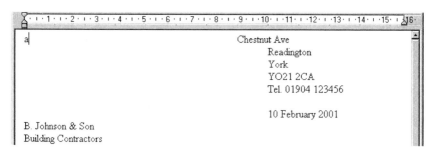

This kind of event is very puzzling to work out exactly what is going on. We see here that the 'a' letter appears in the top left corner, where the cursor was last, but the words 'Chestnut Ave' seem to have mysteriously jumped over, heading towards the left!

The explanation of what you see here is this...

● Because we are in Overtyping mode, the action of typing the 'A' key has inserted a letter 'a', and has overwritten an 'invisible TAB symbol' that was inserted when we pressed the TAB key in the last exercise.

- You may remember that pressing the TAB key was the very first action we did when creating the letter. The TAB key inserts 'invisible TAB symbols' into the document, so that the document knows exactly where next to position text along the line.

- Having overwritten one of them, we now have one less 'invisible TAB symbol' in the first line than we had before, making only seven instead of the original eight. Consequently the words 'Chestnut Ave' have moved back one grey tabbing mark to reflect this fact. Notice that the 'C' of 'Chestnut' is now lined up with the grey mark on the ruler at just less than 9 cm.

Now press the '**A**' **key** again, and see the same thing happen. We now have six 'invisible TAB symbols' instead of seven. And so it would go on ...

Now press the **Insert key** once more. This takes us out of the Overwriting mode and reverts us back to the Inserting mode.

Okay. Now press the '**A**' **key** once again. Notice this time that the words 'Chestnut Ave' didn't move towards the left. This is because we are in Inserting mode, so adding the new letter does not overwrite any of the existing 'invisible TAB symbols'. We still have six of them.

The only time that the words 'Chestnut Ave' will now move back towards the right is if we add sufficient 'a' letters to move the cursor up to (or beyond) the first grey tabbing mark on the ruler. If we do that, then the six 'invisible TAB symbols' (which are still inside the document but now after the 'a' letters) will have to move the text over an additional mark to clock up correct number of grey tabbing marks. Press the '**A**' key several more times and you will see this eventually happen.

Okay. That is sufficient action to demonstrate the mysteries of Inserting mode and Overwriting mode. Now you can understand what happens if you accidentally press the Insert key when you are typing away in Wordpad.

For my own personal working style, I rarely if ever use the Overtyping mode. I usually find it just as quick to stay in the Inserting mode and use the Delete key or Backspace key to remove text that I no longer want. However, the choice is there for you to use it should you prefer.

Now click on the '**X**' button to close the Wordpad window. When you get the **warning message** asking you if you want to save the changes, click on '**No**'. The changes we have made as part of this exercise will then be abandoned, without saving any of them to the file on the Hard Drive. The next time we open the Hard Drive file we shall see that it was not affected.

Note – this effect can be very useful. Suppose you have made a few changes to a document but do not like what you have done and cannot

remember what you had to start with. Do not save, but close without saving. Then re-open the document and you will have what you started with last time.

This concludes exercise 21.

Exercise 22 – Editing with Cut, Copy and Paste

In this exercise, we are going to use the **Clipboard** again. We have met this now on several occasions, and in different circumstances. The Clipboard is a very flexible facility to work with.

We begin at the **Desktop**.

Open Wordpad (you should be competent at this by now!).

From the **Menu Bar**, click on **File**, and then click on '**1 Accept Johnson Estimate**'.

Now the very first thing we are going to do is to save the letter document under a new file name. The advantage of doing this is that once we have done it, the file that we are working on – from that point onwards – is a new file on the Hard Drive, and not the original one. Any changes we make will not alter the original file in any way. If we make a complete sow's ear of the editing, we will always have our original draft version to fall back on.

From the **File menu**, click on the **Save As...** option. When the following **dialog box** appears, the **File name** will be selected and highlighted.

Now I will show you another trick. As the first key that you use when the dialog box appears, press the END key, as shown in the next picture:

Immediately, you notice that the highlight disappears, and the cursor moves to the end of the text. Now press the **SpaceBar key**, followed by the number '**2**' **key**. The text for the **File name** is now shown as 'Accept Johnson Estimate 2'. Then press the **ENTER key** to put our wishes into effect.

Notice that as soon as the dialog box disappears, the blue **Title Bar** of the **Wordpad window** changes its text to show 'Accept Johnson Estimate 2 – Wordpad'. This proves that we are now working with the new file and not with the original.

Okay. Now we are ready to start editing. First we will demonstrate the **Cut** action.

Carefully position the mouse pointer between the end of the word 'premises' and the comma that follows it.

Now begin a drag action by pressing and holding the left mouse button. Maintain the drag while you slowly move the mouse to the right, observing that the text you pass over becomes highlighted blue as you move along. When the pointer reaches the end of '2001', but before you include the following full stop, end the drag action. Your screen should now appear something like the following picture:

> Thankyou for your recent quotation of £1,500 total (including VAT) in respect of the building work required at the above premises, to be completed by 31st March 2001.

Note – **If you have difficulty getting the highlight to end in the right place with the mouse pointer, there is a trick with the 'Arrow' keys that you can use instead. The 'Arrow' keys are the triangular group of four dark grey keys located below the End key.**

First position the cursor at the correct starting point (you can use either the mouse pointer or the Arrow keys to move it there). Now press and hold down the Left SHIFT key, and while you have it held down, press the 'Left' or 'Right' Arrow keys again, as appropriate, to move the highlight back and forth. When you have the highlight ending just where you want it to, release the Left SHIFT key.

This technique also works in circumstances where you may wish to move the highlight across multiple lines. To move between lines, you would use the 'Down' or 'Up' Arrow keys appropriately, while still maintaining the Left SHIFT key held).

Okay. Now that we have the correct text highlighted, click using the mouse pointer on the **Cut button** of the **Tool Bar**, as shown in the next picture:

As soon as you have made the click, then you will see all of the highlighted text suddenly disappear.

The Cut action is now complete. The highlighted text is removed from the document and a copy of it is placed on to the **Clipboard**. Anything that may have previously been on the Clipboard is lost, being overwritten by its new contents.

Now we shall demonstrate the **Paste** action.

Position the mouse pointer immediately after the end of the word 'convenience' in the second paragraph, but before the full stop that follows. Make a click action. As you move the pointer now slightly to one side, you will notice that the cursor is now repositioned, flashing at the point where you made the click.

Note – Again, if you have difficulty positioning the cursor with the mouse pointer, you can make fine adjustments to its position by pressing the 'Arrow' keys appropriately.

Okay. Now click on the **Paste** button on the **Tool Bar**, as shown in the next picture:

Your screen should now show the second paragraph to look something like this:

I wish to accept your quotation and would like you to commence work at your earliest convenience, to be completed by 31st March 2001. Please can you telephone me on the above number to arrange access to the premises.

This is the completion of the **Paste** action.

The Paste action itself does not clear the contents of the Clipboard, so if we wanted to 'Paste' them again somewhere else, we are free to do so. We can, in fact, 'Paste' the contents of the Clipboard as many times as we wish.

Having now successfully made a Cut and Paste, click on the **Save button** ( ) once again on the **Tool Bar** to save the final editing to the new file on the Hard Drive.

The **Copy button** ( ) action is very similar to the **Cut button**. The only difference is that the original highlighted text is not removed from the document when the button is pressed.

I will not demonstrate the Copy button now, but leave you to experiment with it in your own time. Click now on the '**X**' button to close the Wordpad window.

This concludes exercise 22.

9.3   Creating an advertising poster

Another popular use for word processing programs, in addition to writing letters, is making notices or posters. In this section we will conduct an exercise to illustrate the way we can use the flexibility of Font style and Font size to make an advertising poster.

Exercise 23 – Advertising a bicycle for sale

We begin at the **Desktop.**

Click on the **Start Button**, click on **Programs**, click on **Accessories**, and finally click on **Wordpad.** You should then see the **Wordpad window** open.

If the Wordpad window is not already maximised to fill the screen, do so now by clicking the **Maximise button** in the top right-hand corner of the window (the button immediately to the left of the Close button).

To begin our poster, we will use the **default settings** for **Font style** and **Font size** ('Times New Roman (Western)' & '10').

Enter the text as shown in this next picture, pressing the **ENTER key** at the end of each line. Press the ENTER key also to create blank lines. There are two blank lines following the line 'for sale', one blank line following 'One careful owner', and two blank lines following '£100 o.n.o.'. Remember also to press the ENTER key following the last line for the telephone number (you can see the cursor at the beginning of the next line):

We have now entered the text for our poster. The next job is to centre and change the **Font styles** and **Font sizes** for the first two lines.

Position the mouse pointer in front of the 'B' in the word 'Bicycle' and start a **drag** action with the **left mouse button.** Slide the pointer towards the right, and position it after the word 'sale' on the line below. Now end the drag action. You should now see just those two lines highlighted, as shown in the next picture:

Now click on the **Center Button**, located on the Format Bar, as shown in the following picture:

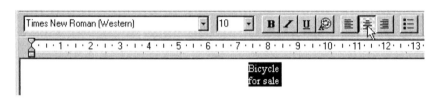

Notice that after the click, the highlighted text moves over into the middle of the page. Now be particularly careful – we need to maintain the text as highlighted for the next action to work properly. If you lose the highlight for any reason, then you will first have to get it back again – by making another drag action over the text – before you perform the next action.

We now click with the pointer on the **Font style down arrow button**, to obtain a drop down list of the various Font styles available. From the list, use the vertical scroll bar to scroll the list backwards so that you can then click to select the 'Arial Black (Western)' option, as shown in the next picture:

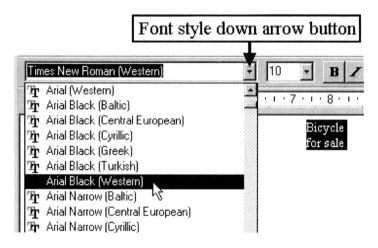

The full list of **Font styles** available on your computer will vary considerably depending on how many styles have been added in by program software overall. The master Windows program itself gives you a basic 'starter' set of styles. Other programs can then add to this basic set, as and when they are installed. You can also purchase special Font packs if you want to increase your choice.

After you have clicked on the selected style, the list will disappear, and you should then notice a distinct change in the appearance of the highlighted text. Again, be careful to maintain the highlight on the text until we have changed the Font size. Now click the **Font size down arrow** and click on the '72' option, as shown in the next picture:

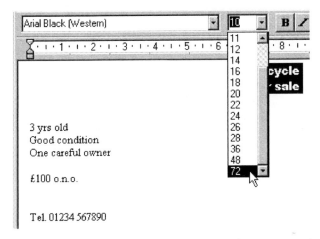

After you have clicked, the list disappears, and you then see a major change to the text, as in the following picture:

I think you can now appreciate why it was necessary to be careful to maintain the highlight on the text. The operations we have just performed of changing Font style and Font size, apply to all of the highlighted area at the time that the changes are made. If the text had not been highlighted, then none of it would have changed.

Having finished with the highlight, we can now remove it. Click anywhere on the page and the highlight should disappear.

We will now change the Font style and Font size for the rest of the text.

This next action is a bit tricky. Carefully position the mouse pointer on the first blank line, after the words 'for sale'. Now make a drag action downwards so as to highlight all the rest of the text, including the blank line after the telephone number. Release the drag when you have it all highlighted. If you have done it correctly, then you will have included two blank lines highlighted before '3 yrs old', and one blank line after 'Tel. 01234 567890', as shown in this next picture:

for sale

3 yrs old
Good condition
One careful owner

£100 o.n.o.

Tel. 01234 567890

Note – If you have difficulty getting the highlight in the right place with the mouse pointer, you can use the same trick with the keyboard 'Arrow' keys that we mentioned in the last exercise instead.

The 'Arrow' keys, remember, are the triangular group of four dark grey keys located on the right side of the keyboard, below the End key.

First position the cursor at the correct starting point (you can use either the mouse pointer or the Arrow keys themselves to move it there). Now press and hold down the Left SHIFT key, and while you have it held down, press the 'Down' Arrow key to move the highlight over all of the remaining text, including the last blank line. When you have the highlight set correct, release the Left SHIFT key.

Take care to maintain the highlight. Now use the mouse pointer in the same way as we did before to click on the **Center button**, as in the next picture:

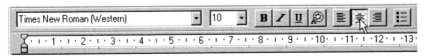

You will then see all of the highlighted text appear in the middle of the page.

Maintain the highlight, and now use the mouse pointer in the same way as before to change the **Font style**. Click first on the **Font style down arrow button** and this time choose the 'Comic Sans MS (Western)' option from the list, as in the next picture:

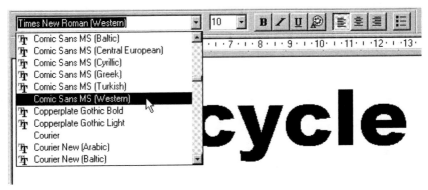

Next we need to change the **Font size**. Click on the **Font size down arrow button**, and choose the '24' option. As soon as you have clicked on it, the list will disappear and you will see the highlighted text change its size.

At this point, we do not need the highlight any more. Another safe way to remove the highlight without disturbing anything else is to press the **End key**, whose location is shown again in the next picture. Press this now:

After we have pressed the End key, the highlight disappears and the cursor is positioned after the last visible part of the previously highlighted text, which is to the right of the telephone number.

We should now save the work that we have done so far. Click on the **File menu** from the **Menu Bar**, and then click on the 'Save **As...**' option. Type the

File name as 'Bike for sale', and then click on the **Save button**. If the file has saved correctly, you should see the blue **Title Bar** of the **Wordpad window** now read 'Bike for sale – Wordpad'.

We have reached the point now where we have finished the basic page layout. In the jargon, we would say that the page has now been 'formatted'. You may have noticed that this word 'format' keeps cropping up for different items! First we:

- **Formatted** a **Floppy Disk**
- Then we **formatted** the **date/time** in our Wordpad letter
- Now we have **formatted** a page!

The final part of producing our advertising poster is to **Preview** it, and check the **Page Setup** settings, prior to actually printing it. If you have a printer, then you can follow the discussion and make a print. If you don't, then you might wish to read it for information only – you may get access to one some day!

From the **File Menu** on the **Menu Bar**, click on '**Print Preview**'. You will then see a new window appear, showing you a view of the page in full, as you might expect to see it on a printed page:

The **Print Preview** facility is a useful one to get an overall view of your work before you start wasting printer paper. If there is anything that you don't like about the overall look of it, you can go back and change it first. Then when you are satisfied, you can go ahead and print it out.

In the view that you now have, take a close look at the positions of the margins as represented by the dotted lines. Check if your text is centred on the page both horizontally and vertically. If the margins are unequal, as we see in the last picture, then you need to change the **margin settings**. You do this within **Page Setup**, which we discuss next.

Now return back to the normal **Wordpad window** by clicking on either the **Close button** from the **Menu Bar**, or the normal '**X**' button in the top right corner.

From the normal **Wordpad window**, click on the **File Menu**, and click on the **Page Setup...** option. We now see the **Page Setup dialog box**, as in the next picture:

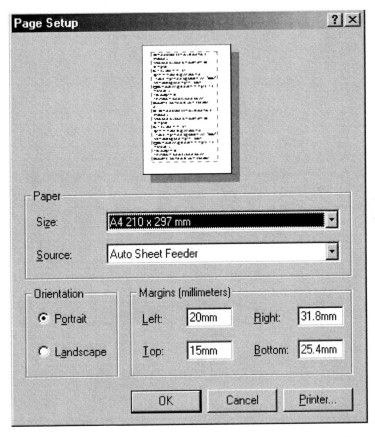

The first thing to do when you see the dialog box is check that the **Paper Size**

corresponds with the paper you are going to use on your printer. If it needs adjusting, then do so now using the **Size down arrow button**, and choose the correct paper size from the drop down list, in a similar manner to the way we changed Font style and Font size.

Notice also that you can alter the orientation of the printing on the paper from **portrait** to **landscape**. This effectively turns the paper through 90 degrees before the text is printed out. The black 'dot' in the small circle indicates which of the two is currently selected. Our advertising poster requires the portrait setting, so if your setting needs altering, simply click on the appropriate word and you will see the 'dot' switch over.

Okay. Now we check the **Margin settings**. The Margin units of measurement and values shown on your own computer may differ from that shown above. If the default setting for the ruler of your Wordpad program is inches not centimetres, then this will be reflected in the units shown here.

For our poster to appear centred on the printed page, the **Left** and **Right Margin values** need to be equal in value. Their combined widths have to be no greater than the width of the Paper Size minus the width required for our text, as seen in the normal Wordpad window. Let us breifly discuss a practical example of checking out the acceptable values for these margins...

> **... For a Paper Size of 'A4', the paper width is 210mm. If we set both Left and Right margins to 30mm each, then their combined width will be 60mm. Subtracting this figure from the paper width leaves a width for our text area of 210 − 60 = 150mm. This resulting value then becomes the text area width as shown by the white portion on the ruler in the normal Wordpad window.**

This next picture shows that 150mm (15cm) is an acceptable value for the text area because the widest part of our text is much less than this:

Bicycle

If your measurement units for the ruler are in inches, you can safely use a value for the margins of 1¼ in.

Note – Read section 9.1 again if you wish to change the choice of measurement units.

Okay. Having decided upon a value for the choice of Left and Right Margins, we must now make the changes. To adjust them, position the mouse pointer over the box that you want to change and notice that the pointer symbol changes its appearance. Right-click to establish a flashing cursor inside the box, and then click on the **Select All** option from the pop-up menu to highlight all of the existing value. Now type your new value on the keyboard, and this will replace the existing value.

When you have both the Left and Right Margins set appropriately, then click on the **OK button** to save the settings. The dialog box now disappears, and you see the normal Wordpad window again.

Go back now and have another look at the **Print Preview** option from the **File Menu**. You should see the text for our advertising poster is neatly centred. Now close the **Print Preview window**.

Finally, we now **Print** the results of our work. From the **File Menu**, choose the **Print...** option. The **Print dialog box** will then appear. Click on the **OK button** and then the printer will make the actual print.

When the printing is finished, close the Wordpad window and admire your work! This concludes exercise 23.

9.4   Embedding drawings in documents

In this final section of chapter 9, we will perform an exercise to show how you can insert a picture or drawing into a Wordpad document, to enhance its information content. Our exercise will first create a simple letter to some friends, advising them that we have moved house. Then when we have the text of the letter prepared, we will insert a copy of the drawing titled 'Map of my house', which we made previously in section 6.3.

Exercise 24 – Inserting a drawing into a letter
We begin at the **Desktop**.

Click on the **Start Button**, then click on **Programs**, click on **Accessories**, and finally click on **Wordpad**. You should then see the Wordpad window open, with a blank page. Keep the **default Font style** set at 'Times New Roman (Western)', but adjust the **Font Size** to '12', as we did in exercise 20.

Now enter the following text to create a simple letter:

Okay. With the basic letter now typed, we should save it to the Hard Drive before we attempt to insert the drawing.

Click the **Save button** on the **Tool Bar** (   ), and the **Save As dialog box** will appear. For the **file name**, type 'House Move', and then click the **Save button**.

We are ready now to insert the drawing. As with many tasks, there are several ways to achieve this. In this exercise, we will use the **copy** and **paste** method. First we will **copy** to the **Clipboard** from the **Paint program**, and then we will **paste** from the **Clipboard** into the **Wordpad program**.

With **Wordpad** still open on the **Desktop**, click on the **Start Button**, then click on **Programs**, click on **Accessories**, and finally click on **Paint**. You should then see the **Paint window** open. If the window is not maximised, then make it so by clicking on the **Maximise button** (the one in the middle of the three in the top right-hand corner).

Now from the **File Menu** of the **Paint** window, click on the **Open...** option. The **Open dialog box** will then appear. Then click on the icon for the 'Map of my house' file, and finally click on the **Open button**. The drawing that we made in chapter 6 should now appear in the **Paint window**.

Choose the **Select Tool** as shown in the following picture:

Now position the pointer just above top left part of the drawing, and perform a **drag** action down to the bottom right, as shown in the next picture:

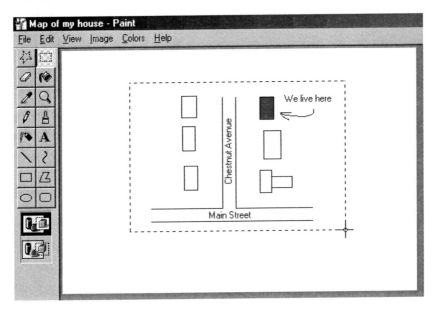

The dashed line then outlines the part of the drawing that we want to copy. Release the drag action.

From the **Menu Bar**, click on the **Edit menu**, and then click on **Copy**. A copy of the area that we selected by the dashed line is now placed on the **Clipboard**.

Close the **Paint window** using the 'X' button in the normal way, and we see the **Wordpad window** again. Even though the Paint program is no longer running, the part of the drawing that we copied to the **Clipboard** is still there upon it.

Okay. Now position the mouse pointer at the beginning of the blank line, just above the words 'Do come and visit as soon as you can.' and click to reposition the cursor at that spot. From the keyboard, press the **ENTER key** twice to create a further two blank lines. Now press the **Up Arrow key** once, so that the cursor moves back to the middle one of the three blank lines which now exist, as shown in this next picture:

Just a quick note to let you know how things are. After what seemed ages, Sandy and I have finally bought the new house and moved in.

Do come and visit as soon as you can.

All our love,

The reason for creating these two extra blank lines is to put a line of spacing between the image that we will now insert, and the surrounding text. We then position the cursor back in the middle because this is where the copy of the drawing will be inserted.

With the cursor now positioned as shown in the above picture, use the mouse pointer to click on the **Paste button** from the **Tool Bar**, as in the next picture:

After clicking on the Paste button, we then see our drawing appear embedded within the letter, and surrounded by a black frame, as shown in the next picture:

Dear Mary and Peter,

Just a quick note to let you know how things are. After what seemed ages, Sandy and I have finally bought the new house and moved in.

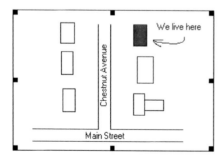

Do come and visit as soon as you can.

All our love,

The black frame that surrounds the copy of the drawing is only temporary, and is indicating that it now has the focus of attention on the page. While this black frame is visible, the object inside it is 'selected' in a very similar way that we regarded text as being 'selected' when it is highlighted blue. When the frame disappears, the object no longer has the focus (if you need to get it back again, then simply click on the drawing).

As an example of the drawing having the focus, let us consider centering the drawing in middle of the page (as we did in exercise 23 with the text of our poster). With the frame now visible, click the **Center button** on the **Format Bar**, as shown in the next picture:

You now see that the drawing moves over into the middle of the page.

Another property of the black frame concerns the eight small black squares around its edge. These black squares are referred to as '**handles**' on the frame. The reason is that you can 'pull' on these handles using a drag action of the mouse pointer. When you do so, the frame size changes, and so does the size of the object inside. In this way, if you wish to, you are able to increase or decrease the drawing size within the letter. We will not change the drawing size now, but you might like to experiment with this later by yourself.

Now click with the mouse pointer at any other part of the page, and notice that the black frame disappears. It thereby loses the focus of attention. Now click back on the drawing, and the focus comes back.

Having inserted the drawing into the letter, we should now save the letter back to the Hard Drive. Click on the **Save button** from the **Tool bar** ( ), and the letter will be saved with the new drawing inside it.

The final task for the exercise is now to print it out. Having made the necessary adjustments to the Page Setup in the last exercise, there should be no need to do this again. You can therefore now click on the **Print button** from the **Tool Bar** as shown in the next picture:

The results of your all your labours will then come rolling out of the printer! Close the Wordpad window using the '**X**' button in the normal way.

This now concludes exercise 24.

10

The End of the Beginning

10.1 A review of progress

We have finally reached the closing chapter of this book, and we have covered a lot of ground since we first began. In order that you can judge your progress along the learning path, we will now review the work we have covered and see if we can summarise the skills and knowledge that you will have now acquired. Then in the next section, we will investigate where you might go from here.

We started at the beginning of the book with a simple assumption that your knowledge of computers was zero. Our first task, therefore, was to introduce the various physical components of a computer and explain what it is that they do. We then progressed to learn how to connect these individual parts together, so that we might switch on the computer and check that it was in working order.

Whenever you switch on a new appliance, it is prudent to know also how to switch it off, and with a computer today it is not just a case of switching off the mains power. We therefore spent chapter 2 learning the correct way to perform these two actions of powering the computer on and then off again.

At this stage, no doubt you were eager to start doing some practical work. But it was important to first understand just a little of how the computer works internally, so we took time out in chapter 3 to discuss computer programs in general. We learnt that they are first installed onto the Hard Drive for long term storage. During the process of running them, they are copied from the Hard Drive into RAM Memory, to take advantage of its much faster speed of operation. We also discussed non-program software, and introduced data files of both input and output types. If you have time available, I recommend that you now go back and re-read chapter 3 once again. There are a few things in there that will probably make a lot more sense with your current experience.

In chapter 4, we had our first real taste of practical work by writing a note, which we then saved as a file named 'Shopping List Number 1'. We used the 'Notepad' program to carry out this task, and in doing so we introduced the use of the keyboard. For those of you who are not familiar with the layout of a typewriter keyboard, I have no doubt that finding the key that you wanted to press was quite a problem. Don't be too worried if you are very slow in finding the keys, everybody is in the same situation when they first begin to learn. I can assure you that it does get much easier after you have written a few complete documents.

The next major learning experience was concerning a novel and interesting device, which we affectionately refer to as a 'mouse'. The mouse is a very useful tool in addition to the keyboard because it allows you to probe around on the inside of the computer. Some of you will have taken to it quite naturally, but others may still be having a problem with actions such as the 'double-click'. It was because this might have been troublesome, that we used the 'right-click' and 'open' technique throughout most of the exercises, as an alternative action instead. If you can become familiar with the double-click action then this is a faster way of working, but it takes a while to truly master it. Do keep practising; you should be able to get the hang of it eventually.

In chapter 6, we learnt quite a lot about the general object known as a 'window'. After all the effort of maximising, minimising, moving and resizing, there is not much concerning a window that you do not now know about. As a reward for your hard work, we then took some light relief playing 'Minesweeper'. This was a good method to get you clicking away with the mouse. I hope you have enjoyed playing this game, and go on to enjoy the other games that are available.

At the end of chapter 6, we started to be more serious by making drawings using the 'Paint' program. This is another simple but effective program to use, and I have surprised many people over the years with the useful and professional looking drawings that you can make with it.

In chapter 7, we learnt more about the basics of the personal computer. We studied the 'Desktop' in detail, and all of the objects within it. We also learnt about a very handy feature called the 'Recycle Bin'. This feature puts your mind at ease to know that if you accidentally delete something, then you have the opportunity to get it back again. Consequently, such actions shouldn't quite be the disaster that they once might have been!

In Chapter 8, we introduced the various forms of 'drive' devices, and we learnt that we use alphabetic letters to refer to them. We also learnt about the inverted tree structure for the storage of files and folders upon drives.

Finally, in chapter 9, we began to achieve some very professional looking work with 'Wordpad'. I think that this is probably one of the most useful parts of the book, and it was a pity that we had to leave it till last. However, we had to build on a solid foundation, and if we had attempted to use 'Wordpad' too soon, then there are many problems that would have surfaced later on. The very last exercise that we did should be very rewarding for future work that you undertake. Inserting drawings into documents is the clear signal that you are no longer a first-timer.

As a conclusion, you now have all the foundation skills of using a modern personal computer. To summarise your progress, I borrow some famous words from a great statesman to say... "You are not at the end of learning about computers. You are not even at the beginning of the end... But you are now at the end of the beginning!"

10.2 Where to go from here

Now that you have the foundation skills of using a computer, there are two different routes along which you can further develop your interest. The first route is to go 'on-line' and use the new technology of the Internet. The second is to learn about more complex programs to work with, in what we call 'stand-alone' operation. Let us look first at what may lie ahead for you 'on-line'.

The term 'on-line' comes from the need to have an electrical line connecting your computer into a network of many other computers. For most people, this 'line' is the humble telephone line, and requires a peripheral device called a 'modem'. You use the modem to dial up to a subscription service that is available from any one of a host of private companies. These private companies have the true connections into the Internet, and you access the Internet only by attaching to (and through) the computers of these companies. They are called Internet Service Providers (ISPs).

In exchange for a subscription payment, the ISP company will issue you with a special username and password. When you want to connect to the Internet, you dial into the ISP computer and establish a data connection to it from your computer (the modem takes care of converting data for use on a voice line). Their computer will then send messages to your computer, asking for the special username and password. If these are correctly entered and vetted as being current, your computer will be connected automatically through the ISP computer into the wider network of the Internet. You are then 'on-line'.

There are several ISP companies now that are providing a dual type of service. In exchange for your subscription payment, not only can you access the Internet, but also you can do so without paying any telephone charges to the telephone company. This can save you a lot of added expense, particularly if you are dialling into the ISP computer on a frequent basis.

What are the services that you can get from the Internet when you go 'on-line'? Well, the two main services are the 'World Wide Web' and Electronic Mail, and we shall briefly discuss these. There are other services, but they are beyond the scope of this book.

With the 'World Wide Web', you start a program running on your computer called a 'browser'. The browser program then allows you to type in addresses of places called 'web sites'. These sites are effectively pages of printed information held on many other computers all over the world. Most of the web site addresses begin with the three-letter symbol of 'www' and have two or three other symbols in the address, separated by 'dots'. For example, "www.yahoo.com" and "www.yahoo.co.uk" are both website addresses. When you have typed in a correct address, the ISP computer will establish a connection for you between your computer and the web site, and then pages of readable information (including diagrams, pictures and photos) will appear within your browser program window.

The following picture shows a browser program running, connected to a typical web site:

There is truly an unbelievable amount of information now available on web sites all over the world. Some of this information is free for you to read at any time, other information requires further subscription payments in order to get access to it. Metaphorically speaking, it is just as though a huge library exists for you to get access to any time of day or night, with millions of shelves and billions of books.

The 'Electronic Mail' (email) service provided over the Internet allows you to create your own documents and to send these to other people who use the Internet. These documents may be letters, notes, drawings, pictures or photos. You use another special program to send and receive email, called a 'reader'.

The way Electronic Mail works is slightly different from the World Wide Web service. Your ISP company, as part of the subscription service, creates a 'mailbox' for you on their own computers. This is just a temporary storage place for your incoming email to be saved into. When someone sends you an email, chances are that you will not be connected to the Internet at that precise moment. The email is therefore stored in this mailbox until you are ready to receive it. Some time later, you dial into the ISP computer and go 'on-line'. When you are connected, you can then use your email reader to collect any email that may be sat in the mailbox waiting for you. At that same time, you can also send out any out-going email to other people. The ISP computer will accept this out-going mail, and relay it forward over the Internet to its destination computer.

Let us now briefly discuss the second route that you might now wish to take, that is, learning about more complex programs in 'stand-alone' operation. We call it 'stand-alone' operation because your computer does not have to be connected to any other computer (it is therefore the opposite of using the Internet). However, more than likely, you will have other peripheral computer devices connected to it.

There are generally three very common jobs that many users wish to perform using more complex program software. These are:

- advanced word processing
- spreadsheet calculations
- maintaining databases.

With **advanced word processing**, a more complex program (than say 'Wordpad') will provide you with further facilities for document production. These facilities will be most noticeable in the enhanced formatting of pages. For example, you may wish to see multiple column pages, text wrapping around graphics, better graphic manipulation, headers and footers on pages, or maybe chapters and sections in your document. A typical Advanced Word Processing program should provide all of these facilities and more.

Desk-top publishing (DTP) programs are a variation of Advanced Word Processing aimed specifically at producing magazines and news letters. This book is produced using a complex program called QuarkXpress 4.2, which lets the editor space out the pages and text and create a file that looks just like the many pages of an opened-out book.

A **Spreadsheet Calculation** program essentially provides you with a viewable 'grid' of squares into which you can put rows and columns of mathematical figures or values. You can then show totals and subtotals for these rows and columns automatically, without having to add the values up yourself! If you adjust any of the figures within the grid of squares, then the totals and subtotals are automatically computed again to reflect the new values. Quite complex formulas can also be applied to the rows and columns of figures within the grid. The following picture shows a typical spreadsheet:

A Database program is a further advancement upon a Spreadsheet program. It holds a collection of other objects that we refer to as tables, queries, forms and reports. These objects can be made to work together in a highly integrated way to achieve an overall objective.

Let us imagine, for example, that you want to enter information in a very simple way, so that the person entering it has little chance of making a mistake. You might then use a 'form' and design it so that information is entered just as you might fill out a paper form. The data from the form can then be automatically stored in one or more tables of values. These tables are at the very heart of the database program, and the linking of tables together is what makes this kind of program very special.

If at some later time you then wish to create a printed report, you can automatically extract information from the tables, manipulating it in a special way, and present it in the report in a very different way to that used for gathering it in the first place.

You can also ask unusual questions from a database at any time. The questions are submitted to the database in the form of a query. The answers to the query can then be presented back to the user, displayed either on a form or printed in a report.

Today, there are many other uses for a computer, in addition to the common tasks we have described.

Digital photography is one of these now rapidly gaining wide acceptance. Modern digital cameras can produce very professional images for downloading into your computer, and ink-jet printers can reproduce these images as quality enlargements, or as selective prints.

Digital scanners can also produce quality images that you can use these images to enhance your documents.

Music is yet another aspect of computers that is undergoing major changes. Special types of player equipment, called MP3 players, have computer type memory to store music in compressed digital form. You can obtain this music direct from the Internet, and then replay it when you are no longer 'on-line'. There are no moving parts to these players, and the quality of the music is the highest you could wish for.

Sadly, we have now reached the end of the book. Whichever direction you now care to take with your new skills and knowledge of the personal computer, I hope that you gain a great deal of fun and enjoyment from it. I have certainly enjoyed writing this book for you to learn the fundamentals from.

APPENDIX 1

If your keyboard does not have a 'Windows Key'

If your keyboard is one of the older styles, then you may find that the Windows Key is missing from your keyboard. You can work around this problem by using the following combination of key presses to achieve the same effect.

First press the TAB key once. Here is where the TAB key is located...

Now press and hold down the ALT key (also shown in the above picture), and with it held down then press and release the S Key. Now release the ALT key. You will now see the Start Menu appear, as shown in the next picture:

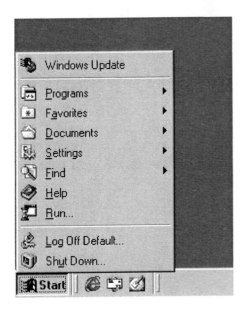

This is the same end result that you would have obtained by pressing the Windows Key, if your keyboard had one.

227

APPENDIX 2

Not switching the computer off properly

If mains power is removed from your computer, either accidentally or deliberately, without first going through the correct shutdown procedure (described in section 2.2), then you will find when you next switch it on that the starting sequence appears to be different.

When you do switch power on and startup the computer again, you will first see the 'Windows' logo screen appear as usual, as shown in the next picture:

However, very shortly afterwards, you will see an unusual blue screen advising you that the Microsoft ScanDisk program is running and it is checking all the files on the Hard drive for errors. This screen is shown in the next picture:

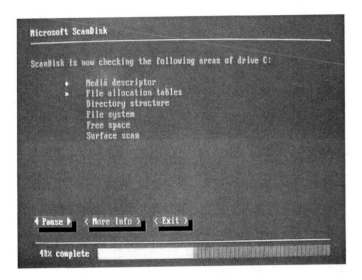

The Microsoft ScanDisk program works its way through all of the files on your Hard Drive, and a yellow progress bar is displayed at the bottom of the screen, showing you the percentage that have successfully been tested. When the Scandisk program has finished, then providing no errors were detected, the monitor screen will return to display the 'Windows' logo screen once again, and the startup sequence will then carry on as normal.

If however errors are detected within some of the files, then the program will advise you, and give you options for resolving the problems. Follow the instructions shown on screen, and where offered, choose the option to 'Fix' the errors automatically. When the errors have been resolved, the startup sequence will continue as normal.

APPENDIX 3

Computer 'crashes'

Modern personal computers are complex pieces of equipment. Whilst every endeavour is made during their design to ensure continued and reliable operation, their complexity inevitably means that, just occasionally, circumstances can arise where something goes wrong. When this happens, the computer may not respond in a predictable manner. In extreme cases it may cease to function altogether. We then say in the jargon that the computer has 'crashed'.

Users normally witness 'crash' circumstances by observing that the mouse pointer starts to behave in a very abnormal manner. Perhaps, when they click on an icon, the underlying program stubbornly fails to run. More often, the pointer symbol will permanently 'freeze' on the monitor screen and fail to move at all in response to any movement of the mouse body.

> **Note – Take care here not to confuse a 'crash' situation with a failure on the part of the mouse itself. Simple things like debris on the mouse mat or dirt in the internal rollers of the mouse mechanism can cause erratic and jerky behaviour of the mouse pointer. Usually a simple cleaning of the mouse ball and mat will remedy things. A computer 'crash' situation however is something altogether more drastic.**

The word 'crash' when used in computing is used figuratively and does not mean that your hardware has suffered any permanent physical damage – unlike, for example, a car crash. It means that something in the master Windows program has happened, either during the start up process or at any other time, which is going to prevent you from doing any more tasks on the computer until the situation is remedied. When a computer has suffered a crash then you have no alternative but to stop working altogether and immediately. If you have work that is not yet saved to disk, then you are almost certain to lose it.

To recover from a computer crash, you will need to shut the computer down in a controlled way (if that is possible) and switch off the mains supply. If the computer won't shutdown normally, then you may have no alternative but to switch off at the mains power point itself. Once you have mains power switched off, then you need to switch it back on again. This action of power off then on again will usually recover from most crash situations. When the power is re-applied, you should notice that the computer starts up once more. If you did manage to power down in a controlled way, then the computer should proceed through the power up stages back to the point where the desktop is again displayed on the monitor. If you could not shutdown normally, then you will notice that the Microsoft Scandisk program runs first (as described in Appendix 2) before the computer displays the desktop.

If simply powering down and powering back up again doesn't remedy things on the first attempt, have a few more attempts before you give in and call for expert help. Each time the power up process takes place the computer will itself try to fix the cause of the problem.

If the computer has a further problem that it cannot fix during the power up phase, you may see messages indicating it is entering 'Safe Mode' or you may see the desktop sceen with 'Safe Mode' written in the corners of the display. You should allow the power up process to complete under these circumstances, and then immediately afterwards perform a normal power down procedure. When you next start up the computer, it should return to normal operation. If it goes a second time into 'Safe Mode' then you have problems that the power down/ power up sequence cannot resolve.

Infrequently, there are times when this simple power off and back on again does not resolve a crash situation. If so then true repair actions are needed – more than likely to the software – to get the computer functioning properly once more. These actions are beyond the scope of a first-timer and you should then enlist the help of an expert.

Index